D0152879

SOUTHERN AFRICA

SOUTHERN AFRICA

An American Enigma

Sheikh R. Ali

PRAEGER

New York
Westport, Connecticut
London

Library of Congress Cataloging-in-Publication Data

Ali, Sheikh Rustum.
   Southern Africa.

   Bibliography: p.
   Includes index.
   1. Africa, Southern--Politics and government.
2. Africa, Southern--Race relations. 3. Africa,
Southern--Economic conditions. 4. Africa,
Southern--Relations--United States.
5. United States--Relations--Africa, Southern.
1. Title.
DT746.A44 1987   968   86-30635
ISBN 0-275-92380-0 (alk. paper)

Copyright © 1987 by Praeger Publishers

All rights reserved. No portion of this book may be re-
produced, by any process or technique, without the express
written consent of the publisher.

Library of Congress Catalog Card Number: 86-30635
ISBN: 0-275-92380-0

First published in 1987

Praeger Publishers, 521 Fifth Avenue, New York, NY 10175
A division of Greenwood Press, Inc.

Printed in the United States of America

∞

The paper used in this book complies with the Permanent
Paper Standard issued by the National Information Standards
Organization (Z39.48-1984).

10 9 8 7 6 5 4 3 2 1

To My Parents
Blessed Be Their Memory

Contents

Preface

This book explores the currents, and undercurrents, of the southern African malaise from 1948 into the end of the second term of the administration of U.S. president Ronald Reagan. The principles and practices of southern African politics are the theme throughout. Events in southern Africa have caught many foreign observers off guard, as the area has become the arena of national liberation struggles in which guerrilla armies, rioting, and killing are commonplace. Many maintain that the situation in southern Africa rivals the Arab-Israeli enmity in its potential to trigger an East-West confrontation.

For the purpose of this study the component units in the southern African subsystem include mainly South Africa, Namibia (formerly South-West Africa), and Zimbabwe (formerly Rhodesia or Southern Rhodesia). On occasion, the former titles, South-West Africa and Rhodesia, are used in the text to convey certain specific meanings.

Complete white control of southern Africa developed gradually, the year 1948 being considered a critical one. The National party, which came to power that year in South Africa, felt that its racial problem could be solved either by integration or by imposing complete white control. The latter and its white supporters prevailed. Therefore, one purpose of this book is to analyze race relations in southern Africa generally and to weigh their impact on the racially conscious Americans.

South Africa tenaciously perpetuates racial inequality—and by minority rule, which explains its unenviable distinction. The world—East and West, Communist and capitalist, rich and poor, black and white, brown and yellow—is generally united today by embargoes and economic sanctions to reform that land of legalized racism.

Southern Africa contains a deliberately polarized society. The difference between races is that of exploiter and exploited. The deprived and abused nonwhite majority remains stigmatized from birth to death. In polarized southern Africa, crisis and conflict, repression and resistance, go on and on. As a middle power, South Africa maintains its hegemonic relations in the region, disdainful of outside powers. Southern Africa's whites, the favored

ix

few, hold all the political, economic, and military powers. The subcontinent's blacks, racially segregated, are moving relentlessly toward revolution.

The issue of southern Africa goes beyond minority rule, as brutal and pervasive as that may be. What is at stake is the political-economic structure within which whites rule and the black majority is condemned to abject poverty. This whole-scale injustice is rooted in the practice of apartheid.

Since World War II, apartheid and racial conflict in southern Africa have received international attention. Many people in southern Africa have tried to eradicate the unjust system of apartheid. They have been helped by individuals, groups, nations, and international organizations. But the direct assistance considered essential for success has been denied the black peoples of southern Africa.

As guerrilla action makes headway in Angola and Zimbabwe, such pressures against the remaining white minority-controlled areas increase. It is in those areas still dominated by white minorities, namely, South Africa and Namibia, that the future looks ominous. They could well be shaken by the uprooting of millions of people.

If widespread racial skirmishes or a civil war should develop within southern Africa, it could draw the two superpowers into the dispute. The Soviet Union would likely side with the black cause, while the United States would be forced to protect its economic interests by supporting the white regime against Communist interference. This could touch off a major political crisis in the United States and possibly race riots. If the United States capitulates in southern Africa, Soviet-backed states could control a vast area there.

The most difficult situation in the region is South Africa. Three times the size of California, it is a richly endowed country. The 1985 population of South Africa was 36 million, of whom 75 percent were black. The white population was 5 million, of whom 2.7 million, or 58 percent, were Afrikaners of Dutch descent. The remaining 2.3 million whites, or 42 percent, were of English origin.

The Afrikaners are fiercely nationalistic. They maintain their supremacy through a policy of racial separation known as apartheid. Apartheid works for them. The term apartheid refers to apartness or separateness along racial lines. Apartheid calls for the permanent inferior position

of nonwhites in South African society. The South African
government believes that political, social, and economic
progress by nonwhites can be accomplished not by integration but by constituting a system of Bantu homelands,
called Bantustans. Several Bantu territories have been
established, but how independent the Bantustans are or
will become is debatable.

By supporting white settlement and the movement of
black Africans onto reserves, the South African government
has extended the apartheid laws to Namibia, and its administration has been increasingly merged with South African government departments. With its relatively small
population and wealth in minerals, Namibia is one of the
few African countries that could be economically independent. Located on the southwest coast of the African continent, Namibia sprawls over an area larger than Britain
and France combined. It is one of the most sparsely popu-
lated countries in the world.

One country in which apartheid thrived was Zimbabwe.
For nearly a century, the white settlers, never more than
4 percent of the total population of Rhodesia, subjected the
native population by means of restrictive discriminatory
laws. Whites controlled virtually every aspect of the lives
of blacks, even determining where they were to live.

Zimbabwe's fortunes will have a lot of bearing on the
future of southern Africa. Many changes are expected.
The new nation must assert black authority in government.
Further, it must be shown that blacks and whites can live
and work harmoniously. It is for the world to support the
Zimbabwean government in its quest for economic independence while encouraging peaceful change in Namibia and,
ultimately, in South Africa if all Africa is to be free.

Because South Africa is at the core of the racial tension in southern Africa, this study treats it accordingly,
although Namibia and Zimbabwe will not be slighted.
South Africa, rich and powerful, dominates southern Africa.
South Africa defends its regional hegemony as being a bulwark against communism and promises to stabilize the region through its military might, proxy war, and economic
control. This claim, as it affects South Africa's foreign
and domestic affairs, is analyzed, too.

To much of the Third World, particularly Africa, the
United States and Britain are leaders in sustaining the
white supremacy regimes in southern Africa. Therefore,

emphasis is placed on southern Africa's relations with Western nations, especially, the United States.

The study is predominantly based on academic research and a review of literature on southern Africa, including official documents, periodicals, and newspapers. Most of the information was gathered between 1977 and 1986. The methodology is divided into two parts: southern African crisis and American policy implications.

The author expresses his appreciation to friends and colleagues for their encouragement. He owes his wife and two sons an incalculable debt for giving up many days of recreation so that the work could be completed.

Part 1
Southern African Crisis

1
Southern African Subsystem

Some understanding of the history of southern Africa offers insight to the politics of the region. The area has long been the scene of movements, meetings, crises, and conflicts among the various peoples who have settled in the region and those who have lived there for centuries.

According to UNESCO (United Nations Educational Scientific and Cultural Organization), "The main but not the only groups inhabiting the area during the first century A.D. were the San and the Khoi."[1] These were later joined by others who intermarried and integrated with the San and the Khoi (or Khoikhoi). When the Europeans came to southern Africa, the San and the Khoi were there.

The Dutch were the first group to settle at the Cape of Good Hope in South Africa in 1652. The Dutch East India Company intended the colony simply as a staging post for India-bound ships. But the ships needed various supplies, including meat, and this brought the Dutch into conflict with the San and the Khoi, who possessed the cattle and refused to supply the intruders. The resistance was broken, and many San and Khoi were killed or enslaved. The settler population increased by births and immigration.

Slavery, already established in the Dutch Empire, was introduced at the Cape in 1657. As the Khoi servants proved unruly and unmanageable, the Dutch masters brought West Indian and West African slaves to the Cape. The early Boers believed that the African blacks were the offsprings of Ham and that they themselves were the descendants of Shem, second and oldest sons of Noah, respectively. In the book of Genesis (9:25), Noah says, "Cursed be Canaan [son of Ham], a servant of servants shall he be to his brethren."[2]   From this Old Testament scripture there developed in southern Africa the idea of blacks as a servant class.   Modern southern African whites justify many of their extreme racial policies toward blacks on this passage.

It was in the first century and a half after the Cape settlement that the conservative Dutch-descended Boers, or Afrikaners, gradually encountered and fought African tribes, including the Bantu.   The second 150 years of Afrikaner history was a period of struggle against the British, who arrived at the Cape after the Napoleonic Wars. The conflict between these two groups led to the Boer War of 1899-1902, which resulted in an uneasy partnership between the Afrikaners and the English in the new Union of South Africa.   But after World War II the Afrikaners took political control of South Africa.

Today, southern African whites, the favored few, hold all the political, economic, and military powers.   The subcontinent's blacks live under a rigorous system of racial segregation.   Slowly, a revolutionary mood is fomenting among the blacks.   Growing numbers of them are demanding an end to racial discrimination and what blacks everywhere else in Africa have received, a black government.

Southern Africa is a subsystem, much like Western Europe, North Africa, the Middle East, or Southeast Asia, and comprises, for the purpose of this study, three territorial units lying mainly south of the Zambezi River. From this river to the north stretches the new world of independent black Africa.   On the south of the Zambezi River, except in Botswana, Lesotho, Swaziland, and Zimbabwe, an overwhelming majority of blacks are ruled by whites. Zimbabwe shed the white minority rule in 1980.   The two African countries still under minority rule--South Africa and Namibia--are geographically at the southern tip of the continent.   Southern Africa as a subcontinent is a contemporary revision of the map of the world.   Here we sketch its components: South Africa, Namibia, and Zimbabwe.

SOUTH AFRICA

The Afrikaners, who speak a Dutch-based language called Afrikaans, are descendants of Dutch, German, and

French Huguenot settlers who arrived in the area between 1652 and 1688. The British settlers acquired the Cape of Good Hope in 1806. The Germans came to South Africa between 1848 and 1858. Today's Afrikaners and other whites of South Africa maintain that they have as much right to the land as the blacks. The blacks, who are the aboriginal population of South Africa, do not deny this right to the whites. But the white minority denies this right to the majority blacks.

South Africa has an area of 454,443 square miles. Its 1985 projected population was 36 million--75 percent black, 14 percent white, 8 percent Coloured, and 3 percent Asian, mostly of Indian and Pakistani extraction.[3] South Africa is a treasure house of underground wealth. It exports 54 minerals, including three-fourths of all the gold produced by non-Communist countries. South Africa is the largest gem diamond producer and mines nearly half of the world's gem diamonds. Located in a continent that is generally underdeveloped and/or developing, South Africa is a most powerful industrial state. Further, it has extensive deposits of platinum, uranium, vermiculite, vanadium, chrome, iron ore, manganese, asbestos, coal, copper, lead, zinc. tin, and sulfur. South Africa produces three times as much steel and generates three times as much electricity as the rest of the African continent. It has as many automobiles and telephones as the rest of Africa.[4]

Considerable foreign investments have been made in South Africa, notably of British, American, German, French, Italian, and Japanese origin. The country's economy is strong and more or less self-sufficient; and its armed forces are considered to be the best equipped and most disciplined in the continent.

No one can measure the wealth of South Africans. But it can be said that, per capita, South Africans are richer than Americans:

> In fact, compared to the life of middle-class
> Americans, the middle-class South African
> white is almost a leisured aristocrat. Hard-
> ly any whites in South Africa do manual
> labor. Not even the postman carries a
> heavy bag. The farmer does not till his
> own land, and South Africa's gleaming gold
> is never shoveled by a white hand. For all
> those jobs, there are blacks.[5]

These advantages do not in themselves make South Africa civilized and humane. Rather, they foster its arrogance in internal race relations, making it the cruelest and most inhumane minority regime in the world. Since the first white settlers arrived, South Africa has suffered internal conflict centered in racial prejudice of the white minority. Whites control the affairs of state by unjust, unfair, and immoral laws, allowing blacks no participation.

The attitude of the South African aboriginal to the growth of white rule has been mixed. Black Africans have opposed white control through both violent and nonviolent means. One of the earlier means of protesting white rule was expressed in religious movements. In recent years Africans have made their opposition felt in the political realm. The founding of the African National Congress (ANC) was the first serious effort to dissolve the tribal divisions in South Africa and to create an "organized" opposition to white domination.

Rarely do South Africans meet members of racial groups other than their own, except as white employers and nonwhite employees. Whites are divided into Afrikaners and British. Their two languages are the official languages in South Africa. In addition, the Coloureds (mixed race), Indians, some Chinese, and Japanese form the South African communities. Oddly enough, the Japanese are officially classified as white, in the hope of cultivating trade and other economic relations with Japan. In South Africa, all white people, even Americans, are considered Europeans.

When the Europeans settled in South Africa, they found the black people there. Centuries before, the black people had migrated southward from central Africa. The vast migration of the Bantu, spilling over subequatorial Africa in the time after Christ, had crossed the Limpopo River in the tenth century; by 1500, its Xhosa vanguard was in the Transkei at the southeastern edge of the African continent.[6]

Anthropologists and historians do not know who the inhabitants of South Africa in remote times were. But when the Europeans settled in South Africa they first met the black people of Negroid descent. "These are supposed to have been the descendants of some of the slaves in America who managed to escape from their cruel bondage and migrated to Africa."[7]

In South Africa the struggle for power is linked with the country's ethnic and racial groups. The main protagonists have been the whites and the blacks and, to a lesser extent, the whites and the Coloureds. Intrawhite politics center around the Afrikaner or Boer-English conflict. White and nonwhite politics each operates in its own sphere. Nevertheless, the power conflict in South Africa could be characterized as a "triangle of forces in which the Afrikaners, the English, and the Africans represent three antagonistic poles."[8]

These three main groups do not compete with one another at the same level, as the blacks are excluded from the parliamentary process. The struggle for power usually takes place between the two white groups, which sometimes follow different methods of achieving opposed objectives. But, in general, the whites agree on the perpetuation of whiteocracy.[9] The blacks, on their side, want to establish a majority rule. This makes the South African political situation unique. White people, numbering about one-seventh of the total population, rule the country in the name of parliamentary democracy.

South African society is made up of varying interests and aspirations and differences in culture, values, and levels of development. To understand South Africa these diversities should be taken into account. Recent political developments inside the country have been concerned with preparing and implementing a new constitution as well as resistance to such a change.

In 1983, two-thirds of the white population in South Africa accepted, through a referendum, a new constitution. The new constitution provides for three separate chambers of Parliament: (1) a House of Assembly for whites with the same composition as the then existing House of Assembly: 166 directly elected members plus 4 nominated by the state president and 8 elected by the members of Parliament (MPs); (2) a House of Representatives for the Coloureds comprising 80 directly elected members plus 2 members nominated by the president and 3 elected by the MPs; and (3) a House of Delegates for Indians composed of 40 directly elected members plus 2 members nominated by the president and 3 elected by the MPs.

The three chambers can only discuss and legislate on what is designated their own affairs. These areas include social welfare, education, art, culture, and recreation, health matters, community development, local government, agriculture, water supply, the appointment of marriage officers, and finance in relation to the chambers' own affairs. The president decides whether a matter is proper to a chamber. Important matters are termed general affairs and are referred to standing committees composed of four whites, two Coloureds, and one Indian. Their decisions must be unanimous. Otherwise, the matter under discussion is referred to the President's Council.

The President's Council consists of 60 members: 20 are designated by the white House of Assembly, 10 by the Coloured House of Representatives, and 5 by the Indian House of Delegates. Ten members are designated on a proportional basis by the opposition parties in the three houses on the basis of six whites, three Coloureds, and one Indian. The rest are appointed by the president. The president is not bound to accept these nominations.

The president is chosen by an 88-member electoral college drawn from the three houses: 50 white, 25 Coloureds, and 13 Indians. Since the whites have an overall majority in the electoral college, the president will be a white person.

The president appoints a cabinet to oversee the general affairs and the Ministers' Council for each house to deal with their own affairs. The cabinet ministers are only responsible to the president and not to Parliament.

This complex constitution has met with sharp criticism, especially from blacks, ever since its promulgation on September 3, 1984. Some objections are that (1) the chambers for Coloureds and Indians are powerless bodies, established to create the illusion of representation; (2) the new dispensation attempts to draw Coloureds and Indians into the white laager, making them junior partners in the white-dominated system; (3) the financial burden of acknowledged state responsibilities, such as housing and education, is shifted to the impoverished communities; (4) the new constitution lays the basis for conscription of Coloureds and Indians into the South African army; (5) the major grievances of the black population, such as the Group Areas Act, the pass laws, separate education, and the homeland policy, remain nonnegotiable pillars of the South African government; (6) the majority black African population is excluded from Parliament; and (7) the new constitution strengthens apartheid, entrenches the white hegemony, and cements racism into the law of the land.

Whites hold elections at regular intervals. In South African elections the outcome is inevitable: The all-white electorate votes overwhelmingly for the Afrikaner-dominated National party. Although several political parties compete, the National party has won by landslides since 1948.

Black South Africans are denied the right to vote in parliamentary elections. They are without the most elementary human rights and opportunities. Unjust laws and regulations block them at every turn. Scores of banning orders on the black people restrict and reduce them to a position of subordination. The white South Africans, claiming to be civilized, cultured, and articulate, conveniently forget that "human beings can never accept the humiliation, degradation, and cruelty of racial domination."[10] Humiliation begets humiliation and tyranny begets tyranny. As doubts beset the white man's rule in South Africa, the government treats nonwhites with increasing harshness and intimidation. As Robin McKown rightly observes: "South Africa today has been likened to a boiling caldron with a lid so tight there is no place for steam to escape. The steam represents the feelings of the oppressed."[11]

Some whites in South Africa would like to alleviate conditions and gain suffrage for nonwhites. In August 1977, the South African government considered some nominal participation by Coloureds and people of Indian origin in governmental affairs.[12] State President Pieter W. Botha is attempting to moderate some features of discrimination, but this is just a tiny step on the long road to justice for the black majority, now more oppressed than ever.

Riots and More Riots

On June 16, 1976, the worst race riot in South African history erupted in Soweto. One hundred and seventy-six people died (all but two of them black) and 1,139 were injured; 1,298 were arrested, and damage to property was put at $50 million.[13] The number of blacks killed in South African race riots in 1976 amounted to 600.[14] In 1977, sporadic riots and demonstrations were suppressed by government cruelty.

Available evidence indicates that South Africa has adopted a calculated official policy to eliminate physically substantial numbers of the country's black leadership.

One of the most prominent victims was 30-year-old Steve Biko, who, in September 1977, was arrested and detained without trial; he reportedly died from a seven-day hunger strike, but many, including progressive news media in South Africa, doubt that to have been the cause. The English-language Rand Daily Mail contended that "people don't die in seven days from a hunger strike."[15] Biko, the twentieth black to die while in police custody in 18 months, helped found South Africa's Black Consciousness Movement. Commenting editorially on Biko's death, the Washington Post said:

> A man with an international reputation, he had personal qualities that had established him as one of the likeliest leaders for the government to deal with if it wished to channel rising black rage away from despair and violence. . . . In a broader context, those in South Africa who prevent blacks developing their own leadership corps and who back off from meaningful dialogue with the black community, are sowing the wind. Without the Steve Biko's they will surely reap the whirlwind.[16]

The newspaper later reported that Steve Biko suffered multiple brain and body injuries before his death in police detention. A special correspondent of the Washington Post, Robin Wright, who filed his dispatch from Johannesburg, reported that "there is already enough evidence to indicate that Biko, 30, probably died of brain damage, such as a hemorrhage, medical experts and well-placed sources said today."[17] However, a Pretoria magistrate cleared South African police of blame in Biko's death. In an unusually sharp statement the U.S. Department of State said, "It seems inconceivable on the evidence presented that the inquest could render a judgment that no one was responsible."[18] A spokesman for the State Department laid the blame on the South African system, which "permits such gross mistreatment and violation of basic human rights."[19]

To be nonwhite in South Africa means to be deprived of almost all the advantages in practically every sphere of life and to be treated as an intruder in one's own country. Apartheid is more than just a set of laws. It is a description of a people's condition of suffering, a social, political, and economic system that sentences a person to a quality of life determined by the color of the skin. Wealth, privilege, and the power to rule are enjoyed by a favored minority. The doctrine of apartheid acknowledges the inferior position of nonwhites in the South African complex. The government supports the political, social, and economic aspirations of the African people not by integration, which it claims would be harmful to the best interests of both white and nonwhite, but by establishing a system of homelands. Despite condemnations throughout the world, the apartheid system has grown stronger, feeding on cheap African labor and massive reinforcement by Western powers and Japan in the form of investments by their multinational corporations.

The internal security law, by which dissent is silenced, permits indefinite confinement without trial. Many people are detained and banned by government orders from leaving their homes, from congregating with more than two people at a time, from publishing anything, from teaching anyone, and from receiving visitors.[20]

Racial relations in South Africa are steadily deteriorating and approaching hostility. Temporarily, majority rule can be denied by force. But once freedom battles begin, the majority will ultimately prevail.

In 1983, the white segment of the South African population was offered a chance to express its opinion about the constitutional proposals through a referendum, but the government denied a similar opportunity to the Coloured and Indian communities. Instead, it was decided that the nonwhite community would be presented with the fact of a new constitution and that the elections for the separate chambers for Coloureds and Indians would take place without previous consultation.

In August 1983, the United Democratic Front (UDF), an alliance to fill a vacuum in black politics, was formed. Its immediate aim was to inform the people about the constitutional proposals and to boycott the elections. A mass campaign was organized, and many other organizations joined the opposition to the constitutional proposals. Within a year of formation, the UDF membership numbered more than 600 affiliated organizations.

The campaign was a big success; only 10 percent of the Coloured community and even less of the Indian community participated in the elections on August 22 and

August 28, 1984. The winner of the Coloured elections was the Labor party, which won 76 seats. The results of the Indian elections were 18 seats for the National Peoples' party and 17 for the Solidarity party.

In September 1984, P. W. Botha was sworn in as South Africa's first president under the new constitution.

The election and inauguration of Botha were marked by unrest and uprisings. Thousands took to the streets to protest rent increases. More than 200,000 students boycotted classes to protest the quality of Bantu education, and mine workers struck for higher wages and the recognition of their trade union. Not only the white minority government but also blacks co-opted by the apartheid system (such as members of the black town community councils) were targets of the dissidents.

The attacks on black traitors and puppets have brought a new dimension to South African unrest. Some councilors have been killed and others have resigned. One of the reasons for targeting these councils has been their increased powers in terms of the new Black Local Authorities Act. This act makes the town councils responsible for collecting rents and service charges and thus they serve as a buffer between the central government and the oppressed. The elections for the councils receive very little support from black South Africans. For example, the elections for the town councils in December 1983 were boycotted by 90 percent of the eligible voters, showing that blacks see through these attempts of the white government to create an image of participation.

The response of the South African government to resistance is violent. Almost the entire leadership of the UDF was arrested in August 1984. Many have been detained indefinitely without any charges. In their violent reaction to the protests, the South African police killed more than 160 persons between August and November 1984.

Recent developments inside South Africa have exposed efforts to modernize and camouflage apartheid through the constitutional proposals. And, as noted, an important facet of recent developments is the growing resentment by blacks against black persons who have let themselves be co-opted into the apartheid system. Thus the struggle for liberation in South Africa is not merely a racial struggle but more and more a struggle between those defending and those opposed to the system of apartheid.

Since the uprisings during the summer of 1984, the daily protests have not ceased. The liberation struggle has rapidly escalated as an increasing number of black South Africans have answered the call of the South African liberation movement, the African National Congress, to sabotage the apartheid system and the township rule. Thousands take part in daily protests, despite the loss of more than 1,700 lives since August 1984.

In the face of armed attacks by the South African police, an increasing number of blacks have retaliated with attacks on government structures with such unsophisticated weapons as stones and gasoline bombs. Unable to cope with the situation, the South African government imposed a state of emergency from July 1985 until March 1986 and reimposed it in June 1986.

The overthrow of the apartheid regime would affect not only southern Africa but the Western world as well. It is perhaps this realization that has caused the United States to seek a peaceful solution to the southern African crisis. Southern Africa's racial problems could affect the United States internally and externally. The plight of the nonwhites elicits sympathy from American civil rights groups. Tolerance of, and in some cases sympathy for, the position of the southern African whites exist in the Reagan administration, including the president himself. Southern Africa presents a unique situation and a unique challenge to American policymakers.

The southern African crisis is not the only threat to human freedom and dignity, but it is the only one in the world based on the color of skin. Later sections and chapters deal with other aspects of southern African politics and its internal and external implications.

NAMIBIA

Namibia is the new name for South-West Africa, which was a German colony before World War I. It was captured by South Africa in 1915. In 1917, the British decided that South Africa should annex the area, but in the peace settlement U.S. President Woodrow Wilson's concept of no territorial aggrandizement prevailed and the territory was formally transferred to South Africa as a mandate of the League of Nations. South Africa assumed the mandate on December 17, 1920.

At the end of World War II, South-West Africa was the only mandated territory that neither achieved independence directly nor was placed under the UN Trusteeship system. South Africa has been trying to incorporate Namibia as part of its territory, but the United Nations has refused to accede to such a request.

Namibia covers an area of 318,000 square miles, inhabited by about 1.15 million people (1985 projection). The racial composition of its population is about one white to seven blacks.[21] The black population is divided into eight or nine tribal and ethnic groups, and, like Zimbabwean blacks, they fight from time to time. South Africa, true to its British and European background, divides the tribes further into political and ethnic lines and rules them.

Nearly two-thirds the size of South Africa, Namibia is fringed by desert and shares a boundary with South Africa. Most of Namibia is semidesert. South Africa has sold land to white farmers who have been encouraged to concentrate development in an area called Police Zone. South Africa follows the principle of separate development along racial and ethnic lines that classify persons as white, native, Coloured, and Asiatic. Their rights and duties depend on the classification. South Africa's policy of apartheid is more rigorously applied in Namibia, where forced labor is evident.[22]

When the League of Nations was dissolved, it did not make any specific provision for the future of the mandate. However, the United Nations refused to accept South African annexation of the mandate. The General Assembly of the United Nations asked for an advisory opinion from the International Court of Justice (ICJ) on the status of South-West Africa. On July 11, 1950, the ICJ held unanimously that the territory remain an "International Mandate" and that South Africa, "acting alone, has not the competency to modify the international status of the territory."[23]

This advisory opinion was accepted by the UN General Assembly, which urged the South African government to comply with that decision. However, South Africa refused to submit reports to the ad hoc committee set up by the General Assembly to oversee matters relating to the implementation of the advisory opinion. The opinion of the ICJ was again sought in 1955 and 1956 in reference to voting procedures in the United Nations regarding reports and petitions on Namibia and the admissibility of oral petitions. On the first issue, it upheld the right of the ad hoc committee to grant oral hearing to petitioners. South Africa refused to accept the court's decision.

On November 4, 1960, two African nations, Ethiopia and Liberia—as former members of the League of Nations— instituted contentious proceedings against South Africa, accusing it of violating the welfare clauses of the mandate. The ICJ rejected South Africa's defense and ruled in 1962 that Ethiopia and Liberia possessed sufficient legal interest in the issue to warrant the judgment of the court. The court held that it had the jurisdiction to hear the case by finding, among other factors, that a dispute existed. In 1966, the court reconsidered the issue of legal interest of the African countries and reversed its previous decision.

South Africa considered itself vindicated by the 1966 judgment, but the general reaction to the court's decision, as viewed by outside observers, came as a result of extraneous reasons. Rosalyn Higgins maintains that the 1966 decision of the court came about because a group of judges, who were in the minority in 1962 when the ICJ determined its jurisdiction, now found themselves—for extraneous reasons—able to command a majority of votes.[24]

The UN General Assembly passed Resolution 2145, terminating South Africa's mandate over Namibia and transferring all administration to the United Nations. South Africa refused to acknowledge the validity of this action. The General Assembly then referred the matter to the Security Council, which adopted Resolution 264, recognizing the General Assembly's termination of the mandate, and the Security Council then requested South Africa to withdraw from Namibia by October 5, 1969. South Africa refused to comply with the request, which prompted the passage of Resolution 276, declaring that "the presence of the South African authorities in Namibia is illegal."[25]

Frustrated by the intransigence of South Africa, the Security Council passed Resolution 283 in which members of the United Nations were urged to refrain from any relations—diplomatic, consular, or otherwise—with South Africa.[26] Again South Africa flouted this resolution. The Security Council then adopted Resolution 284 seeking an advisory opinion from the ICJ. This time the court concentrated on three general issues—judicial review, revocation of the mandate, and the validity of the UN General Assembly Resolution 2145 and Security Council Resolution 276.

In 1971, the ICJ acknowledged that it had no power to review UN resolutions. It also reaffirmed its previous decision, holding that the supervisory functions of the League of Nations were transferred to the United Nations. The court ruled that the failure of South Africa to submit to administrative supervision of the United Nations amounted to breaching the mandate and consequently justified its termination. In addition, the ICJ condemned South Africa's policy of apartheid as contrary to human rights and fundamental freedom and a flagrant violation of the UN charter.[27]

The United Nations grew increasingly hostile toward South Africa. On December 12, 1973, the UN General Assembly recognized the South-West African People's Organization (SWAPO) as the authentic representation of Namibia and granted it associate membership in various UN agencies. SWAPO, whose power base is in the Ovambo tribe in northern Namibia, runs guerrilla operations out of southern Angola.

To cope with the internal situation, South Africa established a multiracial advisory council from various ethnic, regional, and other groups in Namibia. Most significantly, South Africa announced that it would accept both the basic principles of independence and self-government in Namibia. Eventually, the South African Legislative Assembly passed a resolution in November 1974 calling for a multiracial constitutional conference on September 1, 1975. The conference concluded its work by announcing December 31, 1978 as the prospective date for Namibian independence. On a further political level, five Western nations--Britain, Canada, France, West Germany, and the United States--reached agreements in principle with South Africa on how Namibia was to achieve independence by the end of 1978.[28]

In order to work out a detailed formula for the peaceful transition to a majority rule for Namibia, the five Western nations sent representatives to South Africa. Following the meeting, the Western five pursued further discussion with SWAPO, the UN secretary-general, representatives from the five frontline states--Tanzania, Zambia, Mozambique, Angola, and Botswana--and the most important black African nation--Nigeria.

Negotiations among all the parties over the implementation of Security Council Resolution 435 of 1978 have been dragging on for a long time, in spite of elaborate details concerning the deployment of a civilian and military UN peacekeeping force of South African troops and SWAPO guerrillas. But whenever it comes to the signing of a cease-fire agreement and moving forward to the elections, South Africa hedges and raises new issues.

No cause has become so identifiably a UN crusade as independence for Namibia. From its very beginning, the United Nations had sought to exercise authority over the former German colony. So far, the only material achievement from 40 years of effort has been South Africa's gradual "acknowledgment" of the name Namibia, which was bestowed by the UN General Assembly in preference to South-West Africa. Yet, over recent years, a settlement that would include independence and a United Nations-supervised election has seemed temptingly within reach. It was accepted in principle by South Africa, but implementation has proved to be an ever-retreating mirage.

In the meanwhile, South Africa has intensified its efforts to organize a multiracial coalition of conservative parties dominated by white leadership, known as the Democratic Turnhalle Alliance (DTA). The organization is dedicated to the maintenance of status quo. This has led to polarization of political forces in Namibia between SWAPO and the DTA. Although the United Nations adopted a plan to hold a fair and free election in Namibia under UN supervision and control, South Africa held an election of its own in December 1978, which was won handily by the DTA. As expected, SWAPO boycotted this election.

What, then, are the prospects of Namibian independence? Since the attainment of independence by Zimbabwe, attention has been focused on Namibia. There was a time when outsiders placed the fate of the two countries together. But Zimbabwe became free in 1980, and Namibia is still under South African control. What went wrong?

South Africa has imposed an internal settlement similar to the Muzorewa experiment in Zimbabwe shortly before its independence. A so-called National Assembly composed of ethnically based representatives under white leadership and control has been instituted. At the same time South Africa ostensibly continues to leave the door open to negotiations for an internationally acceptable settlement. This is a two-pronged strategy aimed at avoiding international censure while creating an "Uncle Tom" type of administration, which, it hopes, will turn the tide of nationalism. The main consideration for which South Africa is unwilling to install a duly elected black government in Namibia is that it wants to keep the forces of liberation and communism away from its frontiers. This is also to appease the blacks within South Africa proper. The question is whether Namibia's future will be affected by the victory of the liberation forces in Zimbabwe. In Zimbabwe the internal settlement lasted only a year. But in Namibia it has lasted longer. To be sure, there are differences between the two situations, which is to be discussed in the next section.

ZIMBABWE

The Portuguese discovered Rhodesia in the sixteenth century, but soon abandoned attempts to open up the hinterland.[29] When Cecil Rhodes conquered it at the end of the nineteenth century, Rhodesia had been untouched by Europeans for 300 years. Prior to these developments, the region, as pointed out earlier, had been the scene of mass movements of indigenous peoples. The original inhabitants are known to have founded a flourishing civilization at Zimbabwe, well before America was discovered[30]--hence the name the nationalists now give the country.

When Rhodesia became the nation of Zimbabwe on April 18, 1980, the estimated population of the country was 260,000 whites and more than 6 million blacks.[31] The white population agreed that a settlement must come soon, if the loss of population through emigration, already 1,000 a month, was not to become a complete exodus.[32] The whites formed about 4 percent of the total population. Following the British tradition of administration, the Rhodesian white rulers tried to divide the black people and rule them.

Zimbabwe's natural resources, not as great as those of South Africa, include manganese, chrome, asbestos, gold, copper, coal, and precious stones. It has a diversified, well-managed economy.

Technically speaking, Rhodesia was a colony under British legal control. However, Rhodesia was never subjected to firm British control. Conquered by Rhodes in his own behalf toward the end of the 1880s, it was run as a private preserve to seek mineral and commercial concessions from local chiefs. Following his conquest, Rhodes, for whom Rhodesia was named, dreamed, as an imperialist,

of obtaining as much concession in Rhodesia as possible.
As a member of the Cape Parliament, Rhodes procured a
royal charter from the British government for the British
South African Company (BSAC) that gave the company the
rights to administer Rhodesia. "From the first days of
white occupancy, the Europeans implemented laws and ordinances aimed at regulating the African population to
serve white needs."[33]

Negotiations among the BSAC, white settlers, South
Africa, and the British government centered on two points:
the financial settlement to be made with the company and
the future development of Rhodesian politics. The British
government left the choice to Rhodesia by presenting a
referendum on the choice of self-government or joining the
Union of South Africa. Finally, in 1922, the Rhodesian
electorate chose responsible government over union with
South Africa and soon adopted a constitution according
Rhodesia almost complete self-government. Zimbabwe is
now completely independent.

In 1953, Rhodesia (then known as Southern Rhodesia),
Northern Rhodesia, and Nyasaland were united in the Central African Republic. This federation had a brief life-
span. The great black majorities, with voting rights in
the other areas, were suspicious of Southern Rhodesia,
which, from the outset, denied voting and other political
rights to its nonwhite majority. In December 1963, the
federation was dissolved. Northern Rhodesia became the
independent Republic of Zambia, and Nyasaland was granted
independence with its new name of Malawi.

Rhodesia was striving for independence, too. Its
government, headed by Ian D. Smith, was unable to agree
with Britain on the conditions for independence, and on
November 11, 1965, Rhodesia unilaterally declared its independence. But no nation recognized this illegal declaration of independence under white rule but rather independence with black majority administration. In other words,
the issue in Rhodesia was not independence but rather the
postindependent control of the country.

Immediately after the Unilateral Declaration of Independence, the General Assembly of the United Nations called
on Britain to end the rebellion in Rhodesia and asked the
Security Council to consider the situation. The council
imposed sanctions on Rhodesia, including an oil boycott,
and all member countries were requested to implement them.
With its isolation from the international community, Rho-

desia became completely dependent on South Africa.   Rhodesia is bordered by black nations on three sides; its only outlet is through South Africa, on the south.   Rhodesia and South Africa became economically dependent on each other.   Furthermore, bonds of kinship and policies of apartheid united them in their common attitude toward survival in a continent of 50 black countries and an almost all-black population.

On August 31, 1977, Prime Minister Smith returned to power by election--an election in which the white electorate voted for Smith's Rhodesia Front party to enable the prime minister to change the constitution.[34]   This victory by election meant that the prime minister won the majority support of the minority electorate.

The whites feared black majority rule; they regarded themselves as better able to deal fairly with the problems of a multiracial society and claimed that only with white skills and capital could Rhodesia develop rapidly.   African nationalist organizations demanded a universal franchise.   They denied that whites would be abused or driven out.   With neither side having faith in the other, the racial gap steadily widened.

On November 24, 1977, Smith presented his offer to negotiate an internal settlement with black leaders inside Rhodesia as a way to bypass an Anglo-American plan that would involve the guerrilla forces of the Patriotic Front in a transfer of power to an independent, majority-backed government by the end of 1978.

The internal settlement talks, which began December 2, 1977, excluded the Patriotic Front.   But Smith and the three moderate black leaders--Bishop Abel Muzorewa, the Reverend Ndabaningi Sithole, and Chief Jeremiah Chirau--announced on February 15, 1978, that they had reached an agreement on a formula for black majority rule in Rhodesia. The pact provided for universal suffrage leading to black rule with constitutional safeguards for whites.   Many details on the makeup of a transition government remained to be worked out.   The blueprint for black power would be ratified in a referendum by Rhodesia's white voters.   Among the stipulations was a new 100-seat Parliament, in which 28 seats would be reserved for whites for ten years.[35]

A major difficulty was the fact that the proposed settlement did not include representatives of the Patriotic Front, which had, according to various estimates, between 17,000 and 40,000 guerrillas in neighboring Mozambique and Zambia engaged in a war of attrition with the Smith government. As expected, the Front leaders castigated the internal settlement plan and vowed to step up the fighting.

Rhodesia's accelerating economic deterioration, rather than purely political and military considerations, explains why Smith negotiated a settlement based on black majority rule with nationalist leaders. The cost of fighting black guerrillas, the global recession, and the international sanctions had combined to bring the economy to the brink of collapse. Consequently, outward migration of whites rose.

As expected, Smith was not sincere about the transfer of power and did not deal in good faith with the black leaders. Actual control of the government remained firmly under whites. The accord of the prime minister with the nonviolent black leaders proved a fraud.

The guerrilla attacks against Rhodesia that began in 1972 greatly escalated after the internal settlement agreement failed to produce the desired result of black and white cooperation. The Patriotic Front, made up of Robert Mugabe's movement based in Mozambique and Joshua Nkomo's in Zambia, was not a party to the settlement.[36]

On March 3, 1979, the Smith regime and the three moderate black nationalists signed the Salisbury Agreement, which provided for qualified majority rule under which whites would retain considerable power. Broadly speaking, the settlement called for majority rule based on universal adult franchise, a black majority legislature, an independent judiciary, and certain guaranteed rights for minority groups, especially the whites. Twenty-eight of the 100 parliamentary seats would be reserved for whites for ten years. Whites would thus retain enough votes to block any constitutional amendments detrimental to their interests.

After elections in April 1979, the United States-educated Bishop Muzorewa was installed as the first black prime minister of Zimbabwe-Rhodesia, a temporary name given the country to placate the whites. The Patriotic Front denounced the settlement as a fraud and intensified its guerrilla activities inside the country. Several subsequent attempts to negotiate a settlement acceptable to all parties failed.

With the support of the international community, the British undertook to settle the conflict in mid-1979 by arranging the Lancaster House conference in London. Following three months of intensive negotiations, the British government and the concerned Rhodesian parties agreed to an independent settlement internationally acceptable. The agreement, signed on December 21, 1979, called for a new democratic constitution to institute majority rule while protecting minority rights; a short transition period during which Zimbabwe-Rhodesia would return to legality under a British governor; an impartial election; and a cease-fire.[37]

The British government appointed Lord Christopher Soames governor of Rhodesia to preside over the three-and-a-half-month transition period to independence. This interim was punctuated by continuing incidents of violence, but conditions gradually improved as the cease-fire took effect.

The elections were divided into two phases. On February 14, 1980, white voters elected 20 members of Smith's Rhodesia Front to the House of Assembly. During February 27-29, black voters chose the other 80 members. Mugabe's party, ZANU, won 57 seats, while Nkomo's party, ZAPU, won 20 seats. The Parliament is also composed of 40 senators, 10 of whom are whites. Thus the constitution maintained the whites in a strong political position in an independent Zimbabwe.[38]

The Commonwealth Observer Group, which had been assigned an important role at the August Commonwealth Conference in Lusaka, issued an interim report that stated essentially that despite difficult circumstances the elections were free and fair. Other independent reports reached generally the same conclusion. Soon after the results were known, Lord Soames asked Mugabe on April 18, 1980 to form the government as prime minister of independent Zimbabwe.

Among the handicaps facing the country at independence were the damage done by guerrilla warfare; unequal distribution of wealth; a history of institutionalized racial and tribal division and rivalry; lack of control over the military, administration, and economy; and a constitution limiting the new government's power to deal with these problems.

Since becoming prime minister, Mugabe has taken steps that mark him as a pragmatic African socialist and that have helped create a relatively stable situation in Zimbabwe after years of conflict. Mugabe's inclusion of prominent whites in important cabinet, military, and judicial positions, his promise to implement socioeconomic change gradually while building on the economy's strong capitalistic base, and his commitment to reconciliation have been stabilizing factors. Faced with rising black expectations and the problem of resettling an estimated 1 million people displaced during the conflict, as well as the need to integrate the various fighting forces into a unified Zimbabwean army, the government has moved quickly to institute substantive changes and to remove the vestiges of discrimination.

Within southern Africa, Zimbabwe's economy is second only to South Africa's in size and diversity. Its wide range of natural resources and strategic minerals, together with relatively well-developed manufacturing and agricultural sectors, are keys to its future economic strength. The government has been encouraging foreign investment and assistance and has instituted a nonaligned foreign policy. The West has granted Zimbabwe economic and technical aid, which is being used in major reconstruction and rehabilitation programs.

The creation of the independent nation of Zimbabwe has important implications for the southern African region as a whole. Through his public acknowledgment that South Africa "is a reality," Prime Minister Mugabe indicated he will seek to work out a pragmatic relationship with that country.[39] There is also a growing realization within South Africa that it is in its own self-interest to establish a realistic relationship with Zimbabwe. A relatively stable Zimbabwean government is considered preferable to political and economic turmoil with all its negative consequences. The frontline states also have a real interest in ensuring stability in Zimbabwe. These states, especially Zambia and Mozambique, suffered enormously reprisals from the Rhodesian conflict for having offered guerrilla bases and providing shelter and food to refugees.

Zimbabwe's future may depend on South Africa. The South African government has demonstrated its capacity to destabilize the black frontline states, not only Angola but also Mozambique, Zimbabwe's neighbor and ally. South Africa has hitherto carefully avoided interference with Zimbabwe, applying sufficient military pressure to tie down about 10,000 Zimbabwean troops guarding the Mutare-Beira oil pipeline and railway link through Mozambique and supplying arms to the dissident group Super ZAPU, operating in Zimbabwe's western regions. This dual strategy has sent a warning signal to Prime Minister Mugabe and a comforting message to South Africa's beleaguered whites that black majority rule may mean poverty and chaos.

Zimbabwe has been spared the full South African on-slaught for two reasons. Mugabe has prudently refused to allow the ANC to establish military bases within his bor-ders, and Zimbabwe continues to enjoy a special relation-ship with Britain, which supplies arms to the Zimbabwean government. Nevertheless, despite opposition from Britain, Mugabe has imposed full-scale economic sanctions on South Africa.

One of the grim consequences of South African de-stabilization has been the rapid erosion of civil liberties in Zimbabwe and the mounting pressure for a one-party state. Unity talks between the ruling party, ZANU, which won 63 of the 80 black parliamentary seats in the July 1985 general elections, and Nkomo's ZAPU, which got 15 seats, have been drifting unproductively.[40] South Africa finds the situation beneficial as Zimbabwe moves toward a one-party state and inevitable censorship, emasculation of the legislature, and a cult of leadership.

On the other hand, a stable society in Zimbabwe that can accommodate all the races living there would be a model to Namibia and perhaps South Africa. A successful multiracial Zimbabwe would be an example to South Africa of an alternative to racial confrontation. Such a develop-ment would minimize the chances of East-West involvement in the subcontinent's last but most important struggle for majority rule in South Africa.

NOTES

1. Racism and Apartheid in Southern Africa: South Africa and Namibia (Paris: UNESCO, 1974), p. 15.

2. Quoted in N. E. Davis, A History of Southern Africa (London: Longman, 1978), p. 21.

3. Pierre E. Dostert, Africa 1985 (Washington, D.C.: Stryker Post Publications, 1985), p. 88.

4. Leonard M. Thompson, Politics in the Republic of South Africa (Boston: Little, Brown, 1966), p. 1.

5. John Cohen, Africa Addio (New York: Ballantine, 1966), p. 278.

6. Robert W. July, A History of the African People (New York: Scribner's, 1974), p. 281.

7. M. K. Gandhi, Satyagraha in South Africa (Ahmadabad, India: Navajivan Publishing House, 1928), p. 8.

8. Pierre L. Van Den Berghe, South Africa: A Study in Conflict (Berkeley: University of California Press, 1967), p. 98.

9. The Term whiteocracy, coined by the author, means government of the white, by the white, and for the white, as it is in South Africa and Namibia.

10. G. Mennen Williams, Africa for the Africans Grand Rapids, Mich.: Eerdmans, 1969), p. 138.

11. Robin McKown, Crisis in South Africa (New York: Putnam's, 1972), p. 8.

12. New York Times, August 20, 1977.

13. Washington Post, August 7, 1977.

14. New York Times, July 30, 1977.

15. Rand Daily Mail (South Africa), September 14, 1977.

16. Washington Post, September 15, 1977.

17. Ibid., September 18, 1977.

18. Ibid., December 3, 1977.

19. Ibid.

20. National Geographic, June 1977, pp. 780–819.

21. Dostert, Africa 1985, p. 85.

22. John Carey, ed., Race, Peace, Law, and Southern Africa (Dobbs Ferry, N.Y.: Oceana, 1968), p. 18.

23. Ibid.

24. Rosalyn Higgins, "The International Court and South West Africa: The Implications of the Judgement," Internationl Affairs (London), 42 (1966):573–99.

25. UN Security Council Resolution No. 276 (1970).

26. UN Security Council Resolution No. 283 (1970).

27. A. Rovine, "The World Court Opinion on Namibia," Columbia Journal of International Law 11 (1972):57.

28. Washington Post, June 17, 1977.

29. Williams, Africa for the Africans, p. 108.

30. Ibid., p. 109.

31. New York Times, July 25, 1977, and April 18, 1980.

32. Ibid., July 25, 1977.

33. Larry W. Bowman, Politics in Rhodesia: White Power in an African State (Cambridge, Mass.: Harvard University Press, 1973), p. 9.

34. Washington Post, September 1, 1977.

35. Ibid., February 16, 1978.

36. Robert Mugabe headed the faction of the Patriotic Front known as the Zimbabwe African National Union (ZANU) and Joshua Nkomo controlled the Zimbabwe African People's Union (ZAPU).

37. New York Times, December 22, 1979.

38. Richard W. Hull, "The Continuing Crisis in Rhodesia," Current History 78 (March 1980):107-09).

39. U.S. Department of State, Bureau of Public Affairs, The New Situation in Zimbabwe, March 27, 1980.

40. Helen Kitchen, "Africa: Year of Ironies," Foreign Affairs 64 (annual student edition, 1985):572.

2
Apartheid

Race relations has become an important problem not only within southern Africa but in the whole world. Since World War II people subjected to racial discrimination have attempted to eliminate those conditions that have nurtured the injustice. Its victims everywhere have been supported by individuals, groups, nations, and international organizations—thus creating an international environment that has been outwardly against racial discrimination. Unfortunately, the direct assistance that many consider essential to success has not materialized, especially in southern Africa, where this problem is paramount.

Little or no progress has been made in southern Africa because the strength of the established political powers has squelched revolutionary movements. This has been particularly true in Namibia and South Africa. Revolutionary organizations, therefore, have sought to exert pressure throughout the international realm for support of their internal cause.

Despite all that has been said and written of the practice of apartheid in southern Africa, it is by no means easy to define. Etymologically, apartheid means separation. Apartheid is an Afrikaans word—literally, apartness or apart-hate or setting apart or living apart—South Africa's policy of separation of the races. The purpose is to keep South Africa under white domination, control, and supremacy. In practice, apartheid sets up barriers between whites and nonwhites. For example, nonwhites cannot ride in the same bus or train with white people. There are separate toilets, benches, waiting rooms, beaches, and writing and stamping tables in post offices. "For whites only" and "for nonwhites only" are familiar signs seen in much of South Africa. This kind of racial segregation is found in schools, theaters, churches, hospitals, clubs, and institutions.[1] Fundamental to carrying out apartheid is the Population Registration Act, reminiscent of the Nazi laws, which requires every person to have an identity card specifying his or her race.

In southern Africa all peoples are surrounded by walls of containment. They are assigned roles according to their race. The Europeans have arrogated to themselves the master roles of regulating and controlling the norms of human behavior. The racial containment in southern Africa means control over the human mind under conditions of compulsion. Apartheid reflects the aspiration and determination of the white minority to rule over majority. Apartheid is, in other words, a sadistic whiteocracy.

Racial containment is the epitome of apartheid. Racial containment or separate development was legalized in South Africa by the Reservation of Separate Amenities Act of 1953.[2] Much of this legislation was based on laws already on the books. The South Africa of Daniel Malan, Jan Riebeeck, Cecil Rhodes, Paul Kruger, and Jan Smuts had treated its nonwhite population inhumanely.[3] Hendrik Verwoerd, John Vorster, and Botha personally legalized racism in South Africa. Separate development is, in fact, deprivation and dispossession through coercion. The black Africans are separated from other races through coercion and then shunted into kibbutzlike "homelands." The government has taken apartheid a giant step further with its plan to create the so-called independent nations out of black tribes' traditional homelands.

HISTORICAL BACKGROUND

Defending apartheid, a former prime minister of South Africa invoked history and tradition: "It must be appreciated from the outset that apartheid, separation, segregation or differentiation . . . whatever the name . . . is part and parcel of the South African tradition and practiced since the first Dutch settlement at the Cape in 1652."[4] This situation developed as a direct result of South Africa's colonial past. Upon their arrival, the Dutch colonists wrested land violently from the native Africans and sub-

jected them to a master-slave relationship.[5] These colonists today call themselves Afrikaners; they are narrow-
minded and intolerant, resisting absolutely any liberal
ideas of government. Having won the Boer War of 1899-
1902, Britain established the Union of South Africa. British rule was based on compromise and concession granted
to the Boer-Afrikaners. The Afrikaners were a considerable
majority in the white population and they "developed a
more virulent racist nationalism as a result of their experiences."[6]

     In 1948, the National party of the Afrikaners came
to power and has remained in power since. Behind the
rise of the National party was a secret society of the Afrikaners, the Broederbond, founded in 1918. The society is
based on the ideology of white supremacy. Since 1948 all
South African prime ministers and President Botha have
been members of the Broederbond. It created a Nazi-type
organization in 1938, known as Ossewa Brandwag, set up
along military lines. This organization supported Adolf
Hitler's policy during World War 11.[7] A recent prime
minister of South Africa, Vorster, was a member of the
Ossewa Brandwag, which conducted armed sabotage to disrupt South Africa's participation in the Second World War.[8]
Today's ruling party in South Africa is itself identified
with Hitler's policy of extermination of the Jewish race
and other fascist ideology, such as the master race phi-
losophy.[9] It is evident, therefore, that the government in
South Africa is a throwback to Hitler and his Nazi party.

     Briefly, apartheid policy involves the following:

--Consolidating and extending legislation governing the
   separation of blacks, whites, Coloureds, and Asians
--Bringing indirect rule via the chiefs and traditional
   special structures up to date in such a way as to in-
   hibit the rise of an African nationalism
--Emphasizing Afrikaner economic and social control
-- Maintaining racial separation through the medium of
   separate social institutions (language, culture, education) controlled directly by the government or through
   the selective use of state funds.

The aims are to

--Ensure the continuation of white supremacy, while at the
   same time controlling the pace and direction of black
   nationalism

--Guarantee the expansion and competitiveness of South
African business by means of a low-paid, docile, and
highly mobile reserve of workers.

The National party of South Africa has regressed.
Instead of blacks being granted more rights, their citizenship has been revoked and they are forced to organize
their own self-governing homelands, known as Bantustans.

BANTUSTANS

Apartheid policy calls for the full development of
homelands for the Africans, according to their tribal af-
filiations, but to the growing national solidarity of the
Africans, it counterposes fragmentation by retribalization.
The Bantustan project is to implement a well-coordinated
administrative machinery involving blacks in self-government while effectively binding them to the central authority
of the white government. The policy of Bantustan toward
blacks is just another means of maintaining white control
in South Africa. The Bantustan experiment, based on
the whites' need to stem the tide of national consciousness
among the blacks, continues South Africa's traditional policy and practice of white domination.

The land on which the Bantustans are located is that
portion of South Africa still in the possession of the blacks.
The Native Act of 1913 decreed that the right of the Africans to own land was to be limited to the native reserves.
These same reserves are those that have been given the
new name of Bantustans. The black people are denied the
right to acquire a freehold title to land anywhere in
South Africa, including the Bantustans.[10]

In 1951 the South African government passed the
Bantu Authorities Act, which established the Bantustans.
Under the Bantu Homeland Act of 1970, all Africans are
citizens of their respective homelands, whether or not they
reside there. In introducing the plan, the government
proclaimed that it was granting self-rule to the blacks.
It was announced that when the South African rulers had
satisfied themselves that political independence was not
inimical to racial domination, the Bantustans would evolve
into fully independent states. The government hopes that
on the basis of this promise it will appease the blacks in
South Africa, as well as tempering the growing opposition
to apartheid in the outside world.

In sum, the key to a proper understanding of the Bantustans is land. The land dispossession of blacks in South Africa is the most vital aspect of the sustained economic exploitation and political subjugation of the black people. The Bantustans are nothing but the old native reserves under a new name.

The salient feature of the Bantustan plan is that it attempts to use the tribes and the elites simultaneously in such a manner that one supports the other while both shore up the entire system of white supremacy. The white rulers need the tribal people as the pivotal point of the structure of retribalization, which is evident in the scheme. They also need the black elites because they now enjoy popular acceptance in society. The white rulers seek the service of black elites as intermediaries because the elites can sway the masses.

The major tribal groups in South Africa are the Xhosa, Zulu, Tswana, Pedi (North Sotho), South Sotho, Venda Ndebele, Swazi, and Shangaan. South African policy is to give each of these groups a homeland, with the exception of the Xhosa, who have two, Transkei and Ciskei. Together they comprise 13 percent of the land. The remaining 87 percent is controlled by the South African government.[11]

Three of these homelands--Transkei, Bophuthatswana, and Venda--were declared independent in 1976, 1978, and 1979, respectively. None has been recognized internationally. Each has been shunned by both the United Nations and the Organization of African Unity (OAU). An independent commission composed of a former British ambassador to South Africa, two American academicians, and four South Africans has advised against proceeding with independence for the remaining black homelands. The commission, appointed by the government of Ciskei, found that Ciskeians were opposed to independence. Yet it was declared independent by South Africa.

From the outset, Bantustans have had major obstacles. Their small land area is the least desirable, much of it being deficient in water and fertileness. There is no sound industrial base in the Bantustans. Transkei, the showplace of apartheid, suffers from lack of employment and land shortage, low levels of agricultural production, and inadequate housing and public services.[12]

The government of Transkei has an identity of its own, but it is subject to orders of the South African government. The legislative assembly has 109 members, 45 of whom are elected; the rest are tribal chiefs appointed by the South African government. Political parties exist in name only, as all antiapartheid parties and organizations are outlawed.[13] The senior staff of the Transkei government are whites appointed by South Africa. The South African government controls Transkei through the powers of subvention, review, and audit.

Since their arrival in South Africa, the whites have consistently and systematically destroyed the positions, possessions, traditions, and structures of the nonwhite populations. The latter have been forced to serve the white community and have been poorly compensated for the work. The assumptions of the white community regarding the inferiority of nonwhite people are reflected in virtually every aspect of life in southern Africa. The Bantustan policy of apartheid has provided a long-term solution by keeping Africans remote from political power but near enough to be thoroughly exploited economically.

LEGALIZED RACISM

The operational components of legalized racism fall into four converging categories: racial prejudice and discrimination, racial segregation and separation, economic exploitation, and terror. Racism is not bred in brain and bone but is cultured and fed by environment. Racial prejudice is an attitude, a sentiment; racial discrimination is an act, a measure taken to the disadvantage of its victims.

South Africa is the only country in the world that practices legalized racism. It is a crime in South Africa not to be a racist. To comply with the law one has to be a racist. The first step in this direction is to institutionalize clear-cut racial differentiation. Following are a few selective statutes to illustrate the contention that legalized racism is the norm in South Africa.

The Population Registration Act (1950) divides the population into racial categories, and it became compulsory for all citizens over the age of 16 years to possess identity cards and to produce these at the request of an authorized person.

The Bantu Education Act (1953, 1954, 1956, 1959, and 1961) applies apartheid to black education. Separate education was stipulated for Coloureds in the Coloured Education Act (1963) and for Indians in the Indians' Education Act (1965). Under the terms of these acts, education for blacks, whites, Indians, and Coloureds is separately administered and financed. Different curricula are followed. Education is free and compulsory for white children; African children must pay for their schooling.[14]

There is marked inequality in the education systems in South Africa, of which there are four, one for each racial group. For every dollar spent on education for a black child, five is spent on a Coloured student, eight on an Asian student, and ten on a white student. The ratio of students to teachers is 10 to one for whites, 14 to one for Asians, 19 to one for Coloureds, and 33 to one for blacks.

There are laws to control the movement of African workers. President Botha announced in Parliament on April 18, 1986 that pass laws controlling where blacks can live and work would no longer be enforced. He also said that blacks who had been convicted of violating pass laws, and those who are in jail awaiting trial, will be freed. Botha said that passes carried by blacks would be abolished and that a standard identity card would be issued for all races. Many critics, including Archbishop Desmond Tutu, warned that Botha's new proposals, which include identity books that all Africans will have to carry, could mean the same old restrictions under a smoother-sounding name. This type of minor reform is underway in South Africa but designed only to entrench white minority rule.

Blacks are denied political rights. They are not permitted to vote in parliamentary elections. Whereas Coloured and Indian interests are served by their respective elected representatives, black interests are not at all served in Parliament. Political parties are forbidden to have members belonging to more than one race. The South African government has enacted blanket laws banning actions that promote any form of industrial, political, social, or economic disturbance and that threaten public safety and order.

Segregation is even practiced in hospitals, where black and white are treated separately by staff of their racial group. Factories have to provide separate entrances, time clocks, pay offices, dishes and cutlery, washrooms, changing rooms, rest rooms, dining rooms, and so on.[15]

ECONOMIC DIMENSION

With the movement of South Africa from a rural agricultural base to an urbanized industrial foundation, the need for skilled labor has exceeded the supply among the white community. As a result, increasing opportunities have developed in the industrial sector of the economy for the nonwhite population. Thus growing numbers of nonwhites have been attracted to the urban areas.

Whites have reacted to this influx of nonwhites in urban areas with fears of having their civilization destroyed. Their response to this perceived threat is found in the system of apartheid, which the Afrikaner-dominated Nazi-styled National party supported in the 1948 elections and which restored to them power that has not been broken. The system of apartheid has greatly expanded a pattern of segregation, which both the Afrikaners and English had developed over many years.

Increasingly, black Africans are required to work in the white-owned factories, shops, offices, and homes, but only as migrant workers. The migrant workers are mostly unskilled. The pay gaps between white skilled workers and black unskilled workers range from 14 to 1.[16] Not a single black person serves on the board of directors of any significant business organization in South Africa. Few if any of the Anglo-American corporations have black directors. And this despite the fact that there is no legal barrier against black directors.

The ratio of African to European per capita income amounts to more than 1 to 20. South Africa claims that it affords its black population a per capita income equal to or in excess of that in neighboring states. What is pertinent is the remarkably low level of black income in Africa's only economically developed country. With a fair distribution of income, the blacks of South Africa could have the highest per capita income in Africa. It is economic apartheid that prevents them from sharing equally in the resources and wealth of South Africa.

It is naive to suppose that the growing industrialization taking place in South Africa will promote a progressive development in the political thinking of the regime and phase out racism. But there is a paradox: While the white supremacist government finds blacks unfit to run the country, it (the government) stifles the development of a black commercial class.

The industrialization of southern Africa cannot be separated from the rest of the society and treated as if it were a self-generating force. It is an integral part of polity and society. Industrialization in southern Africa is inextricably tied to apartheid. Under the pressure of world criticism, apartheid became refined into the new nomenclature called separate development.[17]

Separate development divides the South African people into separate communities based on race. In the division, the whites retain the instruments and symbols of power, the vast majority of the land (87 percent), and the natural resources. Clearly, under apartheid, the black population is denied the means by which it could develop a pattern of prosperity independent of the white community. In effect, the system maintains the pattern of racial segregation and racial discrimination in a more rigid and arbitrary form. A South African journalist says of the partition of land: "Black opposition to the partition is widespread and intense; there is strong belief that they are being robbed of their birthright to share in the country's wealth. World opinion, too, is solidly opposed, viewing it all as merely old-style apartheid in disguise."[18]

What does this mean in human terms? Nowhere in the world are class-race lines so firmly drawn as in South Africa. Over the years as the South African economy expanded, two sets of laws have developed. One set applies to whites, sometimes also to Coloureds and Asians; it lays down regulations with respect to conditions of employment, wage negotiations, trade unions, and so on. A separate set of laws applies to Africans. These laws deal with such matters as the black African's most intimate, private lifestyle as well as his or her public life in society. It intrudes upon marriage and family life and social and civic rights. This type of "pass law" has been in operation ever since the white people settled in South Africa.

Because of its nature, apartheid cannot be reformed; it must be destroyed. It follows that the political system that perpetuates apartheid cannot be satisfactorily restructured. It must be totally transformed so that a racist society can become nonracist and a system of genocide can become a system of development for all of the citizens. Individuals and organizations around the world are becoming increasingly aware of the monstrosity of this unique system of exploitation.

Because of the incredible injustice to nearly 30 million Africans, the apartheid system in South Africa has been almost universally condemned. Archbishop Tutu, general secretary of the South African Council of Churches, expressed the feelings of the vast majority of Africans about the various proposals and measures designed to reform, modernize, and cosmetize apartheid:

> The government is attempting to give the appearance of reform. They have introduced some multi-racial sport, so-called international hotels and restaurants to serve all races, removed some discriminatory signs, etc., and whites are going into ecstasies about all this evidence of change. Let us dismiss it! All is merely cosmetic and superficial. They are crumbs of concession which have fallen from the master's table. We don't want these crumbs. We want to be there deciding the menu together. We don't want apartheid to be made more comfortable as would be the effect. . . . We don't want our chains made comfortable, we want them removed.[19]

POLITICAL AND ECONOMIC APARTHEID

The politics and economics of apartheid are woven together in a grotesque fabric of black exploitation and systematic impoverishment by a ruling elite of the white minority. This relationship is centered around complete control of the land, labor, and resources in mineral-rich South Africa. It is maintained by total domination of the processes that further the development of the white population and ensure the underdevelopment of the African and Asian populations.

There are six major aspects of political apartheid, all geared to a system of dividing a ruling Afrikaner elite from subjugated blacks:

1. Perpetuation of Afrikaner political domination of South Africa and Namibia
2. Destruction of African political presence in South Africa and Namibia except for a buffer black middle class

3. Banishment of African political presence to impoverished Bantustans
4. Neutralization of the English-speaking minority
   political opposition
5. Co-optation of ethnic minority (Coloureds and Indians)
   potential political strength
6. Subordination of Bantustans to the political will of
   white South Africans

The six major aspects of economic apartheid are tied
to a concept of integration of the means of production that
allows the financial and political leadership to coordinate
the processes of profitable utilization of land, labor, and
resources. This concept of integration ensures that the
lion's share of the benefits will remain with the financial
and political leadership and trickle down to the white
middle classes, leaving the blacks and Indians impoverished:

1. Exploitation of the best land for the white minority
2. Extraction of the mineral wealth of the country for
   the benefit of the ruling elite
3. Protection of white employment privileges and special
   preference for the Coloureds and Indians
4. Recruitment of cheap African labor for industry,
   mines, and agriculture
5. Dispersion of the African family to the nonviable
   Bantustans
6. Encouragement of public and private foreign investment to profit from cheap labor

It is important to grasp the interrelationship between
the politics of apartheid and the development of the South
African economy. For the past 100 years, the political im-
peratives of racial segregation have dominated the economic
requirement of the society.
   One of the best ways to understand this system is to
view the intricate network from a dualistic perspective
that involves special connections between the modernized
urban industrial and rural agricultural sectors with the
traditional urban industrial and rural subsistence agricultural sectors. The modernized sectors dominate white
South Africa, while the traditionalized sectors dominate the
Africans. Since the end of World War II, white South
Africa has been faced with the dilemma of squelching

potential African political power while integrating African labor essential for the economy.

RESTRICTIONS ON THE WHITES

While blacks, Coloureds, and Asians are the major victims of apartheid, the basic liberties of dissenting whites have also been progressively curtailed. Apartheid political control affects all dissidents. Many measures taken by South Africa against dissenters are designed to provide the authorities with a flexible response to acts of defiance. Apartheid has become an outgrowth of the aggressiveness and the search for security and wealth that the white government in South Africa has persistently pursued.

The Suppression of Communism Act (1950), aimed at prosecuting Communists, has provided the government with extensive powers. One of these powers is "banning," which is a sophisticated method of political emasculation.[20] The person served with a banning order is under restriction for the next five years. This restriction includes house arrest, among other penalties. The banned person may not meet with more than one person at a time except for members of his or her family. He or she may not write for publication or be quoted. The government is always watching. For the black African there can be banishment to a remote and lonely area.[21]

A banning order was imposed on Donald Woods, a fifth-generation English-speaking South African who was editor of the East London Daily Dispatch. Woods's crusade over the mystery surrounding Steve Biko's death probably led to his banning.[22] This type of banning makes a person ineffective and reduces him or her into a nonperson. Commenting on the imposition of the banning order on Donald Woods, Time's Johannesburg bureau chief reported:

> Such imposition may seem slight to outsid-
> ers, but each small commandment inflicts its
> own small cut--slowly removing the world
> from the man, slowly reducing the areas
> in which he is free to make even small de-
> cisions. Woods is already treated as
> though he suffers some undiagnosed illlness.
> Friends become nervous about how to ap-

proach him or what to say. People ask
how he is, with the concern they would
show for a patient who is in the hospital.
"Donald" is discussed in the third person,
sometimes even in the past tense. A
friend's affectionate newspaper piece about
him in the Rand Daily Mail read more like
an obituary than a feature.[23]

Other explicit restrictions under law and by min-
isterial and police actions hamper the freedoms to

Choose an area of residence
Not be classified and identified by race
Engage in personal and private conduct as a consenting
 adult
Engage in business or practice professions in areas of
 one's choice
Assemble or even visit with friends and other persons
Select candidates for Parliament and other legislative
 bodies
Travel throughout South Africa
Have a speedy trial upon detention
Enjoy the privacy of one's home without invasion by the
 police
Speak on public policy
Travel abroad
Contribute to charities of one's choice and assist the needy
Read publications
Attend churches of one's preference
Bargain collectively on the labor market
Assign employees to jobs and tasks
House employees on one's own property
Negotiate the sale or purchase of real estate
Select students for schools and universities

APARTHEID AND SLAVERY

South Africa is the world's most condemned nation
because of its legalized inhumane racism. This policy "is
a challenge to the same moral order as slavery in the
Eighteenth Century."[24] It is not only on moral grounds
that apartheid in South Africa is condemnable. There is
also a political aspect: Apartheid has been imposed on

Namibia, and it spread to Zimbabwe before its independence. Thus the situations in South Africa, Namibia, and Zimbabwe have had a common basis: In each case a powerful white minority sought to preserve its privileged position by denying human rights and freedom to the African majority. The apartheid regimes in southern Africa can be viewed as a single problem, because they support each other. South Africa, of course, has the dominant position.

The ingredients for violent conflict are present in southern Africa. Some extreme pattern of violence is likely to result from the continued repression of the nonwhite population by the South African government. Mounting internal strains and external pressures will doom whiteocracy and racial segregation in the near future. Every new repressive measure taken by the South African government, while postponing the explosion, also increases the political danger.

In the United Nations

South Africa was one of the founding members of the United Nations. The first article of the charter drawn up at the first session in San Francisco, by then South African Prime Minister Jan Smuts and others, gives as the purpose of the United Nations: "To achieve international cooperation . . . in promoting and encouraging respect for human rights and for fundamental freedoms for all without distinction as to race, sex, language, or religion."[25]

South Africa and its prime minister achieved fame at San Francisco when he proposed the original draft of the preamble of the charter.[26] But, ironically, South Africa is now the principal defendant in the United Nations; it is in that organization that the international community has been unequivocal in condemning apartheid and has called upon South Africa to amend its policies of racism. Many UN members have expressed concern that a very grim tragedy could befall southern Africa. As early as in its first year the United Nations was called upon to deal with the problem of the discriminatory treatment of persons of Indian origin in South Africa. Every year since 1947, India and Pakistan have introduced in the UN General Assembly motions of censure against South Africa's racial policies. But the years of greatest attention to the South African situation in the United Nations came immediately following the Defiance Campaign of 1952, the Sharpeville incident in 1960, and Soweto's call to arms in 1976.

In 1952, 13 UN members requested the inclusion of "the question of race conflict in South Africa resulting from the policies of apartheid of the Government of the Union of South Africa"[27] on the agenda of the General Assembly. The representatives of these nations justified their request for consideration of apartheid on the grounds that such a policy was creating a dangerous and explosive situation, which constitutes both a threat to international peace and a flagrant violation of the basic principles of human rights and fundamental freedoms enshrined in the charter of the United Nations.[28]

The General Assembly passed resolutions dealing with apartheid every year during the 1950s. The Sharpe-ville incident of 1960 raised the priority of apartheid as an issue and led to its first consideration by the Security Council, at the request of 29 Afro-Asian states. South Africa argued in effect that this was a domestic issue and it posed no threats to international peace.[29]

On November 6, 1962, the General Assembly adopted a resolution calling on member states to take the following steps: break off or refrain from establishing diplomatic relations with South Africa; close their ports to all vessels flying the South African flag; prohibit ships from entering South African ports; boycott all South African goods and refrain from exporting goods, including arms and ammunition, to South Africa; and refuse landing and passage facilities to South African aircraft. The General Assembly vote was 67 in favor, 16 against, and 23 abstentions. The United States, Britain, France, and Japan were among the countries that opposed the resolution.[30] The General Assembly action, while it was the strongest yet taken against South Africa, was only a recommendation and lacked the support of the major Western powers.

Next, the African states took the issue before the Security Council. The Security Council passed Resolution 181 on August 7, 1963. This resolution stated, among other things: "Being convinced that the situation in South Africa is seriously disturbing international peace and secu-rity . . . solemnly calls upon all states to cease forthwith the sale and shipment of arms, ammunition of all types, and military vehicles to South Africa."[31] There were no votes against the measure. Britain and France abstained. Additional resolutions adopted in 1953, 1964, and 1970 have reconfirmed the resolution of August 7, 1963. The 1976 Security Council Resolution 392 strongly condemned the South African government for its resort to a massive slaughter of the African people, including schoolchildren and students.

South Africa has attempted to prevent UN consideration of apartheid by claiming it to be a domestic matter. Both the General Assembly and the Security Council rejected such arguments. The "white redoubt," as southern Africa is frequently called, has been receiving in-depth attention in UN debates.

On October 31, 1977, the United States, Britain, and France teamed up in the UN Security Council and vetoed three African resolutions calling for stringent economic penalties on South Africa because of its repression of blacks.[32] This was the fourth time the three Western powers formed a bloc to veto UN resolutions, all on behalf of South Africa.[33] The first was in 1974 to prevent South Africa's expulsion; and in 1975, they twice vetoed a mandatory arms embargo against South Africa.[34]

But the mandatory arms embargo could not be blocked forever. Two years later, following South Africa's massive crackdown on dissenters, the banning of 18 civil rights groups, shutting down two major black newspapers, and arresting scores of antiapartheid leaders, the Security Council, on November 4, 1977, unanimously voted to impose a permanent mandatory embargo as a first step in bringing pressure on South Africa to eradicate racial discrimination—the first time that a mandatory sanction was imposed against any member nation.[35] In the past the voluntary arms embargo, although fairly well observed, was not respected by countries such as France. But the mandatory aspect of the resolution means that any member that violates it can be suspended or expelled from the United Nations.

However, in denouncing the resolution, South African Foreign Minister Roelof F. Botha said, "The Security Council resolution was based on the most transparently dishonest pretext and without a basis of fact."[36] He termed the action as an incitement to violence.

It is this violence that has increased international concern for the situation in South Africa. Much of the continuing conflict stems from the excessive use of force by South African authorities in maintaining their position.[37] Still the prospect of a political change in this situation appears unlikely despite the embargo, because South Africa is totally self-sufficient in small arms, which is all it needs to control guerrilla warfare and urban terrorism--its most likely challenge in the foreseeable future.[38]

In the long run, if the arms embargo is effective, it may force South Africa to make concessions to the black majority.

Many attempts at imposing an economic sanction against South Africa by the United Nations have not succeeded because of opposition from Western nations, including the United States.

At the Commonwealth

South Africa's racial policy has led to difficulties with the Commonwealth of Nations, the loose association of Britain and most of its former colonies. Of all foreign countries, Britain has had the longest and most complex relationship with South Africa. By the 1960s, the Commonwealth had admitted many Afro-Asian members. Simultaneously, South Africa became a republic. When India, Pakistan, and Ghana achieved the status of republics, their governments applied to remain in the Commonwealth. Thus, when South Africa made this change, it also applied formally on March 15, 1961, at the Commonwealth Prime Ministers' Conference to remain within the "club."

This untimely application to remain within the Commonwealth was made during a period of vocal criticism by Commonwealth leaders. British Prime Minister Harold Macmillan, in a speech to the South African Parliament, indicated that the old patterns of white rule in South Africa must change imminently and more enlightened racial policies must be developed.[39]

As one author observed, the South African withdrawal from the Commonwealth made Britain "freer to adopt a stronger anti-apartheid position in the United Nations, and is saved the embarrassment of trying to restrain other Commonwealth members who want to take drastic sanctions against South Africa."[40] Great pressure has come from the Afro-Asian countries. Following the Sharpeville incident in which 69 black people were killed and 178 injured during a peaceful protest at a police station, this pressure has steadily increased.

At the 1961 Commonwealth Prime Ministers' Conference apartheid became a major issue. South African Prime Minister Verwoerd defined his country's policies but the explanation proved unsatisfactory and the application appeared doomed. Thereupon South Africa withdrew from the Commonwealth and its membership was terminated. Thus the members of the Commonwealth chose racial equality over the retention of one of its original members.

In the Organization of African Unity

Since its founding in 1963, the Organization of African Unity (OAU) has dealt principally with the question of race. It was the African states' common abhorrence of racial discrimination and colonialism that gave birth to the OAU charter in Addis Ababa, Ethiopia. The OAU has inherited the ideas and ideals of Pan-Africanism, one of the most significant elements of which is opposition to racism.

The OAU charter affirms the values of freedom, equality, justice, and dignity, and lists as one of its purposes the promotion of the Universal Declaration of Human Rights.[41] The Addis Ababa conference unanimously agreed upon the need for urgent action and adopted a number of specific measures: create a fund to assist the antiapartheid movement; coordinate activities at the United Nations in this regard; coordinate sanctions against the South African government; appeal to states maintaining regular ties with South Africa to observe the UN sanctions; urge these states to break off all formal ties with South Africa; and attempt to effect the release of all African political prisoners in South Africa.[42]

The foundation of the OAU was established by the charter and two principal resolutions: the Resolution on Decolonization and the Resolution on Apartheid and Racial Discrimination. The two resolutions are largely complementary. This is because the minority regimes in southern Africa have always been viewed by independent African states as colonial. The OAU resolution is one of nonrecognition of the white regimes until majority rule is established.

In the Lusaka Manifesto of 1969 African leaders reemphasized their concern with racism in southern Africa.[43] This was the way that the African nations called attention to the issue of racism as a significant problem requiring international action. Throughout Africa apartheid has become a symbol of "a crime against humanity, a flagrant violation of the principle of the United Nations and a massive and ruthless denial of human rights constituting a threat to peace."[44]

Further, the OAU's policy on apartheid has been threefold: (1) the adoption of measures by the African states themselves; the severance of diplomatic relations with South Africa; the imposition of an economic blockade; the accommodation of refugees from South Africa; support for the liberation movements within South Africa; (2) diplomatic pressure on non-African states and on the United Nations, which has been repeatedly requested to impose economic sanctions on South Africa; and (3) a worldwide campaign to explain and disseminate the true nature and dehumanizing effects of apartheid.[45]

The central issue of apartheid appears to be of international concern, and the OAU regards the declining situation in southern Africa as a serious threat to peace and international security. Both the UN General Assembly and Security Council have endorsed the OAU's stand against South Africa.

Because apartheid violates a value that is formally recognized by all states except southern African white regimes, and because this pattern of rule threatens harmonious race relations around the world, the situation in southern Africa is of global concern. On occasions, the OAU has concluded that blame for the situation in southern Africa lies with the principal trading partners of South Africa--Britain, the United States, France, West Germany, and Japan. The OAU has condemned these unreservedly for their continued economic, political, and military collaboration with South Africa. France, West Germany, and Italy have been cited for selling military supplies to South Africa.

The OAU is willing to discuss Namibia with South Africa but not apartheid. This attitude of the OAU suggests that dialogue alone can effect change by influencing the thinking of South African rulers. However, preparations are being made to continue the armed struggle if peaceful means fail.

The weakness of the OAU is its inability to pose a military threat to South Africa. Also, the organization's effectiveness has been undermined by disagreement among its members as to how to proceed. This disunity is exemplified by the fact that while the OAU unanimously adopted a resolution in 1965 calling for all members to break relations with Britain, only nine of them actually did so. No wonder South Africa feels that it can afford to ignore OAU resolutions, as do many other nations that support the white regimes and carry on normal diplomatic and commercial activities with them. Many of the OAU members themselves scorn the organization's decisions. Such attitudes deter its effectiveness.

If the OAU is to accomplish its objectives in the future, cooperation among its members is required. Only a unified effort of the OAU can bring South Africa to submission. A united OAU in collaboration with the international community can achieve the desired results. The political and tribal differences that divide Africans underscore the difficulties of mobilizing their resentment into concerted action that could topple the white minority stronghold in the south. Usually, the white regimes in southern Africa exploit African disunity to retain their power. But day by day the claims of the southern African governments that blacks are happy with apartheid politics and economics are disappearing; the longer the violent conflict endures, the more African nations and the international community unite.

The OAU can be expected to maintain the diplomatic offensive and to increase its support for liberation movements operating in southern Africa. Some of the formerly moderate members are showing a sincere interest in intensifying the struggle. Nigeria, the oil-rich West African nation, for example, is willing to use oil as a weapon in the southern African crisis and finance states that border on the southern African subcontinent. Nigeria's increasing importance will enhance its capability to pressure the Western nations that support the white regime.

NOTES

1. Robin Mckown, Crisis in South Africa (New York: Putnam's, 1972), p. 52.

2. Ibid.

3. Ibid.

4. Quoted in Evelyn Rich and Immanuel Wallerstein, Africa: Tradition and Change (New York: Random House, 1972), p. 346.

5.   William J. Pomeroy, Apartheid Axis: The United States and South Africa (New York: International Publishers, 1973), p. 11.

6.   Ibid., p. 13.

7.   Ibid.

8.   Ibid., p. 14.

9.   Ibid.

10.   Ibid., p. 17.

11.   National Geographic, June 1977, pp. 780-819.

12.   New York Times, November 10, 1971.

13.   Pomeroy, Apartheid Axis, p. 17.

14.   Western Massachusetts Association of Concerned African Scholars, U.S. Military Involvement in Southern Africa (Boston: South End Press, 1978), p. 22.

15.   See Ibid., pp. 22-24, for other discrimination laws in South Africa.

16.   Benjamin Pogrund, "The Anatomy of White Power: Life Under Apartheid," Atlantic, October 1977, p. 53.

17.   Ibid., p. 60.

18.   Ibid.

19.   Quoted in Baldwin Sjollema, Isolating Apartheid (Geneva, Switzerland: World Council of Churches, 1982), p. 6.

20.   Michael Savage, "Cost of Enforcing Apartheid and Problems of Change," African Affairs 76 (July 1977):53.

21.   Ibid., p. 54.

22.   Time, November 7, 1977.

23.   Ibid.

24.   Donald W. Wyatt, ed., Progress in Africa and America (New Orleans, La.: Dillard University Press, 1972), p. 16.

25.   See section 3 of Article 1, Charter of the United Nations (New York: U.N. Office of Public Information, n.d.).

26.   Thomas Hovet, Jr., Africa in the United Nations (Evanston, Ill.: Northwestern University Press, 1963), p. 23.

27.   "The Defiance Campaign of 1952: Notes and Documents," United Nations, Unit on Apartheid, Department of Political and Security Council Affairs, January 1972, Annex 1, p. 3.

28.   Ibid., p. 4.

29.   United Nations Security Council, Official Records, Verbatim Records, 81 Meeting, March 30, 1960, New York, pp. 8-15.

30.   United Nations General Assembly, <u>Official Records</u>, <u>Verbatim Records</u>, 17 Session, Plenary Meeting, 11, pp. 679-80; Resolution No. 1761, Supplementary No. 17, November 6, 1962, p. 9.

31.   United Nations Security Council, <u>Official Records</u>, 1056 Meeting, Resolution S/5386, Notes and Documents; United Nations Unit on Apartheid, Department of Political and Security Council Affairs, No. 24/70, October 1970, p. 3.

32.   <u>Washington Post</u>, November 1, 1977.

33.   <u>New York Times</u>, November 1, 1977.

34.   Ibid., November 5, 1977.

35.   Ibid.

36.   Ibid.

37.   The following books have recorded the manner in which force is employed by South African authorities. Patrick Duncan, <u>South Africa's Rule of Violence</u> (London: Methuen, 1964); and Muriel Horrell, <u>A Survey of Race Relations</u>, annual ed., 1953-70 (Johannesburg: South African Institute of Race Relations).

38.   <u>Washington Post</u>, October 28, 1977.

39.   Nicholas Mansergh, ed., <u>Documents and Speeches on Commonwealth Affairs, 1952-62</u> (London: Dawsons of Pall Mall, 1968), pp. 347-51.

40.   Pierre L. Van Den Berghe, <u>South Africa: A Study in Conflict</u> (Berkeley: University of California Press, 1967), p. 249.

41.   Vincent B. Thompson, <u>Africa and Unity</u> (New York: Humanities Press, 1969), pp. 369-70.

42.   Ibid., pp. 366-67.

43.   See Moses E. Akpan, "African Goals and Strategies Toward Southern Africa," <u>African Studies Review</u> 14 (September 1971):243-61.

44.   See O. Stokke and C. Widstrand, eds., <u>Southern Africa: The UN-OAU Conference, Oslo, April 9-14, 1973</u>, Vols. 1 and 2 (Uppsala, Sweden: Scandinavian Institute of African Studies, 1973).

45.   Organization of African Unity, Council of Ministers Resolution, September 1967.

3
Repression and Resistance

Since the end of World War II, friction between the races has gradually increased. Life in Southern Africa has been marked by continuing demonstrations, violence, strikes, civil disobedience, terror, and guerrilla warfare between the governments and their nonwhite populations. The white minority controls southern Africa and permits the nonwhite majority no meaningful role in affairs of state.

The period after World War II, especially since the election in South Africa of the National party in 1948, has seen confrontation between the government and the nonwhite population in the form of repression and resistance. The repressive policy of the governments in southern Africa has included such cruelty as the beating to death of prisoners and the deprivation of property and personal liberty and even integrity of character--a policy that seeks to prevent dissent on racial grounds.

Resistance among nonwhites lacks unity in structure and strategy. The African National Congress (ANC) and the Pan-African Congress (PAC), the two oldest black nationalist organizations, were banned in the early 1960s.[1] Based abroad, both remain active and committed to the overthrow of the white southern African governments by force. These and other organizations fighting for the liberation of southern Africa have been operating underground.[2]

The repression and resistance in South Africa show that the long-oppressed and exploited black Africans have risen against apartheid. Opposition has taken various forms, beginning with a demand for a national convention representative of all the people of South Africa.

Government repression was exposed to the world on March 2, 1960, when, at Sharpeville, the police fired on unarmed and peaceful demonstrators protesting the pass laws, killing 69 and wounding 178, women and children included.[3] The Africans reacted with more demonstrations, and a state of emergency was declared by the white government. This was the beginning of the end of peaceful opposition in South Africa.

Neither the ANC nor the PAC was originally behind the Soweto unrest that began on June 16, 1976, over the use of Afrikaans, the official language. Today, many of the important leaders of the overt opposition to apartheid are serving life sentences on Robben Island; others have been killed in jail. One was Steve Biko, a well-known South African black leader. An official state autopsy found that Biko died of brain damage caused by beating.[4] The South African government paid $78,000 to his family in an out-of-court settlement.[5] This settlement was made when it became clear that under South African law the government could have suppressed presentation of the evidence by admitting responsibility, then bargaining with the family over compensation. Still others are rendered politically ineffective by ban, arrest, or exile. Some leaders have fled the country. South Africa's leading white liberal journalist, Donald Woods, who was silenced and banned by authorities, escaped South Africa in disguise and went to London with his wife and children.[6] Increasing numbers of young South African whites, liable for military conscription, are leaving home to avoid the draft.

Educational institutions have become increasingly autocratic, reflecting the need of the repressive state to tighten its grip on black people and produce more obedient students. Independent thought, objective analysis, and freedom of expression are severely curtailed and virtually unlawful. Criticism of the low level of Bantu education and the political system is forbidden. Today's students are resentful of the harsh and desperate authority and social and cultural deprivation.

Today, the conflict in southern Africa is fraught with the conviction by white governments and the nonwhite peoples that their differences can be resolved only by force. The governments have stressed repeatedly that they are not willing to compromise on apartheid. The nonwhites have no alternative but to fight for their basic human rights to achieve freedom and dignity.

Following the establishment of the Organization of African Unity, the activities of the ANC and PAC came under the supervision of the National Liberation Committee of the OAU in Dar es Salaam. The liberation movements of southern Africa include such leading organizations as the Zimbabwe African People's Union (ZAPU), the Zimbabwe African National Union (ZANU), and the South-West African People's Organization (SWAPO). In the first combined guerrilla action in 1967 in Zimbabwe the ANC and ZAPU sustained heavy losses. The Rhodesian army was supported by a contingent of South African police and equipment.[7]

The government of South Africa has been responding to the guerrilla threat by increasing the military forces and expanding the police state apparatus. At its disposal is the most up-to-date equipment. The Terrorism Act of South Africa allows the government to detain without trial and to torture. Rhodesia's similar problems led it to develop closer relations with South Africa and to adopt similar tactics to thwart any opposition to the regime.

In South Africa, one sees an unprecedented spirit of rebellion and restlessness among the oppressed African population. The student rebellion has spread from Soweto to other centers of population. Begun on June 16, 1976, it is continuing in different forms and in various locations. Demands raised in the rebellions show that no changes short of the overthrow of the apartheid regime can make up for the decades of suffering and hardship.

In Namibia, the people have rejected the occupationist South African scheme for a Bantustan type of independence. SWAPO, the leading liberation front in Namibia, harbors no hope of a democratic solution through the United Nations or any other international organization and is prepared for an inevitable armed struggle. For SWAPO, the complex situation has a simple solution: the consolidation of the armed struggle and a united front of the masses. In general, the prospect looms of such struggle and favors the Namibian people against South African occupation.

The leadership of the liberation movements in southern Africa remains nonrevolutionary, despite rhetoric to the contrary. The ANC retains the greatest following in South Africa. SWAPO still enjoys the confidence of the majority in Namibia. The major problem of these organizations is that they are slow in channeling their support to armed struggle.

CRISIS OF LEGITIMACY

The death of Steve Biko, who died a hero's death in September 1977, probably laid the foundation for the end of white rule in South Africa. The world community has imposed a mandatory arms embargo and a partial economic sanction against the apartheid regime, weakening the white position more than ever before. Futurists wonder whether it will drive the whites back into the laager (armed camp), taking an inflexible position of defiance. In fact, the government and the white population face the current situation with deeper concern than ever before. South Africa runs counter to the universal renunciation of racist principles. Southern Africa is in danger of coercion, both internally and externally. The New York Times, editorializing under the heading "Courting Disaster in South Africa," said:

> The South African Government seems deter-
> mined to create precisely those conditions
> that will transform its largely moderate
> black opposition into an extremist and vio-
> lent force. . . . For a while now, the
> regime will not have to confront the persis-
> tent, well formulated and articulate black
> demands. In time, however, if it holds to
> its present course, the Government will
> have to cope with worse, with violent rheto-
> ric and violent deeds. And it will need
> even more violent methods to prolong the
> suppression.[8]

The white oligarchy in southern Africa has had trouble since their usurpation of power. Upon establishing their authority on a foundation of white hegemony, they were confronted with the test of legitimacy to make their rule acceptable to the local people. The problem of how to make the white domination acceptable to the blacks involved two elements: steering the black people toward democracy--a government of, by, and for the people--and their administrative and physical control--the police function performed by the state.

To control both, the white rulers have had to look outside, to their homelands and other countries in Europe, for artificial social control for the great majority of the people. The imported solutions to the southern African problem have consisted mainly of such "laws" as apartheid. Stephen S. Rosenfeld, an editor of the Washington Post, wrote: "In essence South Africa is like Russia, or becoming so. The unmistakable scent of police is in the air. There is the same emotionally draining quality to one's personal encounters, the same conspiracy of privilege and tradition against conscience and change, the same unequal struggle by good people against a hard state authority."9

The country is ruled by whites, a numerical minority consumed by fear of the effects of radical change. These rulers hold the franchise as their exclusive preserve. The "subject" communities, having suffered continuously under the existing system, are excluded from the government and its agencies. The exclusion of blacks from all aspects of power, even nominal, is complete. They are, therefore, vengeful.

While maintaining "legitimacy," the rulers seek to cull the allegiance of the vast majority of the population. The white overlordship has had to devise for the blacks a special kind of institutional fiat, which it hopes serves the interests and aspirations of the black population. A great variety of devices has been used to subdue the blacks. Among the earliest was the system of indirect rule through chiefs, a British strategy employed in empire building during the colonial days.10 The white overlordship in South Africa has supplemented this strategy with such ploys as Bunga Councils, advisory boards, Native Representative Councils, and, most recently, the Bantu Authorities, which are projected as being the independent Bantustans.11 In 1984 the South African government enacted a new constitution extending political rights to the Coloureds and Asians, while denying such rights to the black majority who do not live in the set-aside tribal Bantustans.12

This sort of disguised rule by the whites has yielded doubtful results. The history of southern Africa reveals an unabating restlessness. Time and again the blacks have rebelled against the indirect rule and their appointed chiefs' attempts to implement tax collection, forced labor recruitment, stock culling, mass removals, and so on. Well known are those in Sekhukhuneland, Zeerust, Pondoland, and Northern Natal in the 1950s and 1960s. The numerous boycotts and mine workers' strikes in Durban and Johannesburg in 1972 and 1973 and the Sharpeville

and Soweto rebellions are examples not only of a growing
anger among the people but also of a determined opposition
to racial prejudice and domination.

It is against this background of turbulence that the
government's elaborate repressive measures become clear.
The massive use of force by the minority government is, in
itself, the most direct proof that efforts to secure order
peacefully have failed and that white rule is in jeopardy.

The white rulers cannot exert direct influence on the
population. Makeshift arrangements for disguising the co-
ercive nature of the state have eroded rapidly, one after
the other, and the state power has been forced to show itself as a hostile force. In this regard the segregationist
regimes in southern Africa fall short of the legitimization
process that, in a democracy, holds the majority population in a consensus of common norms, guaranteeing the
supremacy of the ruling elites. In the absence of this
kind of popular democratic base, white dominancy depends
on a small minority base.

Another impediment to the development of an effective
mechanism for legitimization of power is the system of
superexploitation itself. Evidence of this superexploitation
is the denial of wages, high rates of malnutrition and in-
fant mortality, labor regimentation, and all forms of human
degradation, including apartheid. Further, almost every
issue of an economic or political nature that the Africans
take up from time to time with the white oligarchy invariably leads to direct confrontation with the government.
Every issue inexorably tends to bring into focus the central issue of power. The factor restraining the development of a false consensus to white dominancy has been the
growth of sociopolitical and economic consciousness among
the blacks and the development of black nationalism.

BLACK CONSCIOUSNESS

The reactions of the black people to the growth of
settler colonialism in southern Africa have included the
development of a positive black consciousness movement.
Following their conquest by Europeans the blacks have objected to white rule with and without violence.

It was through the African religious movements that
the blacks began to register their opposition to white
rule.[13] At the turn of the twentieth century, black oppo-

sition to white domination began to manifest itself in the
political realm.   Black influence in politics was the greatest in the Cape because of the qualified franchise then
held there.   Throughout southern Africa, blacks looked to
the Cape model as worth emulating.   In the Cape, blacks
could vote with whites.   A similar policy was adopted in
Natal province, but the authorities' failure to implement it
resulted in a condition for the blacks similar to that in
the Orange Free State and Transvaal, where they had no
rights to vote.   At the end of the Boer War in 1900, self-
government was returned, but it failed to bring any relief
for blacks outside the Cape.   From this time onward black
political consciousness grew significantly.

African National Congress

The establishment of the Union of South Africa and
the formulation of a native affairs policy provided further
stimulus to a closer union of Africans.   The Native National Congress was formed, which became the African National Congress of South Africa.   Many of the founders
were men of high caliber who had studied in England and
the United States.   Some were lawyers.[14]
The ANC was the first national African movement in
which a serious effort was made to eliminate tribal divisions.   Initially, the ANC moved cautiously toward limited
objectives.   However, with the founding of the Youth League,
new leadership developed that pressed for sweeping change
and the use of more militant tactics.   The major function
of the ANC was to unify the blacks.   The political leadership and the white elite structure did not attempt to extend
the Cape native policies into the northern areas of the
country.   Instead of liberalization in the former Boer republics, their past policies were continued by the British
government.   It was an opportune time to direct the collective efforts of the blacks toward reorganization of native
policy.
The objective was set forth by P. K. I. Seme (his
efforts were responsible for the formation of the ANC) in
the call for a conference: "The demon of racialism, the
aberrations of Xhosa-Fingo feuds, the animosity that exists
between Zulus and Tongas, between the Basuta and every
other native, must be buried and forgotten. . . .   We are
one people.   These divisions, these jealousies, are the

cause of all our woes and of all our backwardness and ignorance today."[15]   The conference was intended to discuss the problems of the black people and submission of African opinion and grievances to the government.   In his keynote address, Seme told the gathering about the objectives:

> We have gathered . . . to discuss a theme
> which my colleagues and I have decided
> to place before you.   We have discovered
> that in their land, Africans are treated as
> hewers of wood and drawers of water.   The
> white people of this country have formed
> what is known as the Union of South
> Africa--a union in which we have no voice
> in the making of laws and no part in their
> administration.   We have called you to this
> Conference so that we can together devise
> ways and means of forming our national
> union for the purpose of creating unity
> and defending our rights and privileges.[16]

Although the ANC was the first black national organization worthy of its name, its weak structure limited its potential as an effective body, and consequently, the leaders held little influence over the operation of the organization.   Despite its formal constitution, the ANC was loose and ill-defined.   Very little control was exercised over the local bodies--some had adopted a militant policy, while others followed a moderate policy.   As a result, the organization failed to operate as a potential agent of change in South Africa.[17]

While the leadership of the ANC consisted mostly of urban, educated blacks, some tribal chiefs also participated.   Government pressure, however, forced them to withdraw.[18]   The ANC was unable to attract membership in the rural and tribal areas during its early years.   While only a small fraction of the people joined, "the statements of its leaders had become a conditioning factor in the thinking of many thousands of Africans who never took out membership. . . ."[19]

The South African government's arrogance prompted the ANC to seek external support, sending two delegations abroad to secure British intervention in South Africa so as to reverse the policies of discrimination followed by the

government. The first deputation to London submitted
petitions to King George, the Parliament, and the colonial
secretary. In each of these petitions the ANC delegation
stated the problems of racial discrimination and its effects on the black population. They emphasized their
concern for the future if the Land Act was to be implemented.[20] No positive response was received, just sympathy.

When the South African government failed to indicate
any interest in improving race relations, the ANC officials
decided to visit London again for British support; however,
nothing was done to remove the color barrier from South
African society. The delegation made some valuable contacts with private British organizations, such as the Anti-
Slavery and Aborigines Protection Society, Brotherhood
Societies, and various church groups. The public in general received the delegations well, and the British press
gave good coverage, intended to arouse public support and
sympathy for the plight of black South Africans. One
member of the delegation, Sol Plaatje, remained in England
for some time and, before returning to South Africa, visited the United States, where he made contact with the
National Association for the Advancement of Colored People
(NAACP).[21] He also visited Canada.

The appearance of the delegations before private
groups did provide some basis for linkage with international politics. On an individual basis also, some members
of the ANC had attended international gatherings to seek
support for black causes. One such member, Josiah Gumede,
attended a conference sponsored by the League of Nations
against imperialism in Belgium. From this meeting Gumede
went to Moscow to establish contact for the first time with
the Soviet Union. Gumede, who became president-general
of the ANC in 1927, was impressed by the Soviet concern
for equal rights regardless of race.[22]

The period immediately before, during, and after
World War II was transitional in many respects. During
this time the ANC structure was revised and its membership
base was broadened, making it a stronger organization.
A new constitution, adopted in 1943, and the establishment
of the Youth League in 1944 were reflections of the new
vitality of the ANC. While the constitution provided for
greater centralization, the Youth League brought young
blood into the organization.

The younger members were in significant contrast to the conservative middle-class Africans who had dominated the ANC from the beginning. Their pressure for the adoption of more radical methods of operation intensified after World War II. The Youth League rejected moderation and compromise and advocated the broader mass scheme reflected in the Program of Action.[23] The establishment of the United Nations and the development of nationalism throughout the Afro-Asian world gave rise to some ambitious demands. Such demands as one man one vote, equal justice, freedom of land ownership, and the repeal of the pass laws were promulgated.

After failing in an attempt to obtain control of the ANC, the more radical group seceded in 1959 and founded the Pan-African Congress.[24] The ANC planned a vigorous campaign against the pass laws. But PAC forestalled the ANC and launched a campaign against the pass laws on March 21, 1960: "On that day large numbers of Africans presented themselves at police stations in different parts of the country without passes, inviting arrest, in the hope of clogging the machinery of justice and causing a labor dislocation."[25]

Sharpeville Massacre

At Sharpeville, police resorted to shooting at the crowd, killing and wounding many people. Both the ANC and PAC called for a day of mourning. Work was stopped in many major cities and an impressive demonstration took place in Cape Town. The government reacted by declaring a state of emergency. It mobilized the armed forces and banned the ANC and PAC. The government arrested 98 whites, 36 Coloureds, 90 Asians, and 11,279 blacks, jailing another 6,800 blacks for violating pass laws and other ordinances.[26] With these measures and by physically assaulting hundreds of black people, the government forced their return to work and crushed the demonstration.

Following this massacre, three underground revolutionary movements emerged in South Africa: the Spear of the Nation, an offshoot of the ANC; Poqo, an offshoot of PAC; and the African Resistance Movement (ARM). The Spear of the Nation worked to disrupt communications, power lines, and government offices, hoping public order would gradually collapse. Poqo planned the mass killing

of white people.   ARM began to commit acts of violence.
The government responded by outlawing all of these organizations and by enacting more repressive legislation and
instituting mass arrests.[27]

In December 1960 black leaders of all political groups
in South Africa convened. Their purpose was to develop
ways and means for the black people to present their interests to the South African polity. One of their principal
acts was the creation of a Continuation Committee composed
of representatives of each of these groups. They were
united on the following points: the removal of apartheid,
the immediate establishment of a nonracial democracy, and
the effective use of nonviolent pressures against apartheid.

In 1961 the Spear of the Nation, or "Umkhonto we
Sizwe," was established to develop a new strategy ranging
from a renewed effort at nonviolent resistance to revolution.
The leader of Umkhonto we Sizwe, Nelson Mandela, said:

> Firstly, we believed that as a result of
> government policy, violence by the African
> people had become inevitable and that un-
> less responsible leadership was given to
> canalize and control the feelings of our
> people, there would be outbreaks of terror-
> ism which would produce an intensity of
> bitterness and hostility . . . which is not
> even produced by war. Secondly, we felt
> that without violence there would be no
> way open to the African people to succeed
> in their struggle against the principle of
> white supremacy.[28]

Sabotage, widely reported in South Africa between
1961 and 1966, was attributed to or publicly claimed by
Umkhonto. In addition Umkhonto adopted guerrilla warfare
and terrorism tactics, employing the accumulated experiences gathered over years in its struggle against oppres-
sion.

Political awareness among blacks in southern Africa
has also been facilitated by developments on the world
scene. In recent times oppressed peoples in different
parts of the world have risen in victory against colonial
powers. These victories, of course, served to inspire with
a new sense of understanding and brotherhood in the
struggle against injustice and racial hatred.

In December 1968, a group of black South African students met at Marianhill in South Africa to discuss the formation of an all-black student organization.   Although the response of the participants was cautious, Steve Biko persuaded them to form the South African Students Organization (SASO), which was established in July 1969.   With Biko as its first president, SASO developed a program that, more than any other single effort, has encouraged the spirit of resistance among South Africans today.   The manifesto of SASO defines the concept of black consciousness:

> Black consciousness is an attitude of mind, a way of life.   The basic tenet of black consciousness is that the black man must reject all value systems that seek to make him a foreigner in the country of his birth and reduce his basic human dignity.
>
> The black man must build up his own value systems, see himself as self-defined and not defined by others.
>
> The concept of black consciousness implies the awareness by the black people of the power they wield as a group, both economically and politically, and hence group cohesion and solidarity are important facets of black consciousness.
>
> Black consciousness will always be enhanced by the totality of involvement of the oppressed people; hence the message of black consciousness has to be spread to reach all sections of the black community.

From the beginning, SASO was fearless in a way no political group in South Africa had been since the ANC and PAC were banned in 1960.   The response of the white government has been a strong new level of repression, by most accounts unparalleled in South Africa.   The ranks of every dissident organization have been thinned by the banning and detention of people of all races.   The resilience of black people, particularly in the face of such harassment, has been remarkable.

Biko's Murder

A total of 45 political detainees, held without trial, have died in South African police custody. Four hundred people are serving sentences for political offenses, and a thousand others have been arrested. The most notable killing, that of Steve Biko, the president of SASO and the leader of the Black Consciousness Movement, has been described earlier. Postmortem tests showed that Biko died of massive brain injuries while in a South African jail.[29] Commenting on Biko's murder, the Washington Post reported:

> Biko, 30, considered a creative leader by
> blacks in all of South Africa's tribes, was
> seen as a man of moderation who might
> have been able to bridge the growing gap
> between black and white. His death under
> disputed circumstances appears to be un-
> leashing anger and bitterness among blacks,
> many of whom hold that the government is
> responsible for the death of a political
> moderate.[30]

By killing the leader of the Black Consciousness Movement, perhaps the white rulers of South Africa were attempting to obscure the right of the majority there. But, in the meantime, black militancy grew in protest to the mysterious slaying of Biko. The South African government launched a massive crackdown on dissent against its racial policies. Eighteen civil rights groups were banned, including the most powerful black organizations, the Black Peoples Convention and the Soweto Students Representative Council. The government also shut down major black newspapers and arrested Percy Qobozo, editor of the World, and scores of black and white antiapartheid leaders.[31]

The primary objective of the black people is not independence in southern Africa but majority rule, a difference often misunderstood by outsiders. However, the struggle between blacks and the white governments of southern Africa has become prominent internationally. Central to this conflict has been the element of force; the element of violence has been the second most important consideration in the internationalization of the problem in southern Africa.

Violence and New Constitution

Violence in South Africa has been at a high level since the inauguration of the new constitution in 1984, which, as noted in Chapter 1, is flawed because it grants only limited political rights to the country's Coloured and Asian populations and none to the black majority. Adding to black unrest have been school boycotts by students protesting inferior education; a nationwide recession, with skyrocketing black unemployment and spiraling inflation; increased rents for black housings; and killings, bannings, police brutality, and the detention of black leaders, some of whom have been charged with treason.

The rigid system of labor control requires all blacks to carry "passports" that dictate where the African can legally live and work. They must be kept up to date with regular endorsements and are subject to scrutiny on demand. More than 200,000 people are arrested under this law every year. South Africa has the highest prison population in the world with 440 jailed for every 100,000 of the population. The equivalent figure in the United States is 189. Forty percent of the South African prison population consists of pass law violations, thus committing "crimes" that only blacks can commit.[32]

In July 1985, the South African government declared a state of emergency in 36 magisterial districts to stem the tide of violence. Under South African law a person can be detained without a charge and held incommunicado indefinitely. Detention is used to silence opponents of apartheid who have broken no law, and many disappear without any public report.

More than 1,700 people, most of them black, have been killed since a new wave of violence began in September 1984 in an effort to end apartheid. Law enforcement officers, who already enjoyed ample authority to search, seize, and arrest, were granted even more extensive powers under the emergency regulations. More than 8,000 people, 2,000 of them under the age of 16, were arrested under the emergency provisions.[33]

South Africa imposed a nationwide emergency on June 12, 1986, and rounded up about 1,200 people in an attempt to quell black rioting. The emergency was proclaimed just before the tenth anniversary (June 16) of bloody protests in the huge black township of Soweto, outside Johannesburg. The intensive policing frustrated plans for a massive cam-

paign of violence. Yet the subdued protests brought to 42
the number of people killed during the first few days of
the emergency. During this time, Archbishop Tutu, who
met with President Botha, for the first time in six years,
said: "This is not likely to help restore law and order."
The message has proved quite prophetic; violence continues
unabated.

Repression and resistance in South Africa is an every-
day fact of life for the vast majority of the population.
People are constantly arrested for crimes for which only
black people can be blamed. Violence will continue until
apartheid is destroyed. It is not a system that can be
modified or reformed into acceptability because it is fundamentally and by definition racist. The only way to right
the wrong in South Africa is to do away with apartheid.

The white ruling elites cannot offer more than pseudo
rights to the blacks in southern Africa without undoing the
whole structure of white privilege, which they are not
willing to do now. South Africa is not willing to include
all its population in the benefits of civilized law. South
Africa's economy and polity are based on a near-slave
condition artificially created to suppress the black people.
Southern Africans are laboring under a misapprehension
that the growth of black consciousness will help them to
gain their fundamental human rights, such as racial
equality. Without armed struggle or civil war, however,
such equality can hardly be achieved under the present
conditions of segregation. The cost of fighting is considerable, in fact, prohibitive. But there is no alternative.

The legitimacy of armed struggle in South Africa cannot be challenged on moral grounds. The long consistent
and persistent determination of the black African people of
South Africa and Namibia to establish their rule has
evoked enough world sympathy. It is time to launch the
last battle and the sooner the better for the world and
the people of southern Africa.

NOTES

1. In preindependence Zimbabwe, the African National Congress was the only legal nationalist movement.
2. For a discussion on the history of the ANC, see
Mary Benson, The African Patriots (New York: Encyclopaedia Britannica Press, 1963).

3. Leslie Rubin and Brian Weinstein, Introduction to African Politics: A Continental Approach (New York: Praeger, 1974), p. 123.

4. Washington Post, October 26, 1977.

5. Durham (N.C.) Morning Herald, July 29, 1979.

6. Washington Post, January 7, 1978.

7. Rubin and Weinstein, Introduction to African Politics, p. 124.

8. New York Times, October 20, 1977.

9. Washington Post, October 21, 1977.

10. The South Africa Act of 1909 was a British statute that created the Union of South Africa out of the four self-governing colonies--the Cape, the Orange Free State, the Transvaal, and Natal. It provided the constitutional framework of the Republic of South Africa.

11. The Representation of Natives Act No. 12 of 1936 introduced a scheme of separate representation for the blacks. This act was abolished in 1959. The Bantu Authorities Act of 1951 discarded the white representation of blacks in a white parliament and in turn introduced the "self-rule" for blacks in the Bantustans.

12. New York Times, October 20, 1977.

13. See James W. Fernandez, "African Religious Movements: Types and Dynamics," Journal of African Studies 2 (December 1964):534.

14. Peter Walshe, The Rise of African Nationalism in South Africa (Berkeley: University of California Press, 1971), pp. 31-34.

15. African National Congress: A Short History (London: Publicity and Information Bureau, ANC, 1971), p. 9.

16. Walshe, Rise of African Nationalism, p. 34.

17. Edward Roux, Time Longer Than Rope, rev. ed. (Madison: University of Wisconsin Press, 1966), p. 112.

18. Walshe, Rise of African Nationalism, p. 244.

19. Ibid., p. 240.

20. The Land Act provided that the African rights to own land outside the reserve areas would be abolished.

21. Mary Benson, South Africa: The Struggle for a Birthright (New York: Funk and Wagnalls, 1969), p. 24.

22. Ibid., p. 62.

23. Nelson Mandela, No Easy Walk to Freedom (New York: Basic Books, 1965), pp. 18-20.

24. On the origin of the Pan-African Congress, see Benson, South Africa, chapters 21-22.

25.   Leonard M. Thompson, Politics in the Republic
of South Africa (Boston: Little, Brown, 1966), p. 179.
    26.   Ibid., p. 180.
    27.   Ibid., p. 182.
    28.   Mandela, No Easy Walk, p. 164.
    29.   Washington Post, September 26, 1977.
    30.   Ibid.
    31.   Ibid., October 20, 1977.
    32.   Sunday Times (Johannesburg), April 12, 1981.
    33.   Time, March 17, 1986.

4
Militarism and Nuclearism

The fundamental principle of South African military policy was formulated in the 1977 government White Paper on defense. It said: "The principle of the right of the white nation to self-determination is not subject to discussion."[1] Thus any discussion of South Africa's military posture must start from the special situation created by apartheid, not only in South Africa itself but in the region as a whole.

MILITARISM

South Africa is the continent's strongest country militarily and economically. The traditional concept of national security interests, threat perceptions, and defense may apply only to a limited extent where the military policy of that country is mainly concerned with maintaining a system of minority rule. The greatest threat to peace in southern Africa is its racial policies that deny human rights to the majority and the minority governments' use of strong repressive means to safeguard their interests.

The defense policy of South Africa is to uphold apartheid by military means. A shift in the military strategy occurred in the 1970s, when the outward policy of promoting cooperaton among conservative African states in the 1970s gave way to a posture of "Fortress Southern Africa."[2]

South Africa is the cornerstone of white supremacy in the southern African subcontinent. To maintain this position South Africa has built itself, with the help of Western nations, into military superiority in the region. Defense spending is 18 percent of the national budget, about $3 billion a year.[3] In the 1984–85 budget, $2.95 billion was allocated for defense. White children begin military training at the age of 12. South Africa has 86,000 men on active duty, with about 260,000 serving in the active reserves. An estimated 300,000 white schoolboys and -girls are in cadet training.[4] Measures have been taken recently to increase the recruitment and utilization of white women and extend the service duration from 12 to 24 months.

In matters of arms supply and manufacture, South Africa procures between $200 million and $300 million worth of armaments a year. It is completely self-sufficient in the manufacture of small arms and even exports small arms. Many sophisticated arms in the South African arsenal—jets, armored cars, and missiles—are produced with French, Italian, and British help.[5]

The production of armaments has accelerated since 1968 by the creation of the Armament Development and Production Corporation, or Armscor. It was established with an initial capital of $150 million. The most important South African firm in the manufacture of arms and ammunition, African Explosives and Chemical Industries, is a huge corporation with 14 subsidiaries in which some British and American companies hold stock.[6] Since the United Nations imposed its arms embargo of 1977, Armscor engages 1,200 private contractors to satisfy the country's military needs. Although South Africa's military machine is by far the strongest in Africa, a rising tide of nationalism and unrest could cause the country to lose the war while winning every battle. White southern African survival may ultimately depend less on guns than on goodwill.

The defense force is segregated, composed of whites, except for laborers and the Coloured Corps. The Coloured Corps was established in 1963 for light duty, such as drivers, storemen, clerks, and stretcher-bearers. In 1965 the South African Navy accepted Coloured recruits on a permanent basis. Recently, South Africa has formed armed African and Eur-African troops to augment its white forces. These troops are supervised by white officers and deployed with regular white units in attendance.[7] Without fanfare, the navy has become the most integrated branch of the armed forces, with Coloureds and Indians accounting for 30 percent of its manpower. Nonwhite officers often are in charge of white sailors.

In addition to the permanent force--army, navy, and air force--South Africa has an army combat group, formed in 1966 on orders of the Supreme Command. Its strength is a security secret but it comprises some of the best trained troops, equipped with the most modern weapons available, and assured of full and adequate air support in any emergency. The unit is readily available.

The Citizen Force was originally composed of volunteers and citizens drawn by ballot. In 1967 the ballot system was abolished and compulsory military training was introduced for all fit male citizens from the age of 17. Those in the standing force, police, and prison department were exempted. Training takes place in nine periods--12 months during the first period, 26 days during each of three periods, and 12 days during each of five periods. An estimated 130,000 men are enlisted in the Citizen Force.

South Africa has a large police force. Mobile police units, specially trained in guerrilla warfare, guard strategic parts of South Africa. The police force is fully capable of maintaining internal security and of coordinating with the defense forces in matters of external security.

The UN Security Council, on November 4, 1977, imposed a permanent mandatory arms embargo on South Africa. By unanimous vote, the 15-member council approved a resolution that, for the first time in the history of the United Nations, applied stiff punitive sanctions against one of its members.[8] But the arms ban came too late to hurt South Africa. In the words of the Washington Post: "The Western arms embargo on South Africa now in the making has come far too late to have any significant effect on that country's ability to wage conventional or guerrilla war against other African countries or its own black population in the foreseeable future."[9]

By all available indications it appears that the arms embargo has not adversely affected South Africa's military superiority in the region, because "on their part, the South Africans have been building up inventories, arranging hidden arms purchase channels and strengthening their own manufacturing capabilities."[10] However, as the New York Times said: "It will be measures like these (end to Export-Import Bank credits and discouragement of American investments), more than the arms embargo, that may begin to affect thinking among white South Africans."[11]

Furthermore, in addition to aircraft and support equipment sold to South Africa through various loopholes

in the embargo, arms have been bootlegged to South Africa.
Such illegal transactions have involved the delivery of U.S.
weapons to countries not covered by the embargo, from
where they are rerouted to South Africa.   Such smuggling
of arms to South Africa from Europe and America continues.
U.S. undercover agents arrested two British subjects and
four Austrian airline crewmen on May 13, 1981, on charges
of violating the Neutrality Act and the embargo regulations.
The agents seized the million-dollar cargo as it was being
loaded on a Boeing 707 bound for South Africa at a pri-
vately owned terminal at Houston International Airport.[12]

NUCLEARISM

As early as 1949 the South African Atomic Energy
Board (AEB) was established, and the first uranium plant
was opened in 1952.   South Africa is the world's third
largest supplier of uranium.   By 1965, South Africa was
emphasizing the following objectives of policy: the development and exploitation of the country's uranium resources;
research into the use of atomic energy as a cheap method
of producing electricity; and production of radioactive iso-
topes and the development of new uses for them.
In July 1957, South Africa and the United States
reached a ten-year agreement on the peaceful uses of
atomic energy.   The agreement resulted in the U.S. Atomic
Energy Commission's making available for South African
purchase up to 500 kilograms of 20 percent enriched uranium
for use in a materials-testing reactor and research quanti-
ties of U-233, U-235, and plutonium.   In September 1960,
agreement was reached on three NASA (National Aeronautic
and Space Administration) facilities in South Africa.
In 1967, the West German government began training
South African nuclear scientists and nuclear technicians in
Bonn.   The Soviet Union and East Germany have charged
that a secret treaty exists between South Africa and West
Germany to produce nuclear weapons.[13]   This may serve a
dual purpose: South Africa is developing nuclear weapons
and will use them when necessary; and as Germany could
not develop its own nuclear weapons at home because of
restrictions imposed by the World War II victors, it may
under mutual understanding transfer nuclear weapons from
South Africa and use them for its own purposes or at least
have them ready for the future, if needed.

The South African AEB has asserted that it has the resources to make atomic bombs.[14]   In addition, in 1970, Prime Minister Vorster announced that South Africa had developed a new uranium enrichment process and was setting up a plant to produce nuclear fuel.   This plant is the sixth of its kind in the world, after those in the United States, the Soviet Union, Britain, France, and the Netherlands.

South Africa's potential as a nuclear power is the result of its connections, secret and open, with the four major Western powers--West Germany, the United States, Britain, and France.   These four powers have been helping South Africa variously in methods of producing concentrated uranium weaponry.   In 1975 the South African government issued its own version of its atomic advances in a 32-page advertising section in Business Week, entitled "Dynamic South Africa":

> South Africa has invented its own nozzle enrichment process which will be used at a $1 billion plant due for completion in the Eighties.   It will produce 2400 tons of uranium oxide at a cost expected to be 30% less than the gaseous diffusion and centrifugal separation processes.   The venture is aimed at creating a capacity to market South Africa's huge uranium reserves in refined forms as well as making a meaningful contribution to worldwide scientific and technological development.[15]

This claim, coupled with South Africa's arrogance in signing the nuclear Non-Proliferation Treaty (NPT), suggests that the Pretoria administration is intent on retaining its option to go nuclear.

On August 8, 1977, the Soviet Union said that South Africa was on the verge of creating a nuclear bomb and called for urgent international efforts to block such a development.[16]   However, South Africa categorically denied this report and emphasized that its uranium enrichment program and other developments are only for peaceful purposes.   Admittedly, that is what other nations claimed before they embarked on their programs of nuclearization.

In 1977, a U.S. reconnaissance satellite spotted something unusual in the Kalahari Desert.   The photointerpreters, however, could not be sure. Commentators Rowland Evans and Robert Novak, in their column in the Washington Post on South Africa's nuclear bomb, said that "the South Africans are either near or at the point of building a bomb."[17]

South Africa is confronted by growing international condemnation of its policy of apartheid and the prospect of eventual total isolation from a world committed to equality. It is against this background that South Africa's activities and growing capabilities in the nuclear field are of particular concern. South Africa's past assurances of interest in only peaceful uses of nuclear energy are ambiguous. Although South Africa has adhered to the partial test ban treaty, it has repeatedly refused to support creation of a nuclear weapon-free zone in Africa. This refusal to cease acquiring nuclear weapons is particularly ominous because South Africa has the technical capability to make those weapons. These concerns have grown with the 1977 discovery in the Kalahari Desert of what was reported to be an underground nuclear weapons test site and the detection by a U.S. reconnaissance satellite in the area of the South Atlantic in 1979 of a double flash of light resembling the signals from an atmospheric nuclear explosion. The strong reaction of the world community to those two events shows that South Africa's nuclear capability is considered a grave threat to international peace.

Uranium Production

South Africa's nuclear energy activities began at the end of World War II, when, at the request of Britain, South African Prime Minister Jan Smuts secretly surveyed his country's potential uranium resources. Production of South African uranium began in 1952.[18] Initially, the development of uranium production was the responsibility of the prime minister and several high officials. After the Atomic Energy Act of 1948, control over uranium production and export passed to the South African AEB.

With one of the largest uranium deposits in the world, South Africa has accounted for about 16 percent of world production. Peak production in South Africa in 1959 resulted in 5,850 metric tons. As the British and American demand waned, production of South African uranium dropped. When demand for uranium went up in the world, South African uranium production peaked up from 1975 (see Table 4.1).

TABLE 4.1

Uranium Production in South Africa and Namibia

	(1) South African Uranium Production (metric tons)	(2) World Total Production (except USSR, Eastern Europe, China)	(3) 1 as Percentage of 2	(4) Internal South African Consumption of Uranium (metric tons)	(5) Uranium Production in Namibia (metric tons)	(6) 5 as Percentage of 2
Pre-1975	70,076	428,775.2	16.3	--	0	0
1975	2,488	19,068.1	13.0	--	0	0
1976	2,758	22,089.8	12.0	--	654	3.0
1977	3,360	28,851.7	12.0	--	2,339	8.0
1978	3,961	33,900.1	11.7	--	2,697	8.0
1979 (planned)	5,195	38,379.0	13.5	--	3,692	9.6
1980 (est. attainable)	6,500	50,100.0	13.0	576	4,100	8.1
1985 (est. attainable)	10,600	98,000.0	10.8	374	5,015	5.1
1990 (est. attainable)	10,400	119,300.0	8.7	374	5,015	4.2
2000 (est. attainable)	10,000	n.a.	n.a.	n.a.	4,615	n.a.

-- = little or no internal consumption.

n.a. = not available.

Source: United Nations, South Africa's Plan and Capability in the Nuclear Field (New York, 1981), p. 6.

The South African AEB began research on uranium enrichment in 1961. Knowledge of this research was restricted to only a few members of the South African cabinet, until Prime Minister Vorster announced in Parliament that South Africa had succeeded in developing a new process.[19] Parliament provided funds for the construction of a pilot enrichment plant at Pelindaba, and the Uranium Corporation (UCOR) was created to carry on further development.

Started in 1959, the National Nuclear Research Center at Pelindaba is the main nuclear research organization. Pelindaba's centerpiece is a 20-megawatt (thermal) research reactor called SAFARI-1, similar to that at Oak Ridge, Tennessee. It was purchased from the United States under the Atoms for Peace Program and its reactor operators were trained as part of that program at the Oak Ridge National Laboratory. Fueled with approximately 14 kilograms of high-enriched uranium per year, the reactor first went critical in March 1965.[20]

The United States supplied the necessary fuel reloads; the cooled spent fuel was sent to the United States and Britain for reprocessing. However, since 1975, the United States has not authorized shipments of fuel, and in 1976 it cancelled preexisting contracts and the refund of South African deposits. Underlying this decision was South Africa's unwillingness to sign the nuclear Non-Proliferation Treaty.

South Africa's plans to become a supplier of nuclear fuel in the 1980s have been modified with its decision not to construct a commercial-size enrichment facility but only to expand the pilot plant for its own domestic requirements. By contrast, transfer in the future by South Africa of uranium enrichment technology to another country cannot be ruled out. The impact then would depend on the specifics of such a sale, whether with or without safeguards and the degree of South African concern about the potential end use of its technology by the buyers. The adverse nonproliferation cost could be high.

Recent plans call for the expanded facility to be built with a capacity of 200 to 300 tons SWU (separate work unit) per year. If designed and operated for that purpose, this additional capacity could produce about 1,000 to 1,500 kilograms of high-enriched uranium per year, enough to make several dozen fairly sophisticated bombs.

Beginning with the development of its uranium mining and extraction industry, South Africa's nuclear energy activities have expanded steadily since World War II. On its own, South Africa is one of the largest uranium producers in the world. By its occupation of Namibia, South Africa has added to its considerable share of the international uranium market. Critical details about South Africa's unsafeguarded enrichment facility are highly classified by that country. Thus it is difficult to assess fully South Africa's actual development and capability in the military nuclear field.

South Africa's official and semiofficial statements on nuclear weapons acquisition have been ambiguous and tell little of its intentions and plans. A discussion of this topic must take into account the very special situation arising from South Africa's international isolation because of its apartheid policy. The diplomatic and political costs of South African acquisition and deployment of nuclear weapons are high and may be disastrous if those weapons are used. Nevertheless, tenaciously preserving the apartheid system, South Africa's government has not weighted the cost-benefit ratio. South Africa must have tried to justify the acquisition of nuclear weapons as a last resort to attempt to preserve white supremacy by intimidating neighboring countries or as a device to demoralize black South Africans and, conversely, to buttress the morale of the white population. The extreme dangers of nuclear weapons in general take on especially ominous dimensions in the hands of a government clinging to the unpopular stand of apartheid.

New details of South Africa's nuclear program show that Pretoria has the capacity to produce nuclear weapons. Signals received by two U.S. underwater sensors in the South Atlantic in 1979 suggest that there was a major explosion off the coast of South Africa. Many analysts believe South Africa accomplished this nuclear feat in collaboration with Israel. In a secret report to the U.S. National Security Council, dated June 20, 1980, the Central Intelligence Agency raised the possibility that the "mystery flash" of 1979 was part of a tactical nuclear weapons test in the South Africa-Israel-Taiwan program.[21] The advantage of tactical weapons to the three nations is that they could be used for limited, defensive purposes to forestall invasion from aggressive neighbors. South Africa could repel an attack from the black African nations, Israel from the Arab countries, and Taiwan from China.

In summary this means that South Africa certainly has the immediate capability of producing atomic nuclear bombs; that despite denial, South Africa is capable of producing a nuclear bomb; that the Pretoria government is telling the African nations and the world that by trying to join the "segregated nuclear club" South Africa is attempting to polarize segregation among the co-nuclearists; and that it wants nobody to doubt its policy of nuclearism.

The long Western commitment to partnership with South Africa in its nuclear development forms the background to the 1977 and 1979 concerns about whether South Africa is indeed a nuclear power. Of more importance is the fact that almost certainly it can be if it so chooses. Of course, nobody doubts that if South Africa becomes embattled and is threatened with annihilation by black Africa, the white regime would use nuclear weapons to defend itself. Developing a nuclear capability adds substance to the argument. However, such a policy would only deepen the hostility of the world toward South Africa and possibly hasten the demise of white rule in all of southern Africa.

Traditional concepts of security interests and perceptions of threat may apply only to a very limited extent in a situation where the greatest threat actually stems from a racist regime's denial of basic rights to an overwhelming majority. South Africa is prepared to take drastic measures to preserve its interests and privileges. Such a situation clearly invites illogical response and actions by South Africa.

The proliferation of nuclear weapons in any country is a matter of serious concern to the world. The introduction of nuclear weapons to the African continent, and particularly in such a volatile region as southern Africa, not only would thwart worldwide efforts at nonproliferation but would also undo many years of effort to spare the African continent from the nuclear arms race and to make it a nuclear weapons-free zone. The possession of nuclear weapons by South Africa leads to a sharp escalation of instability and tension in southern Africa and increases the nuclear threat to all humankind. The support of other states in South Africa's acquisition of nuclear weapons is at variance with the efforts made by many countries and the United Nations to prevent the proliferation of nuclear weapons throughout the world. By choosing to produce its own nuclear weapons, South Africa has issued a challenge to all peoples.

The reaction of the world community to the reported Kalahari test site and its persistent concern about the event amply testify to the great concern with which the world regards South Africa's capability and plans in the nuclear field. As long as South Africa seeks nuclear weapons, thereby frustrating creation of a nuclear weapons-free zone in Africa, its capacity and plans in the field will continue to be a matter of concern to the world community.

NOTES

1. White Paper on Defence, 1977 (Pretoria, South Africa: Government Printer, 1977).

2. Robert S. Jaster, South Africa's Narrowing Security Options, Adelphi Papers No. 159 (London: International Institute for Strategic Studies, 1980), pp. 27-30.

3. Newsweek, September 29, 1980.

4. Ibid.

5. Washington Post, October 28, 1977.

6. Britain's Imperial Chemical Industries has the largest share, followed by the Anglo-American subsidiary De Beers.

7. Christian P. Potholm, The Theory and Practice of African Politics (Englewood Cliffs, N.J.: Prentice-Hall, 1979).

8. Washington Post, November 5, 1977.

9. Ibid., October 28, 1977.

10. Ibid. (editorial), October 29, 1977.

11. New York Times (editorial), November 5, 1977.

12. Durham (N.C.) Morning Herald, May 14, 1981.

13. William J. Pomeroy, Apartheid Axis: The United States and South Africa (New York: International Publishers, 1973), p. 66.

14. Ibid.

15. Business Week, November 10, 1975.

16. New York Times, August 9, 1977.

17. Washington Post, October 20, 1977.

18. A. R. Newby-Fraser, Chain Reaction: Twenty Years of Nuclear Research and Development in South Africa (Pretoria, South Africa: Atomic Energy Board, 1979), pp. 22-25.

19. Ibid., p. 91.

20. Ibid., pp. 50-53, 62.

21. Jack Anderson, "South African Flash Still Mystery," Durham (N.C.) Morning Herald, September 16, 1980.

5
Economic Trends

South Africa not only dominates southern Africa politically and militarily but it also maintains economic hegemony in the region. The vital statistics of South Africa--steel production, electricity, transportation network, telecommunications, and industrial, commercial, and financial development--are comparable to those of most European countries. South Africa's national product is three times larger than the combined total of its neighbors. Accounting for only 3.6 percent of the continent's landmass and 6.1 percent of its population, South Africa produces or possesses 40 percent of all goods and services in Africa, 41 percent of all Africa's automobiles, 33 percent of all trucks, 44 percent of all tractors, 52 percent of all telephones, 95 percent of all gold, 94 percent of coal reserves, 94 percent of vanadium, 87 percent of antimony, 87 percent of steel, 69 percent of wool clippings, 79 percent of chrome, 73 percent of uranium, and 25 percent of building cement.

A brief recapitulation of the contemporary sociopolitical crises in South Africa is in order before we discuss the economic malaise in the land of plenty.

In recent years, growing political differences in South African society--within the ruling elite itself as well as in the confrontation between the classes--have become discernible. Within the ruling group, differences among interest groups are escalating. The government is coming under increasing pressure from two sides. Having introduced the constitutional reforms, it now faces insatiable demands from industry. Workers stand ready to fight for their rights and, along with strikes, industry is suffering heavy losses in production. Consequently, within the existing apartheid structure, industry seeks certain rights and privileges for some of South Africa's black population in order to keep workers happy and production uninterrupted. At the same time the government contends with pressure from the right wing hard-liners, who resist change within the existing system.

The fundamental conflict between the ruling class and the majority population is becoming apparent. The growing unrest has manifested itself in the following manner:

In 1983 the United Democratic Front (UDF), an alliance primarily of black organizations, was launched. Its efforts succeeded in the rejection of the elections for the tricameral parliament in August 1984. This umbrella organization also successfully nullified community council elections in 1983-84 and called on persons elected to resign.

In 1984 major strikes increased. On the whole, the number of working days lost tripled in comparison to the 1983 figure.[1] The increased political motivation of workers to strike is seen in three political boycotts between September and November 1984. The general strike in November in the Transvaal region was observed by 70 percent of the workers. The workers in the gold mines also joined the strike in February 1985.

Apart from the workers' struggle, other evidence of an overall increased readiness of black South Africans to demand their rights is apparent, such as the continued protests of students and renters and the rise in political protests with the formation of numerous organizations. The formation of the End Conscription Campaign (ECC) in 1984, including church-related as well as other organizations, is another sign of the mounting open opposition to the war South Africa wages not only in Namibia and Angola but also at home. In 1985, the widely publicized struggle of the Crossroads people against their forced removal to Khayelitsha had to be suspended at least temporarily. These indicators, taken together, demonstrate the intensifying determination of the South African people to struggle toward a nonracial, democratic South Africa.

In 1984-85 South Africa was in a state of civil war. Military and police occupied South African townships and secured the homes of tens of thousands of people, using tear gas, batons, whips, rubber bullets, and bullets against a population in revolt. The economy was suffering

from the effects of antiinflationary measures, including
spending cuts and raised interest rates. Consequently,
unemployment rose. The slowing down of economic activity
created a massive turnaround in the current account balance. An annualized deficit of more than R2 billion
(1 U.S. dollar = 2.60 South African rand) in the third
quarter of 1984 was replaced by an annualized surplus of
R5.4 billion in the second quarter of 1985. Important contributions came from gold exports. The average return on
foreign investment in South Africa has slid from 20 percent
at the beginning of the decade to a current 5 percent.

PHASES IN ECONOMIC DEVELOPMENT

South Africa has passed through various phases in
economic development. Until 1974-75, the one word that
best described South Africa's economy was growth. Slow
in 1975, the South African economy in 1976 entered its
first deep recession since World War II, which continued
unabated in 1977.[2] Steadily mounting inflation, declining
growth rate, and rising unemployment, especially among
the majority black people, imposed certain strains on the
economy and were reflected in a slowing down of business
and other economic activity, a drop in savings, and some
lowering of living standards.[3] Profound doubt and defiance pervaded the air. As Time said, the worst was yet
to come: "At the seemingly endless stream of seminars on
the national destiny, the questions are inevitably asked:
What will South Africa be like in a year? In two? In
five? And there is an all-too familiar answer: Worse."[4]
Real gross domestic product (GDP) declined the first
and second quarters of 1976, compared to the previous respective quarters. At an annual rate, projections put this
decline at 1.5 percent.
The economic downturn in South Africa resembled in
many respects the recession in the United States, Western
Europe, and Japan following the Arab oil embargo in 1973.
The recession was accompanied by a further deterioration
in the balance of payments with the deficit in the first
half of 1976 reaching more than $2.4 billion annually. A
decline in the net capital inflow contributed to foreign exchange reserves falling by 26 percent in the first seven
months of 1976 and led to the government's imposition of
an import deposit scheme in August. International pressure

on South Africa to change its racial policies and the worldwide recession prompted the government to tighten up on
import licenses and foreign exchange regulations in 1976–77.
The inflation rate was between 10 and 15 percent. While
the budget for 1976 was aimed at stimulating exports and
curtailing imports, the deficit in the balance of trade remained large, attributed partly to the increased cost of
imports. The fall in the price of gold, which is South
Africa's largest export, and the increase in defense expenditure contributed to the decline of the foreign exchange
reserves and the balance of payments.[5]

Additional adverse factors on the economy in 1976
were the conflicts in neighboring countries and the continued political unrest and violence in the black urban
townships of South Africa. While the latter had only a
marginal physical impact on the industrial and commercial
life of the country, it contributed to pessimism in business,
particularly among overseas investors.

After the most severe economic downturn of the postwar period in the mid–1970s, South Africa recovered in 1978.
With a weak American dollar pushing the price of gold up
from $50 an ounce to $225 at year's end, South Africa
reaped a bonanza.[6] A hundred years after the first strike
of gold on a rocky ridge near Johannesburg, the kingpin
of South Africa's economy is still gold. Its price has
more than doubled since 1978, and South Africa's 35 active
gold mines produce close to 700 tons, 50 percent of world
production.

The South African economy continued its upturn in
1979 with real GDP increasing by 3.7 percent. As the gold
price climbed, the gross national product (GNP) rose more
rapidly than GDP, increasing by 5 percent in real terms
during 1979. Growth was fairly evenly distributed among
the various sectors, with manufacturing, non–gold mining,
and services performing particularly well, while agriculture
and commerce fell from the previous year. The inflation
rate climbed to 14 percent from 11 percent the previous
year due to higher prices of oil. South Africa's international trade position strengthened considerably in 1979 as
the value of gold exports rose 55 percent. The country's
current account surplus doubled to $3.7 billion.[7]

Gold accounts for a third of the country's exports.
This governs the nation's economic health. Thus the country passed through an almost effortless boom in 1979,
achieving a record growth of 8 percent in 1980.[8] The

momentum of this economic upswing carried over into 1981 at about a 5 percent rate. There are, however, some problem areas. South Africa may lose skilled labor, which would constitute a major constraint, as economic growth in the major industrialized countries will eventually have an impact on South African mineral exports.

Most of the bad economic news for the West concerns the gold market. Beyond that, cheaply produced industrial products like South African–made BMW automobiles are also providing a competitive edge. In any crisis in the world, such as in the Middle East or Poland, worried foreigners begin to stock up on exports of raw and precious South African minerals and thus hype the South African economy.

South Africa has decided to give top priority to improving the balance of payments through a tight monetary and fiscal policy in lieu of a general recovery. Government spokesmen say that any economic recovery must be export-oriented rather than internally stimulated. However, as black unemployment increases, thereby adding potential fuel to the political unrest, the government will come under mounting pressure to shift to more expansionary economic policies. Needs for defense and infrastructure improvements in black areas will add to the pressure for increased government spending. The problem is to coordinate the balance of payments while stimulating the economy. To do so a solution is sought in the private sector for greater use of selective import controls.

Many white South Africans feel the country is going in the same direction as Zimbabwe because of the continuing unrest and dissent of the majority. The whites are shifting money and valuables to foreign banks.[9] For the first time, more whites are leaving the country than are entering it. South Africa has been passing through a political as well as economic crisis. Despite its official criticism of apartheid, the U.S. government helped South Africa to obtain $463 million from the International Monetary Fund to combat its economic problems.[10]

In 1982 and 1983 South Africa suffered negative real economic growth, a phenomenon the country had not experienced in the post–World War II period. The economy reached its low in early 1983 and then moved into a cyclical upswing fueled by a rising dollar price of gold and other positive developments in the balance of payments. Monetary policy was relaxed, and government expenditure increased substantially. However, what appeared to be the long-awaited export-led recovery turned into an unsustainable consumption-led recovery. The upswing, halted by August 1984, led by a downturn in agriculture.

In spite of a downturn in the second half of 1984, the South African economy grew by 4.5 percent for the year as a whole. The strength of the first half, based on rapid rises in consumer and government spending, quickly waned under the onslaught of drought, low gold prices, a three-percentage-point increase in the general sales tax, and tight financial measures introduced in late August. Even with a cooling economy, the inflation rate continued to rise at a double-digit pace. The tighter financial policies, however, choked the boom in consumer spending and by year's end, the current account appeared to have moved into surplus.

The economic slowdown continued into 1985. Assuming the government lives up to its commitment to limit spending severely and resists premature relaxations of monetary policy that characterized the recent past, an export-led recovery could accomplish an economic turnaround during 1986. In light of the above, one may make an obvious conclusion that, within very broad limits, South Africa's vital economic interest has set few serious constraints on the development of policy toward other nations as well as at home.

FOREIGN INVESTMENT

South Africa maintains an open door policy for foreign investments, which play very active roles in the country's economic development. While the government has assumed an increasing role in areas considered strategic, the private sector, following the U.S. model, generates three-fourths of the GDP.[11]

Britain is South Africa's principal partner in development. West Germany is the second ranking supplier, with the United States third, followed by Japan, France, and Italy. Together, the United States and Western Europe have investments of about $20 billion in South Africa.[12] Of late, the governments of these countries are discouraging investment in Namibia, under South Africa's occupation. There is an increased awareness in the Third World and among progressive elements in the Western world that foreign investors, particularly from the developed countries, are playing a key role in the South African economy.

Some 260 American companies have investments in South Africa. A few of the large American corporations involved in South African development are Ford, Chrysler, Kaiser, Firestone, Goodyear, Union Carbide, U.S. Steel, Chase Manhattan Bank, First National City Bank, Chemical Bank, Standard Oil of California, Texaco, Mobil, and Standard Oil of New Jersey.[13]

The American companies are bound by U.S. law to avoid discrimination, but they cannot always do so if they have to do business with South Africa.[14] In November 1977, shortly after the UN arms embargo was imposed on South Africa and in the wake of a threat of world trade and economic sanction against it, the South African government notified businesses that it had reactivated World War II powers under which it can require firms to manufacture and sell to the government certain items it considers strategically important. This measure is meant to be implemented should the government feel a squeeze on essential items as the result of any future trade sanctions.

While the Carter administration was reviewing its commercial relations with South Africa and had recalled the American commercial attaché from the consulate in Johannesburg, U.S. companies operating there launched an American Chamber of Commerce with a view to fostering trade and commerce between the two countries.[15] The strategy had been discussed for several years, but its organization was now seen as a response to fears of increased international pressures on business. The move to form the chamber was followed by an announcement by an American firm, Polaroid, that it was withdrawing from the South African market.

Investment is not a one-way affair. It is equally important for both the investors and invested country. The feeling that the foreign investors could wreck the South African economy by removing their investments is not correct. It would hurt the South African economy, but not fatally; at the same time, it would also hurt the investors. Some observers agree that foreign influence on South African events is becoming more limited as the South African economy becomes less susceptible to outside pressure.

U.S. investments in South Africa have not had a significant effect on America's balance of payments. A large percentage of the U.S. profits from such investments have been reinvested in that country. U.S. financial involvement in South Africa stands at about $14 billion, including bank loans, shareholding, and $2.5 billion in direct investment by 260 American corporations.[16]

British economic ties with South Africa are very large. British investments in South Africa are at least three times as large as American investments there and show an average yearly return, after taxes, of 10.5 percent.[17] South Africa, like West Germany and Australia, takes about 5 percent of Britain's exports, exceeded by only the United States, which takes 12 percent.[18]

Although southern Africa has not become a major public issue in the United States, even for most black Americans, a serious crisis there could have severe effects within the United States. In the event of widespread racial conflicts within southern Africa, there would be strong pressures on the United States to take sides, either to protect American investments or to help stop what could become a black bloodbath or to help protect neighboring African states if they were involved. Furthermore, it seems that a race war in southern Africa would exacerbate racial problems in the United States.

Contrary to American verbal denunciation of the apartheid government, U.S. trade and investments in southern Africa are not shrinking. For the past 25 years, U.S. returns on investments in South Africa ranged between 15 and 20 percent.[19] The United States has a stake in demonstrating in its southern African policy some consistency between principle and practice.

The United States, like most other Western and Third World nations, has a legitimate interest in the present as well as the future of southern Africa. Controversy about the prospects for southern African society is now focused on the question of whether the demands of a rapidly growing economy will increasingly force socioeconomic and political change. The debate is made particularly intense because of the obvious relationship between this change and whether U.S. investment in the southern African economy can play a liberalizing role.

The question, then, is whether economic growth can bring equality. Some say that social pressures for liberalizing the societies will grow since economic development will require more and more black workers and laborers. Others see very little causal relationship between economic development and liberalism. They hold the view that apartheid gains strength as the economy does. "When the economy is good the rulers can enforce their repressive laws."[20] Far from undermining white supremacy, economic growth is constantly reinforcing it. Foreign investments stabilize the economies and governments in southern Africa, which enables the whites to reinforce their power structures.

SULLIVAN PRINCIPLES

How should the world react to companies doing business in apartheid South Africa? Should investment in such companies be stopped on grounds that they abet racism? There is a proinvestment side and an antiinvestment plea also. A University of Pennsylvania Trustee Committee made the following recommendations:

> We hope that by continuing in most cases
> to hold the stock of companies doing busi-
> ness in South Africa, we can help to hold
> all such companies accountable to a high
> standard of conduct . . . rather than in-
> discriminately selling our shares to other
> probably less concerned owners and turning
> our backs on the problem.[21]

The presence of American businesses in South Africa could be a positive thing--if they can be persuaded to seek equal treatment for black workers. But how are the companies to be held accountable? There is a scheme for that.

The so-called Sullivan principles were enunciated by the Reverend Leon H. Sullivan, a black pastor in Zion Baptist Church in Philadelphia who is the founder of Opportunities Industrialization Center, a job training program. Sullivan encouraged U.S. companies to implement these principles in their South African facilities and thus break down the apartheid regulations that allow discrimination against nonwhite employees. Briefly these principles are the following (a fuller description of the principles is given in Appendix A):

1. Nonsegregation of the races in all eating, comfort, and work facilities
2. Equal and fair employment practices for all employees

3. Equal pay for all employees doing equal or comparable work for the same period of time
4. Initiation and development of training programs to prepare blacks, Coloureds, and Asians in substantial numbers for supervisory, administrative, clerical, and technical jobs
5. Increasing the number of blacks, Coloureds, and Asians in management and supervisory positions
6. Improving the quality of employees' lives outside the work environment in such areas as housing, transportation, schooling, recreation, and health facilities.

Sullivan has since amplified his code with a new principle calling upon U.S. firms in South Africa to oppose apartheid actively. He has maintained that his goals are not antithetical to the divestment movement, but are actually in conjunction with it.

As of September 1985, 153 American companies endorsed the principles.[22] Since then, three-fourths of the companies report that their eating, toilet, work, and locker room facilities are desegregated. Many companies have adopted common medical insurance and pension plans for all categories of employees. Many are also hiring black professionals and providing financial assistance for housing.[23]

Since 1977, when 12 signatories agreed to the Sullivan code of conduct, 153 of the 260 American companies operating in South Africa are participating and following the principles. Upon his election to the board of directors of General Motors, Sullivan asked GM to stop doing business in South Africa. But he was later convinced that economic sanctions would not diminish South Africa's racial problems and would, instead, hurt the black workers employed by U.S. corporations.

Basically, the Sullivan principles condemn apartheid and require its signatories to operate on a desegregation basis. They also require participating companies to submit to audits to determine if they are living up to the principles. These audits have shown that 99 percent of all plant facilities operated by participating companies are fully desegregated in production, dining, rest rooms, and so on; that the average annual pay increase for whites since 1980 has been 16 percent and for blacks, 20 percent; that the percentage of blacks in supervisory roles has increased from 16.7 percent in 1979 to 21.2 percent in 1983;

that corporate-sponsored tuition and scholarship programs benefited 5,077 blacks in 1979 and 35,523 in 1983; and that corporate contributions for black employees' education, training, health, and entrepreneurship programs have increased from $70 per employee in 1978 to $339 per employee in 1983.[24]

Editorializing on the Sullivan principles, a North Carolina newspaper wrote:

> One might have reason for criticizing some American businesses for their work in South Africa--particularly if they are cozying up to the white leadership to take advantage of South Africa's blacks. But the Sullivan Principles companies have made a rare business decision that places their ethical strategy on par with their economic goals. That seems worthy of applause rather than scorn.[25]

The South African economy is the most sophisticated in Africa. Yet it relies on American computers and other high technology. South Africa could probably develop these technologies over a period of time, but the cost would be prohibitive. The consumer market in South Africa is not large enough to warrant research and development of high technology. In the face of worldwide economic sanctions, the South African economy could not adequately meet the demand for spare parts of high technology equipment, despite the government's stockpiling of such parts. Except for selling its mineral resources, South Africa is unable to develop a large foreign market for its products. However, faced by an economic boycott from without, the South Africans would have to intensify their efforts to achieve self-sufficiency in the most crucial sectors of their economy.

Economic sanctions could also be expected to weaken the white minority's support of apartheid. If the apartheid system cannot deliver the high benefits the white population is used to receiving, the loyalty of the greatest beneficiaries might wane. The divisions among whites may fester, further fragmenting the nervous white population. (For further details about economic sanctions against South Africa, see Chapter 8.)

DIVESTMENT

Divestment is the withdrawal of funds from corporations and banks that do business in South Africa. The divestment movement in the United States began a decade ago when college students pressed trustees to sell stock in companies doing business in South Africa. Although much has been achieved since that time (see a partial list of schools ending investment in South Africa in Appendix B), apartheid still reigns supreme in South Africa, aided¨ by the confused investment policies of many U.S. colleges and universities.

The most significant aspect of U.S. investment in South Africa is its importance in maintaining apartheid. U.S. corporate support of South Africa is important for apartheid's survival as shown by the strategic areas covered by these firms:

Computers: U.S. firms control 70 percent of the computer market. IBM supplies computers to the South African government to monitor the pass system (IBM plans to sell business).

Motor vehicles: Both Ford and GM supply vehicles to the military and police in South Africa (GM plans to sell business).

Heavy machinery: Caterpillar Tractor supplies the government with bulldozers that are used to flatten homes in black communities during removal.

Military hardware: United States-made electronic sensors and infrared detectors and tracking equipment are available in South Africa.

Money: Many American and other international banks lend millions of dollars to South Africa (see Table 5.1).

South Africa was torn again by bloody protest and riots in 1985 and the first part of 1986. As these protesters burned government buildings and other installations, American companies doing business in South Africa hopelessly watched as one of their favorite arguments against divestment—that their presence in South Africa helps change apartheid—also went up in smoke. This was most untimely for the companies, and especially for the South African government.

Business Week comments: "For U.S. companies, disinvestment is no longer just a possibility; it has become

TABLE 5.1

Bank Loans to South Africa, Mid–1982 to End 1984,
Grouped by Nationality

Nationality of Parent Bank	Number of Banks	Number of Loans	Amount of Loans (millions of U.S. $)
1. United Kingdom	26	34	1,957.6
2. Switzerland	20	37	1,520.4
3. South Africa	12	24	1,382.3
4. West Germany	48	27	1,235.0
5. France	23	22	1,094.8
6. United States	20	20	1,079.9
7. Austria	8	19	959.7
8. Belgium	7	19	927.7
9. Italy	11	18	884.7
10. International	6	20	848.5
11. Luxembourg	4	17	802.5
12. Nationality not available	9	14	744.2
13. Canada	2	11	516.8
14. Japan	1	5	264.2
15. Liechtenstein	1	5	225.7
16. Vatican City	1	5	171.9
17. Netherlands	1	4	163.8
18. Spain	1	2	145.0
19. Finland	1	1	57.8
20. Portugal	1	1	50.0

Source: Eva Militz, Bank Loans to South Africa: Mid–1982 to End 1984 (Geneva, Switzerland: World Council of Churches, April 1985), p. 15.

fact."[26]   Indeed, there has been a steady increase over
the past five years in legislation introduced across the
United States aimed at ending the investment of public
funds in companies supporting apartheid.   Since the beginning of 1985, the pace has accelerated, with a record 30
bills introduced at the state level and many more in city
councils.   Even the U.S. Congress, which has been cool to
the idea of divestment, has seen more than 41 separate
bills, 10 of them aimed at economic sanctions against South
Africa.   President Reagan, who has opposed sanctions, ordered implementation of most of the antiapartheid provisions of a bill in 1985.

The South African government used to pretend that
the divestment movement would have no impact.   While
still enforcing the Internal Security Act that makes it a
crime of treason to speak out for divestment, it has placed
the South African business community on alert.   A group
of prominent South African business leaders flew to Lusaka,
Zambia, on September 13, 1985 to talk with Oliver Tambo,
the ANC's president-in-exile.   The business leaders wanted
to end the violence and begin negotiating on black rights.[27]

The passage of divestment legislation in five
states--Connecticut, Maryland, Massachusetts, Michigan,
and Nebraska--prohibits the investment of state funds in
banks and companies supporting apartheid.   By the end of
1984, state and municipal measures had mandated the withdrawal of more than $2 billion in public funds from com-
panies dealing with South Africa, and several hundred
million dollars have already been divested.   Five other
states and 32 cities in the United States have some kind
of divestment policy.   New Jersey, for example, has more
than $10 billion in its state employee retirement system,
and it is selling some $2 billion in South African invest-
ment because of a state divestment law passed in August
1985.

There is a growing trend toward getting rid of
South African holdings among campuses in the United
States.   Since the spring of 1985, when scores of campuses
erupted in antiapartheid protests, about 20 colleges and
universities from coast to coast have adopted policies of
total or partial divestment of South Africa-related investment.   They include Columbia University, Rutgers University, University of Iowa, University of Arizona, Barnard
College, Duke University, and Harvard University (partial
divestment).

In 1981 375 American companies were doing business with South Africa. As of November 1986 there were about 260 American companies in South Africa with a total investment of less than $2.5 billion. American employment of South Africans, both black and white, had fallen to 65,000 in 1986 from 90,000 in 1982.[28] In the face of escalating strife and continuing crisis, "nearly every American corporation in the country (South Africa) has an escape plan."[29]

ARGUMENTS AGAINST DIVESTMENT

Then there is the argument against divestment. Paralleling the argument that the United States should impose economic sanctions on South Africa is the suggestion that American institutions should divest from U.S. corporations in South Africa. Opponents of divestment argue that blanket economic sanctions would be counterproductive.

The U.S. government maintains the position that rather than disengage from South Africa and the region, the United States should be seeking even more ways to make a positive difference. Contrary to conventional wisdom in unofficial circles, the U.S. government believes that American direct investment in South Africa could hardly provide the kind of leverage that could, by itself, bring apartheid to an end. The United States accounts for less than one-fifth of the 10 percent capital derived from foreign sources.[30] Ninety percent of investment in South Africa comes from South Africa's own sources. Even if American firms departed South Africa, little would change so long as there were British, German, Japanese, or, more than likely, South African companies willing and able to produce what American enterprises now produce. Gone would be the benefits of investment the American companies have provided under the Sullivan principles.

Many Americans, including some black Americans, are not persuaded that divestment is an effective strategy for accomplishing the goal of equality. J. A. Parker, head of the Lincoln Institute of Research and Education, states:

> I have visited South Africa a number of
> times during the past decade. On each
> visit I am impressed by the beneficial im-
> pact American business is having on race

relations.   The vast majority of blacks
with whom I speak in South Africa oppose
disinvestment.   They argue that if such a
policy were ever adopted, blacks would be
its victims.   The only blacks who seem to
support such a policy are revolutionaries
who reject peaceful change and want only
power for themselves.[31]

Walter Williams, a professor at George Mason University,
argues :

To the extent that foreign investment and
trade produce jobs, black and white South
Africans benefit from economic relations
with the U.S. . . .   South African blacks
are indeed mistreated at the hands of the
state.   But if we're going to help, shouldn't
we make sure our "help" doesn't hurt?
Trade sanctions would hurt.   In fact, most
who might be called black leaders in South
Africa are strongly against disinvestment. . . .   There's an admission given
to medical doctors, primus no nocere.   It
means "first do no harm," which we would
be well-advised to heed in our policy toward South Africa.[32]

One of the arguments against economic disinvestment
in South Africa is that it hurts blacks hardest, the very
people it is designed to help.   But black leaders, black
trade unions, and a growing number of ordinary blacks
say they are prepared to make the sacrifice necessary to
undo apartheid.   Some other arguments against divestment
include the following:

1. A university invests its funds through a governing
   body responsible for the financial solvency of the institution.   The governing board seeks to optimize the
   return on assets while minimizing the risk of the entire
   portfolio.   When the university trustees divest stock-
   holdings to help achieve South African equality, they
   endanger the quality of investments and violate their
   responsibility as trustees.

2. A university must be committed to moral neutrality. A university must continue to educate and research without deference to morality. Precedents respecting moral positions are unhealthy for the university as an institution.
3. The sale of assets from a university portfolio cannot have any real effect on the position of any corporation. The market system dictates that each seller finds a buyer, thereby negating any net withdrawal of capital. The university holds more power over the corporation by exercising its right to vote through its shares of common stock.
4. A university should not be allowed to be a platform for practicing national and international politics. If an academic institution turns out to be political, it may fail as a seat of objective learning.
5. An educational institution must continue its moral and political neutrality. The teachers and taught must seek truth in a free and unfettered atmosphere.

Overall, the current divestiture movement has had some popularity, but it has not created any big impact on the operation of American corporations in South Africa.

IMPACT ON AFRICA

Despite international economic sanctions and a ban on trade by the Organization of African Unity, trade links exist between South Africa and 47 of the 50 black mainland and island African states. South Africa's exports to the rest of Africa represent 5.5 percent of all exports, while imports from Africa represent approximately 2 percent of all imports.[33] In addition, South Africa's relations with neighboring states range from technical cooperation to developmental aid to tourism. Trade relations have been growing because South African products are well suited to ecological and general conditions in Africa. Neighboring states also enjoy the added advantage of lower transport costs and quick delivery in comparison with competing overseas products.

Other than being a supplier of manufactures, South Africa has become an important source of food grains for many African countries, such as Zambia, Zaire, Kenya, and Tanzania. In view of the decline in per capita food production in most African countries over the past two decades and the poor prospect for greater outputs, the significance of South Africa's commercial farming sector is considerable.

South Africa buys groundnuts, coffee, tea, bananas, tobacco, cotton, and hardwoods from African countries. Virtually all roads and railways in southern Africa lead to South Africa and its modern port facilities. South Africa is linked by air, road, and rail to all neighboring states. The landlocked states, such as Lesotho, Botswana, and Zimbabwe, are heavily dependent for their imports and exports on South African transportation facilities. Even the economies of Zaire and Zambia rely greatly on South Africa's rail and harbor facilities for their imports and exports.

About 350,000 foreign African blacks are legally employed in South Africa. They come mostly from Lesotho, Mozambique, Malawi, Botswana, and Swaziland. An estimated 1.2 million blacks from these countries work in South Africa illegally. If employment opportunities were to be reduced further by economic sanctions and divestment, South Africa would not be able to employ these foreign workers. If sanctions were to be effective, they would undermine South Africa's capacity to supply nations of southern Africa with grains, machinery, equipment, and consumer goods. Alternative sources could be found elsewhere but would be more expensive. Also, longer delivery time would compound the problems some of the southern African countries have been facing.

It seems that divestment and sanctions will affect the general welfare, living standards, and stability of millions of people in southern Africa. Who will get hurt most? Usually the poor, and in this case the poor happen to be the blacks. However, no freedom has ever been won without sacrifice. South Africa's blacks cannot be an exception to this general principle.

Obviously, it is possible that greater awareness among foreign investors and businesspeople of the issues involved in investing and trading in southern Africa can lead to greater knowledge of the working conditions in the subcontinent. However, a disengagement of foreign economic interests can make a major contribution toward raising the political consciousness of democratic public opinion everywhere in the world, and that will, in itself, be an important contribution to the liberalization of southern African society.

The question here is the length of time that the majority blacks are willing to endure the insult of apartheid. How gradually they will accept the easing of their lot will determine the price everyone involved will pay for black rights. An active but patient approach may well eradicate prejudice as well as bondage. Should emancipation erupt or simply ensue? Can violent revolt beget true tranquillity? Some say the United States, like Canada and Australia, could have avoided much suffering by sliding off the captor's knots without cutting the rope. Perhaps. Left to themselves by the outside world, South Africans of all races might learn how much they really need each other. Only time will tell.

NOTES

1. *Financial Mail* (Johannesburg), December 21, 1984.

2. *Time*, November 21, 1977.

3. Encyclopaedia Britannica, *Book of the Year, 1977* (Chicago, 1977), p. 620.

4. *Time*, November 21, 1977.

5. Ibid.

6. *New York Times*, February 4, 1979.

7. U.S. Department of Commerce, "Foreign Economic Trends and Their Implications for the United States," July 1980; and "Overseas Business Reports: Marketing in South Africa," November 1984.

8. *Washington Star*, August 3, 1980.

9. *Washington Post*, December 25, 1977.

10. Ibid., December 24, 1977.

11. U.S. Department of Commerce, "Overseas Business Reports: Market Factors in South Africa," March 1977.

12. *Washington Post*, November 11, 1978.

13. A complete list of these corporations is available from the American Committee on Africa, 198 Broadway, New York, NY 10038.

14. *Time*, November 21, 1977.

15. *Washington Post*, November 24, 1977.

16. Brooke Baldwin and Theodore Brown, *Economic Action Against Apartheid* (New York: American Committee on Africa, n.d.), p. 1; and *Business Week*, November 23, 1985.

17. *Economist* (London), June 5, 1971.

18. Ibid., June 29, 1968.

19. Clyde Ferguson and William R. Cotter, "South Africa: What Is to Be Done," Foreign Affairs, January 1978.

20. Washington Post, October 29, 1977.

21. Quoted in Bulletin, January 25, 1980.

22. Business Week, September 23, 1985.

23. Washington Post, December 4, 1978.

24. Durham (N.C.) Morning Herald, August 14, 1984.

25. Ibid.

26. Business Week, September 23, 1985.

27. Ibid.

28. Ibid.

29. Ibid.

30. U.S. Department of State, Bureau of Public Affairs, "Promoting Positive Change in Southern Africa," Current Policy No. 789, January 24, 1986.

31. Quoted in Embassy of South Africa, Process of Constitutional Change Underway in South Africa (Washington, D.C., 1985).

32. Ibid.

33. Embassy of South Africa, South Africa and Africa: Cooperation and Development (Washington, D.C., May 1983); and Christian Science Monitor, March 25, 1983.

6
Foreign Policy

South Africa's foreign policy is determined largely by its domestic makeup and its unique political and social structure. The fundamental question to be raised at this point is: What aspects of domestic policy does the foreign policy seek to advance? The answer is the domestic policy of apartheid--that classic selfish system of rule which maintains that the skin color of a person is the indicator of his or her worth.

This may sound peculiar, since one usually thinks of foreign relations and internal affairs as belonging to distinct spheres. In general, however, foreign policy is an extension of domestic policy. The acts that a state performs in its relationship with other states are meant to gain the objectives which that state pursues in its domestic policy. This is because a nation is first of all an entity in its internal environment before it becomes an international participant. A nation's survival depends primarily on its internal environment before it becomes an international personality.

In the case of South Africa, the policy of apartheid is most critical to its survival at home where the white regime is a minority. It is only this "policy of skin color" that the regime has to sustain at home and propagate abroad. South Africa bases its politicomilitary and economic strategy at home and abroad on the premise that white skin is good and black skin is bad. This color prejudice in South Africa is the root cause of all socio-political and economic ills in the southern African subcontinent.

Discussing South Africa's foreign policy, a British journalist who has visited South Africa many times quoted one senior member of its Strategic Planning Staff who described the centrality of the foreign policy of South Africa in the following words: "South Africa's national security is dependent upon its relationship with the international community, which is determined by its relationship with black Africa, which in turn is governed by its relationship with its own black population."[1]

In other words, South Africa's foreign policy is determined by its relationship with the black population at home. Since 1948, when the National party came to power in South Africa, the elevation of apartheid into a symbol of survival for the white regime has made domestic policy a crucial factor in determining South Africa's foreign relations. Although apartheid existed in South Africa before the advent of the National party, criticism of it by outsiders was not widespread.[2] Soon after World War II, a large number of African states were on the verge of independence and those in power were sensitive to that possibility. Few other states have had to face such hostility to their domestic policies as has South Africa over the last 38 years.

OUTWARD-LOOKING POLICY

To put it differently, South Africa's foreign policy is determined by its relationship with the black peoples in the southern African subcontinent. Detente and dialogue are the two concrete means by which South Africa struggles to maintain white rule. The campaign is waged by the white government of South Africa seeking friends in its war against the blacks. Detente is the prolongation of that war by other means. The white rulers in South Africa have enlisted the aid of significant sections of the black elite within its own frontier but have failed to win over the black people. Therefore South Africa looks for friends in black African states. In extending its friendship, South Africa is asking the African nations for approval of the concept of apartheid.

Prime Minister Vorster embarked on an aggressive policy designed to win friends in Africa. The effort was to establish more normal relations with the rest of Africa. Under the euphemism of dialogue, the South African government offered trade, tourism, investment capital, and development loans to African states that would, in effect, curtail their opposition to apartheid.

This strategy has caused consternation among some sectors of the white people in South Africa, who fear that dealing on an equal level with black African states will ultimately lead to erosion of apartheid at home. However, this was made an election issue in 1970, and the ruling National party won again. This confirmed the support of the majority of whites in South Africa toward the policy of apartheid.

A more serious source of challenge that arose in the 1960s lay in a revised approach by the South African government in its relations with African states. A number of factors have been thought to motivate South Africa. One was suggested by Vorster in 1966, when he announced his outward-looking policy--a policy he believed would "prove to the world that racial groups with different policies can live together alongside one another in the same geographic area."[3] In other words, South Africa regards this outgoing policy as one means to limit African criticism of apartheid and to eliminate external support for the revolutionary movements. Another factor might have been to reverse its situation of isolation in Africa and in world affairs. Third, the requirements of economic expansion are vitally linked to South Africa's policy toward black Africa. It is because South Africa needs the system of cheap labor migration from neighboring Malawi, Lesotho, Botswana, Mozambique, Zambia, and Tanzania. Fourth, Africa is a logical market for South Africa's industrial production. Additional factors could be listed, but it is apparent that there are important benefits to be derived from this outward-looking policy for South Africa, if successful.

Until 1966 South Africa had no formal relations with any of the independent African states. While this situation was largely a by-product of apartheid, by then it had become clear that such a dissociation was undesirable. The first manifestation of outward-looking policy was marked in September 1966 by a visit to Pretoria of Lesotho's prime minister, Leabua Jonathan.[4] South Africa established formal diplomatic relations with Malawi, then trade relations, and welcomed visiting cabinet ministers from Malawi.

When the prime minister of Lesotho visited South Africa, "Hotel and restaurant prohibitions were conveniently waived so that he could be housed and fed in white areas."[5] The same arrangements greeted the state visit of Hastings Kamuzu Banda, president of Malawi, in August 1971.[6] Further, to accommodate black diplomats, South Africa has established diplomatic enclaves in Cape Town and Pretoria so that black envoys can live among the affluent white areas rather than among the poor people of the Bantustans.

South Africa's rationale and motives for developing externally were related to a growing sense of isolation, the need for maintaining the status quo, an image as a regional power, frustration, and strategic considerations.[7] South Africa was looking for a new way of dealing with black consciousness at home and with black nations in the region. The image white South Africa conveyed was one of multifaceted benevolence in economic, diplomatic, and good-neighbor relations. The object of this approach was to convince black African states that differences within the domestic realm should not be permitted to preclude relations in the economic and diplomatic areas.

South Africa had begun its external relationship with a number of African countries and had established a muted dialogue with them. As pointed out earlier, Pretoria had full diplomatic relations with Malawi, a working relationship with Botswana, Lesotho, and Swaziland, and friendly contacts with the Ivory Coast and Senegal.[8]

South Africa developed a patron-client relationship with its bordering neighbors, particularly the "captive nations," like Botswana, Lesotho, and Swaziland. At first, South Africa was hostile to the grant of independence to these nations, as indeed it was the grant of independence to Africa in general.

Under the guise of peaceful dialogue, the greatest potential for the success of this new direction in South African foreign policy developed. In November 1970, President Felix Houphouet-Bigny of the Ivory Coast was made spokesman for a group of African states that called for the OAU to withdraw from the confrontation policies and enter into dialogues with South Africa. The states that joined in this proposal included many of the former French colonies, plus Ghana, Uganda, and Malawi. This behavior of the African states could be explained as a response to their fear of communism and to their hope of deriving economic and technical benefits from their cooperation with the most developed African state in the south: "In the broadest terms their argument was that as the tactics already used to attack apartheid had not succeeded, there was no point in continuing with them. As an alternative, peaceful contact could be used as a means of convincing and persuading the South Africans to change their policies."[9]

In the 1971 meetings of the OAU, the proponents of this position indicated that the OAU should sponsor dialogue as a means of moving South Africa from its policies of apartheid. They further regarded this proposal as a potentially more effective instrument for avoiding the excesses of confrontation.[10]

The proponents of continued conflict and confrontation, most notably Tanzania and Zambia, were opposed. In an obvious attempt to discredit South Africa's opponent and the chairman of the 1971 OAU meetings, Vorster disclosed that secret negotiations with President Kenneth Kaunda of Zambia had been underway since 1968, which Kaunda denied. In the recriminations that followed between the African nations and South Africa, the latter revealed that other African states had been meeting South African envoys regularly over two years concerning the possibilities of opening trade relations.[11]

The proposed dialogue never took place, at least not publicly. The fact that such an issue could be debated indicates that support for conflict and confrontation and the total isolation of the racist regime in international affairs had decreased in the late 1960s and early 1970s.

Very few African nations were prepared publicly to support a dialogue with South Africa, as there was an ambivalence among the black nations. This can be detected in the famous Lusaka Manifesto, drawn by 14 East and Central African nations in April 1969 and subsequently endorsed by the OAU and the United Nations.[12] This document is still the basis of Africa's strategy toward South Africa.

The African leaders declared in the Lusaka Manifesto: "We do not advocate violence. . . . We would prefer to negotiate rather than destroy, to talk rather than kill . . . but to give the peoples of those territories all the support of which we are capable of in their struggle against their oppressors."[13] The African nations rejected apartheid. South Africa, the manifesto said, ". . . is an independent sovereign state and a member of the United Nations. . . . On every legal basis its internal affairs are a matter exclusively for the people of South Africa."[14]

However, South Africa rejected the Lusaka Manifesto as a basis for any dialogue with the African nations. In retrospect, it seems a lost opportunity for South Africa. But, in the light of the current state of the political situation in southern Africa, it is simply not possible to describe the Lusaka Manifesto as a call for the peaceful settlement of southern African racial problems.

In embarking on external negotiations with the African states, South Africa sought to bring them to its side. This quest was prompted by two sets of interrelated considerations. First, it was only by being at detente with the black African nations that the white south could mollify the Western nations and the Third World countries. The Western powers are solicitous of the African states, like the rest of the Third World, and see to it that these countries are not unduly offended and antagonized. Linked with this was the fact that South Africa exhausted its resources for pacifying the blacks at home, so its appeals to other blacks in Africa was for them to pacify South African blacks from outside. It was clearly South Africa's aim in detente and dialogue to use the African states as a shield against world disapproval of apartheid.

Black African nations are relieved when UN trade sanctions against South Africa, which they publicly promote, are vetoed by the Western nations. The reason is simple: African nations get food and other essentials from South Africa. According to the Economist (May 16, 1981), 47 black African nations buy maize and wheat from South Africa, and this trade is carried out openly. Covert trade in South African arms and other items with black Africa is also booming.

ENTENTE CORDIALE

Few states have been so isolated morally and diplomatically as are South Africa, Israel, and Taiwan from the rest of the world. The reasons for their relative political isolation vary: South Africa, for its racial apartheid; Israel, because it is opposed by Arab and many Third World countries; and Taiwan, because most nations now recognize mainland China.

Israel

It may be pointed out that Israel is the only Jewish state in the world and South Africa has the ninth largest Jewish population in the world--118,000 Jews, who are among the most affluent. Some of the prominent Israelis were born in South Africa, such as Abba Eban, the well-known Israeli foreign minister.[15] These are added reasons for South Africa and Israel to have an entente cordiale.

In 1948, soon after Israel was created, South Africa recognized the new state even before Britain, which had administered Palestine under the League's mandate. In 1949, South Africa voted for the admission of Israel into the United Nations. Besides the United States, South Africa may be the only country to give permission to its Jewish citizens to join the Israeli air force whenever the need arises.[16] Along with cooperation from West Germany, France, Britain, and the United States, South Africa is being helped by its friend Israel to build atomic bombs.[17] South Africa also bought an undisclosed number of Reshef gunboats equipped with Gabriel missiles from Israel.[18]

Both South Africa and Israel fear the gradual loss of Western support for their policies, and that is precisely the reason for their desire to build nuclear weapons. According to commentators Rowland Evans and Robert Novak, Israel already has 16 bombs in its arsenal.[19] If necessary, Israel would sell some of these bombs to South Africa.

In economic matters, Nathan Weinstock states that Pretoria is one of Tel Aviv's main trading partners, but their relations do not end there. Writes Weinstock:

> The preposterous South African Jewish community, which sympathizes with the fascinating ways of Zionism--a fact which is accounted for by the political context--is one of the main financial backers of the Zionist movement. It follows that Israel, eager to make use of these contributions of capital, must win the favor of the Pretoria authorities for fear that they may obstruct the transfer of Zionist funds.[20]

In citing further evidence of this collaboration, Weinstock says: "Thus in June 1967, South Africa authorized the transfer of Zionist funds, proceeds of collection for

Israel: $18 million. In exchange Tel Aviv agreed to invest part of that sum in South African government stock."[21]

Although South Africa took a neutral position in the Arab-Israeli war of 1967, as it had done at the time of the Suez crisis, in the outpouring of pro-Israeli sentiment the Pretoria administration permitted volunteers to work in civilian and paramilitary capacities in Israel. South Africa also released to Israel more than $28 million held by the Zionist group.[22]

Trade relations between South Africa and Israel--as well as Taiwan, another "outcast" nation--have increased dramatically. In the last decade South African imports from Israel have increased fourfold and its exports twelvefold. South Africa has participated in several ventures in Israel, including the construction of a railroad, a steel rolling mill, and a hydroelectric plant.

An exchange of visits between high-level officials has cemented the South African-Israeli relationship. In 1976, South African Prime Minister Vorster visited Israel. Israeli Finance Minister Simcha Ehrlich came to South Africa in February 1978. These and other visits signal that, even in the face of mounting international hostility to the politics of the two governments, they do not intend to desert each other. They are not fair-weather friends and have never wavered in their loyalty toward each other. They are friends in need. Despite their differences, the two countries have gravitated into this close friendship because of the fear of annihilation from hostile forces. As apartheid and Zionism become targets of more and more UN resolutions, South Africa and Israel grow closer. Mutual isolation has strengthened this friendship.

The South Africa-Israel-Taiwan grouping has been labeled as the entente cordiale to resist the economic and political pressures mounted against each by other governments. The steady increase in South Africa's trade with Israel and Taiwan benefits the economies of all three.

Taiwan

South Africa has some 8,000 ethnic Chinese. At present, the Chinese are in limbo in South Africa's race structure, being exempt from discrimination. When the Taiwanese visit South Africa, an understanding has been reached that they, like Japanese visitors, will be considered white but are to avoid entanglement in South Africa's apartheid policy.[23]

Friendship, including diplomatic recognition by South Africa, means a lot to the Taiwanese, for there are now only a few countries that have not severed official relations with Taiwan in favor of formal ties with Communist China. To cement a growing friendship, South African Prime Minister Botha (now president) made a state visit to Taiwan in October 1980, and the Taiwanese premier returned the visit.

With Taiwan, the upsurge in trade has been impressive, reaching $300 million. South Africa is cooperating with Taiwan in the production of electronic equipment to assist private mining ventures in each country, and it is coordinating in the marketing of steel.

Cooperation between the three outcast nations took time to develop. In the past, Israel and Taiwan joined the UN condemnation of South Africa for its policy of apartheid. Until 1973, Israel cultivated the black African nations. Following the Arab defeat in the 1973 war with Israel, African nations cut off relations with Israel. After that, Israel and South Africa became closer. Taiwan warmed up to South Africa after it was expelled from the United Nations in favor of China.

Persistent reports have South Africa, Israel, and Taiwan cooperating in the production of a tactical nuclear weapon for use in the event of invasion from their hostile neighbors. However fanciful these reports may be, it is certain that the three disenchanted nations, in countering boycotts, are emerging militarily powerful out of all proportions to their size, technologically and economically more developed than all other nations in their respective regions. Thus they hope to maintain their military and economic superiority in their respective regions and thereby protect their vital political interests.

NONRELATIONSHIP WITH THE THIRD WORLD

Despite efforts to gain approval from the Third World, South Africa has become more and more isolated. It is also the most hated nation in the Third World. South Africa has full-fledged diplomatic relationships with four Third World nations--Malawi in Africa, Brazil in Latin America, and Taiwan and Israel in Asia.

South Africa has been suspended or expelled or has withdrawn from various international organizations in which the Third World has the dominant influence. The Commonwealth of Nations and some of the specialized agencies of the United Nations, such as the International Labor Organization and UNESCO, are but a few examples.

The major areas of conflict between the Third World and South Africa are apartheid and the issue of Namibia. The Third World, inhabited largely by the black, brown, and yellow peoples, has been most forthright in its condemnation of the few million white people there. Just about 5 million, the South African ruling class, is not only rejecting the moral judgment of almost the whole world but also that of the International Court of Justice in the case of Namibia, which is currently under South Africa's occupation.

At the United Nations, the Third World has been arguing persuasively for application of sanctions. As apartheid has become a byword throughout the world, the South African regime is slowly collapsing under denunciation by the Third World. In the interest of the whites themselves and the preservation of civilization, Third World leaders have been trying to bring the ruling elites in South Africa to their senses.

Apartheid has circumscribed South Africa's position in the Third World. South Africa must win respectability before it can coexist in the Third World. White nationalism and settler colonialism in southern Africa have further complicated South Africa's bid to open dialogue and widen its influence in Africa, Asia, and Latin America.

In spite of its policy of apartheid, South Africa made some headway in its efforts to penetrate the subregion adjacent to its borders. Responding to pressing needs in Malawi, Botswana, Lesotho, and Swaziland, South African banks, industries, capital, and aid attempted to shore up weak economies, for a price. The price has been received but very minimally. For Africans throughout the continent, including these four nations, apartheid became a symbol of "a crime against humanity, a flagrant violation of the principles of the United Nations and a massive and ruthless denial of human rights constituting a threat to peace."[24] It follows, then, that South Africa is despised by black Africa.

In Asia, like Africa, South Africa had little or no luck. It was only with Lebanon and Iran under the late

shah that it was able to establish consular links. South
Africa has, of course, had diplomatic relations with Israel
and Taiwan. Both Lebanon and Iran permitted trade relations on favorable terms. Lebanon benefited by the
South African tourist trade, and Iran sold oil for hard
cash. South Africa has taken a number of steps to reduce
its dependence on the import of oil, including developing
synfuel from coal. During the 1973 Arab oil embargo,
Iran, which sold oil to Israel, continued to supply oil to
South Africa. After the fall of the shah, Iranian leaders
stopped supplying oil to South Africa. While maintaining
a hostile image, "the Arab oil countries have purchased
large amounts of gold from South Africa over recent years--
presumably in exchange for oil."[25]

On the treatment of Asians, which include mostly
Indians and Pakistanis, India first referred the issue to
the General Assembly of the United Nations on June 2,
1946 for its consideration. It was asserted by the Indian
delegation that South Africa's internal situation was of international concern. On becoming independent in 1947,
Pakistan joined India in condemning the South African
racial policy. It was one of the few issues on which the
two had a common policy.

The antiapartheid stance was given support by 13
members of the United Nations that requested the inclusion
of an item on the agenda of the General Assembly entitled
"the question of race conflict in South Africa resulting
from the policies of apartheid of the Government of the
Union of South Africa." The group alleged that the policy
of apartheid was creating a dangerous and explosive situation in the world that threatened international peace. They
also pointed out that the segregation practiced by South
Africa was in flagrant violation of the basic principles of
human rights and fundamental freedom as set forth in the
UN charter.

In the early years of the debate at the United Nations, the United States and other Western countries supported the South African position. Increasingly, they became aware that such a policy would alienate most of the
UN members from the Third World. The United States was
particularly concerned about its own pluralistic, multiracial population. As the Western world adopted a politically
"neutral" attitude toward the South African apartheid, the
issue of whether South Africa's treatment of its nonwhites
was a matter of international concern or solely domestic in

nature became more pronounced. As pointed out earlier, it has become one of the most important international issues, not only to the Third World but to the world at large because of South Africa's policy of intransigence and non-relationship with the Third World.

The South African government continues to make friendly overtures to the other continent of the Third World, South America, where it has diplomatic relations only with Brazil. South Africa had contracts with the Inter-American Development Bank to provide capital goods and financial and technical advice for modernization of Ecuador's railway and water and sewage systems as well as its bridge building and fishing industry development.[26] South Africa has direct relations with Brazil. These relations are based on very profitable trade policies for the Latin American country. For example, in the case of Brazil, "of the $10 million worth of goods exported last year to Africa, about $8.5 million were purchased by South Africa."[27]

South Africa's relations with Latin America have other implications. A common interest is defense and nuclear development.[28] The chairman and other high officials of the South African Atomic Energy Board have visited Argentina and Brazil to discuss nuclear development. Both Argentina and Brazil have a high potential of becoming nuclear powers in the near future. South African collaboration in this area will be mutually advantageous.

COMMUNIST PHOBIA

To outsiders, South Africa unequivocally identifies its principal enemy as communism. The government is doing this to attract the attention of the anti-Communist Western countries, particularly the United States. South Africa has remained an insular country, isolated from the main current of world politics, ever since it crystallized the policy of apartheid. It attempts to focus world attention on South Africa by raising the bogey of international communism, while it is more apprehensive of internal subversion from the black people who are denied their elementary human rights. The core of South African policy is designed to prevent the development of radical nationalism in the region of southern Africa. Any opposition to government policies at home is labeled Communist inspired.

In the same way South Africa has tended to identify threats to its survival as Communist supported.

The Communist threat is all over the world. In that sense, of course, the threat exists in southern Africa. Otherwise, there seems to be no special concern about communism in white-dominated southern Africa. As an observer of Chinese Communist affairs notes, southern Africa is not unique for Communist revolution: "The situation in Southern Africa, where the majority of the countries have been under metropolitan or white minority governments, presents the Chinese with the opportunity to exploit conditions of extreme stress, but they do not confine their hopes of violent revolution to these areas."[29]

As regards Soviet infiltration into the southern African region, it is "largely the result of uncompromising resistance by the white governments in the region to legitimate black demands."[30] Southern Africa labels any hostile demonstration against it as being the work of Communists. It may be true in some cases, but this does not detract from the fact that to prove communism today irrefutable evidence is required. However, South Africa regards China and the Soviet Union "as a twin-headed monster bent on South Africa's destruction."[31] To outsiders, this type of policy seems to be conspiratorial and overdrawn.

The Pretoria government actually has been preoccupied more with the threat of black revolt than with the so-called Communist menace. It combating the black threat, authorities have invariably blamed the Red menace.[32] This is because government authorities in southern Africa are not willing to distinguish between black consciousness and their proud sense of identity and international communism.

The Soviet Union is quite explicit in its advocacy of armed conflict in Africa. Moscow supplies arms to friendly groups. Motivated by a new sense of power, the Soviets have exploited the convergence of interest in Africa with Cuba. When the Chinese Premier Zhou Enlai visited Tanzania in June 1965, he announced that Africa was "ripe for revolution."[33] He may have been right, but part of the continent was also ripe for crushing revolution. The South African government's own propaganda against revolution and Pretoria's unsuccessful military intervention in Angola bear testimony to the policy of the white south.

As far as the direct Communist threat to southern Africa is concerned, the exiled Communists can be said to form the spearhead of separations.[34] South Africa has outlawed its Communist party for its subversive activities. Another organization, the ANC, which was suspected of having links with the Communist party, has also been banned. After being banned, their primary objectives have been to have South Africa isolated in both political and economic terms and to gain political, economic, and military support for their efforts within South Africa.

Under present conditions, a stimulant for greater world attention on southern Africa would be an increase in Communist activity. There does not seem to be any reliable evidence that the Communists have successfully penetrated southern Africa; however, the turmoil there proves ideal for Communist exploitation. Southern Africa's protest movements are a natural reaction to oppressive action and exploitation of the people by a handful of elites. When the people organize protest movements, rulers jump to the conclusion that it is caused by Communists.

RELATIONS WITH THE WEST

Seldom, if ever, has any country been subjected to such a barrage of hostile criticism as South Africa, as a result of the white rulers having established a master-slave relationship there. From the outset, the white oligarchy developed a narrow and intolerant community that resisted any liberal ideas of society or government. In the 1960s Prime Minister Verwoerd was preoccupied with hostility abroad. Speaking before the House of Assembly in April 1964, Verwoerd took an essentially defensive and isolationist posture when he said:

> The crux of the problem is whether it is more important to be in the good books of world opinion than it is to make up your own mind as to how best you can ensure your survival as a white race in this country. I do not want to push aside the nations of the world. I should like to seek the friendship of others; but I can seek that friendship only within the limits of the right that South Africa herself must have to formulate her own policy in respect of what is to happen within South Africa.[35]

From time to time South Africa finds itself in a dangerously beleaguered position. There was a time when the Western nations blocked firm action for change in South Africa. Their financial involvement in apartheid, through trade with and investment in South Africa, dissuaded the United States, Britain, France, and West Germany from siding with the African bloc when they demanded positive action. South Africa takes full advantage of their dilemma and is emboldened by the weakness of UN resolutions against apartheid. However, in the hardening of world opinion after the Sharpeville massacres, the Soweto riots, and Biko's killing, the attacks on apartheid have increased, and South Africa's Western friends are becoming cool.

From the very beginning the friendship between the West and South Africa was forged in war, as in both world wars South Africa joined the Allied powers. This military cooperation was resumed in 1948, when South Africa took part in the Berlin airlift and again in 1950 when Pretoria sent troops to Korea. Following the end of World War II, many of the Third World (particularly African) states became independent. At the same time, an aggressive racist policy was developed by South Africa. The relations between the Western nations and South Africa were cooling as the West began to show increasing interest in the newly independent nations.

South Africa's whites have been subjected to constant criticism because of their refusal to grant independence to Namibia, the treatment of the Asians, and apartheid. All three are linked to racial segregation. They have led South Africa to difficulties in the United Nations and other international forums. Initially, the greatest blow to South African policies came from Britain. This was to be expected because of South Africa's longstanding historical and economic links with the British. South Africa's policies had been the subject of a number of crucial speeches by members of the British cabinet. Perhaps the best known of these addresses was that now called the "Winds of Change" by the British Prime Minister Harold Macmillan, delivered during a visit to South Africa in February 1960 to a joint session of Parliament. Macmillan indicated that the nature of the new world was such that differences in approaches to dealing with the destinies of free men could no longer be sheltered behind national boundaries. The old patterns of white rule could no longer be maintained indefinitely and more enlightened racial policies must be developed.[36] The statement appears to be representative of the thinking of a majority of democratic nations in the West, including the United States.

Diplomatic relations with Britain have been shaky. The British Conservative party has offered a better deal for arms sales than the Labour party. While the British have vacillated, the French have seized the opportunity to sell arms to South Africa, defying the 1963 voluntary arms embargo imposed by the United Nations. True to its policy of opportunism in international affairs, France has been deeply involved in the joint manufacture of arms inside South Africa. Mirages and Impala jets are manufactured by France in South Africa.[37] France also provides the bulk of South Africa's helicopters, alouettes, super frelon missiles, and submarines. France also built South Africa's first nuclear power plant, outside Cape Town, at a cost of $1.2 billion,[38] and sold nuclear reactors to South Africa.

The other major European power, West Germany, has also provided substantial assistance to South Africa. Its principal source of enriched uranium comes from the plant at Pelindaba, South Africa, which utilizes the West German enriching process.

Despite American criticism, South Africa made it clear that it wished to retain its friendship with the United States. In 1965, Verwoerd told the House of Assembly:

> It is our desire to continue having the greatest degree of friendship with the United States. We do our utmost to come to a good understanding with them, even in respect of policy where we know they differ from us. We try to let them understand the reasons for our standpoint. . . . We have the right to expect not to be asked to buy their friendship by abandoning our interests and our customs in this country.[39]

The Americans had neither the traditional ties of the British nor the warm friendship of the French with South Africa, but generally their relations have been based on contradictory national interests. The United States supported the arms ban against South Africa and disagreed with the British and French governments on their arming of South Africa. Even then the ambivalence of U.S. policy in South Africa vis-à-vis the Franco-British policies on arms sales was evident. The United States, while respecting the 1963 UN arms embargo, sold South Africa some arms and spare parts.[40]

"America's relations with South Africa involve mutually contradictory American national interests."[41] The total U.S. investment in South Africa amounts to $14 billion.[42] The U.S. government maintains that a cessation of this American investment in South Africa in order to bring pressure to bear on apartheid might impel South Africa to turn to other sources of investment. It could cause some damage to America's economic interests and handicap a dialogue with South Africa.

On becoming prime minister in 1966, Vorster told the House of Assembly that "we shall, as we have always done, go out of our way to preserve and maintain friendly relations as far as possible and to the best of our ability" with the United States. However, he challenged the United States, which he said was unable to solve its own racial problems, and questioned whether it could advise South Africa on the subject.[43]

There is considerable sympathy for South Africa in the United States, stimulated by organizations like the American Southern African Council.[44] The American government seeks to avoid difficulties and complications. It wants to avoid a general conflict situation in southern Africa, partly because of its economic and military interests and partly because of America's experience in Vietnam. Americans are sympathetic to the opponents of apartheid but do not want to become directly involved.

To demonstrate opposition to apartheid and to support change toward racial justice, the United States has imposed significant restraints in relations with South Africa. In 1977 the United States joined the United Nations in imposing a mandatory arms embargo on South Africa. In February 1978, the United States tightened restrictions on exports destined for the South African military, police, and other apartheid-enforcing agencies. In December 1984, the United States joined other UN Security Council members in voting for an embargo on imports of arms and ammunition produced in South Africa.

The United States opposes apartheid by refusing to recognize the independence of Transkei, Venda, Ciskei, and Bophuthatswana. The United States rejects the homeland policy because it is an extension of apartheid that forcibly expatriates South African blacks.

The United States has supported the Sullivan principles in business in South Africa. The United States has established an assistance program within South Africa aimed at improving educational and training opportunities for disadvantaged South Africans. During the 1984–86 period, the United States spent $30 million to bring black South Africans to study in the United States.[45]

To indicate America's displeasure with the continued high level of violence and the slow pace of reform in South Africa, President Reagan in September 1985 announced further restrictions on U.S. ties with the South African government. Reagan carefully tailored his actions to avoid punitive measures that would disrupt the country's economy and hurt those South Africans disadvantaged by apartheid. Instead, he attacked the apparatus that enforces apartheid. The new measures were somewhat similar to those contained in legislation that had been approved by the U.S. House of Representatives. Still they were different in that they did not include a ban on new investment but did include restrictions on nuclear and computer sales and on bank loans to the South African government. They also banned arms imports from South Africa and imports of Krugerrands after consultations with American partners in the General Agreement on Tariffs and Trade. A new requirement ordered U.S. firms doing business in South Africa to adhere to the Sullivan principles or forfeit marketing assistance from the U.S. government anywhere in the world.

In 1984–86 South Africa came under greater pressure from an increasingly hostile press and Western community. Until 1985, foreign investors had viewed South Africa as a stable country, but with the increase in racial tensions, doubts surfaced. The U.S. government showed its concern over the slow progress in ending apartheid, though it remained opposed to blanket economic sanctions. Instead, it favored a program of selective sanctions to exert pressure on South Africa. It remains to be seen whether South Africa bows to external pressure and modifies or dismantles its apartheid economy.

NOTES

1. John de St. Jorre, "South Africa: Up Against the World," Foreign Policy, no. 28 (Fall 1977):53.

2. In some respects, apartheid existed in South Africa ever since the white rule was established there, but more directly the seeds of apartheid were sown in the 1909 constitution.

3. South African House of Assembly debates, September 21, 1966.

4. Larry W. Bowman, South Africa's Outward Strategy: A Foreign Policy Dilemma for the United States (Athens: Ohio University Center for International Studies, 1971), p. 6.

5. Ibid., pp. 6-7.

6. Ibid., p. 7.

7. Kenneth W. Grundy, Confrontation and Accommodation in Southern Africa (Berkeley: University of California Press, 1973), p. 241.

8. St. Jorre, "South Africa," p. 59.

9. James Barber, South Africa's Foreign Policy: 1945-70 (London: Oxford University Press, 1973), p. 269.

10. Washington Post, August 19, 1971.

11. For a summary of these charges and counter-charges, see "South Africa-Zambia," Africa Research Bulletin, April 1-30, 1971, pp. 2070-73.

12. Barber, South Africa's Foreign Policy, p. 271.

13. St. Jorre, "South Africa," p. 62.

14. Ibid., p. 63.

15. Gail-Maryse Cockram, Vorster's Foreign Policy (Pretoria: Academia, 1970), p. 55.

16. The Americans can join the Israeli armed forces without fear of losing their citizenship.

17. Rowland Evans and Robert Novak, "South Africa's Bomb," Washington Post, October 20, 1977.

18. Ibid., October 28, 1977.

19. Ibid., October 20, 1977.

20. Quoted in George T. Tomeh, "The Unholy Alliance: Israel and South Africa," distributed by the Arab Information Center, Washington, D.C., n.d.

21. Ibid.

22. Richard Stevens, "Zionism, South Africa and Apartheid: The Paradoxical Triangle," Arab World, February 1970.

23. Los Angeles Times, October 19, 1978.

24. O. Stokke and C. Widstrand, eds., Southern Africa: The UN-OAU Conference, Oslo, April 9-14, 1973, Vols. 1 and 2 (Uppsala, Sweden: Scandinavian Institute of African Studies, 1973).

25. Chicago Defender, July 17, 1980.

26. Cockram, Vorster's Foreign Policy, p. 82.

27. Ibid., p. 83.

28. Ibid., p. 87.

29. G. W. Choudhury, Chinese Perception of the World (Washington, D.C.: University Press of America, 1977), p. 58.

30. St. Jorre, "South Africa," p. 55.

31. Ibid.

32. Ibid.

33. Choudhury, Chinese Perception.

34. Eschel Rhoodie, The Paper Curtain (Johannesburg: Voortrekkerpers, 1969), p. 161.

35. South African House of Assembly debates, April 27, 1964.

36. Nicholas Mansergh, ed., Documents and Speeches on Commonwealth Affairs, 1952-62 (London: Dawsons of Pall Mall, 1968), pp. 347-51.

37. Washington Post, October 28, 1977.

38. Ibid.

39. South African House of Assembly debates, June 17, 1965.

40. Washington Post, October 28, 1977.

41. U.S. Department of State, Bulletin, April 12, 1965.

42. Brooke Baldwin and Theodore Brown, Economic Action Against Apartheid (New York: American Committee on Africa, n.d.).

43. South African House of Assembly debates, September 21, 1966.

44. See Vernon McKay, in William A. Hance, ed., Southern Africa and the United States (New York: Columbia University Press, 1968), p. 24.

45. U.S. Department of State, Southern Africa: U.S. Policy in Brief (Washington, D.C.: December 1985).

Part 2
American Policy Implications

7
American Interests

Before we discuss American interests in southern Africa, a brief outline of U.S. policy toward Africa is in order. Historically, American interest in Africa has been exercised by proxy through the European imperial powers that controlled Africa--Britain, France, Portugal, Spain, Belgium, and the Netherlands. Until World War II, American contact had been fragmentary. Yankee traders had participated in the lucrative slave trade, and in 1822, the United States was instrumental in establishing Liberia as an independent country; American delegates attended the Berlin Conference of 1884-85 at which the boundaries of many African countries were agreed upon. American missionaries, philanthropists, and educators were long active in the African continent.[1] Beyond these sporadic encounters, American interest in Africa was minimal.

Today United States–Africa relations are influenced by considerations of trade, access to minerals, strategic and humanitarian concerns, and certain other pragmatic reasons. First, Africa has political clout. In addition to its own bloc of 50 nations, in concert with other nations of the Third World Africa constitutes two thirds of the membership of the United Nations. The continent, therefore, plays an important, often decisive, role in most international forums. Second, Africa is strategically located; many African countries possess good ports, airfields, and controlling positions in relation to major waterways. Africa is rich in important natural resources--oil, copper, diamonds, gold, bauxite, uranium, cobalt, and many

others.   Fourth, the continuing minority rule in southern
Africa makes it a potential arena for superpower confrontation.   Africans themselves do not wish their continent to
be used as such a battlefield.   Furthermore, Africa requires Western capital investment and technology, while
the West needs African raw material.   The North-South tension based on the affluence of the industrialized capitalist
world and the poverty of the nonindustrialized Third World
countries, if not resolved, could create overt hostility toward industrialized Western nations.   Last, Africa is particularly important to black Americans, who are increasingly concerned about the white minority rule in southern
Africa and other socioeconomic and political problems on
the African continent.

Elements of U.S. policy involving southern Africa
have shifted from time to time, depending on the various
administrations, changing congressional attitudes, and
shifting circumstances in Africa itself.   Present American
interests in Africa, more widespread than in the past, go
back no further than World War II, when American military planners became conscious of the strategic significance
of Africa.   Africa was the last continent "to be discovered
by the United States,"[2] remaining the "dark continent"
more for America than for any other country.   As late as
1958 the United States had more Foreign Service officials
in West Germany alone than in the whole continent of
Africa.[3]

America, with a black population of mostly African
origin, needs to develop mutually beneficial relations with
Africa.   The politicoeconomic and strategic importance of
Africa has forced the United States to pay greater attention
to a part of the world it largely ignored earlier.   Speaking before the annual convention of the National Association for the Advancement of Colored People (NAACP) at St.
Louis in 1977, former U.S. Secretary of State Cyrus Vance
noted the importance of the African nations in world affairs and their relationship with the United States:

> The role of the African nations at the
> United Nations, and in other multinational
> bodies, is pivotal.   One-third of the U.N.
> member states are African.   Africa's min-
> eral and agricultural wealth already pro-
> vides a substantial portion of our imports
> of such commodities as copper, cobalt,

and manganese for our industries, and cocoa
and coffee for our homes. And Africa supplies
38 percent of our petroleum imports.[4]

Southern Africa has additional significance, often
obscured by discussions of its complex internal problem of
race relations. South Africa's strategic geographic position, its dynamic economy, and substantial military capabilities are important variables in the calculations of
world politics and may become more important in the future.
In the southern African subcontinent, which is thoroughly
dominated by a single rich and powerful state, South
Africa, the United States is involved in the economic structure and, to a degree, is supportive of the politicomilitary
interests of South Africa. This policy is keyed to the
forces of status quo rather than to the forces of liberalism
and change.

White South Africa, like pre-Zimbabwe Rhodesia, is
a European nation transplanted to the soil of black Africa.
Its position is like a fish out of water. Being rootless,
the South African government is determined to follow its
oppressive policy of apartheid and thus has turned the
southern African system into a vast police state. For the
United States, the list of professed American principles
flouted by southern African society would appear to be a
compelling reason for concern. Racial equality, one man,
one vote, individual rights, freedom of the press, freedom
of thought, and above all, democracy and human rights,
are all abused by South Africa. U.S. policy toward southern Africa must be seen as an important test of the American government's response to a most difficult international
problem: protection of human rights. This type of policy requires firm and clear opposition to racial and social
injustice in southern Africa.

Addressing the United Nations in March 1977, U.S.
President Jimmy Carter made his commitment on human
rights firm:

> We in the United States accept this re-
> sponsibility in the fullest and the most
> constructive sense. Ours is a commitment,
> and not just a political posture. I know
> perhaps as well as anyone that our ideals
> in the area of human rights have not al-
> ways been attained in the United States,

but the American people have an abiding
commitment to the full realization of these
ideals. And we are determined, therefore,
to deal with our deficiencies quickly and
openly. We have nothing to conceal.[5]

The United States was the closest ally of South Africa
in both world wars. South Africa also assisted the Western
victors in World War II in the Berlin airlift. In the years
immediately following World War II, the Truman administration recognized South Africa's strategic importance and
directed U.S. policy to promote South Africa's economy.
The U.S. and South African missions were raised to embassy
level in 1948. The American friendship with South Africa
was again manifested during the Korean War when they
fought together. President Reagan has sounded the theme
of a new tilt in U.S. relations with South Africa. He
asked, "Can we abandon a country that has stood beside
us in every war we've ever fought."[6]

Growing American interests and involvement in
southern African affairs can be attributed to three factors:
(1) the verbal opposition to racial discrimination for the
purpose of protecting human rights, (2) the prosperity of
the American economy, which is to some extent dependent
on South Africa's minerals, and (3) military collaboration.
The United States has conflicting interests in southern
Africa, and there has not been a crisis in which one or
the other of these stakes was not fundamentally threatened,
thus forcing choice between them.

Apartheid emerged as a government policy in South
Africa while Truman was president of the United States.
"The Truman foreign policy was bold, innovative and effec-
tive--but not on African question."[7] To be sure, South
Africa had long cooperated with the United States in world
affairs. For example, Smuts worked closely with the Americans on the drafting of the charter of the United Nations.
But the harsh racial discrimination and inequalities that
had flourished in South Africa throughout his tenure were
most offensive. Smuts, probably the leading racist of all
South African leaders, was reported to have said in a
speech in New York that the Negro was "the most patient
of all animals, next to the ass."[8]

South Africa wanted to formalize the military relationship that had developed between the two countries during World War II and suggested the formation of an all-

African political and defense charter as a bulwark against communism. South Africa would cooperate with neighboring states (presumably the then European colonial powers in Africa) with the aim of preserving European civilization in Africa. There is no public record to indicate whether the Truman administration encouraged the South African government to believe that Washington might some day become a formal, rather than an informal, ally. But South Africa devised defense plans of its own in the event of Communist aggression, and these received approval in Britain and the United States.[9] South Africa reached an agreement with the United States for reimbursable military assistance under the Mutual Defense Act.

The South African government seemed to believe that its European background could somehow overcome the geographic barrier and thereby it could gain access to a "southern" North Atlantic Treaty Organization type of arrangement. When South Africa pushed for such a pact, it aroused little interest in Western Europe and the United States.[10]

The United States, while avoiding a formal, open military alliance, gained token South African assistance in the Berlin airlift and in the Korean War and a favorable settlement of the lend-lease debt.

SOUTH AFRICA

From the time of the establishment of a consulate in Cape Town in 1799, the United States has maintained official relations with the various governing entities. Important trading partners and wartime allies, the two countries are now adversely affected by South Africa's policy of apartheid. Brutally enforced, apartheid laws are in conflict with racial justice and human rights that are so much a part of American policy.

In order to demonstrate opposition to apartheid and support for nonviolent evolution toward racial equality, the United States has imposed many restrictions on its relations with South Africa. Among these are support given to the United Nations-imposed embargo on arms sale, police weapons, and equipment. In deference to the wishes of black Americans, the United States has imposed a ban on American naval ship visits to South Africa. The Reagan administration has imposed a partial economic sanction on South Africa.

In the field of trade, U.S. law requires that in order to qualify for Export-Import (ExIm) Bank services, nongovernment purchasers in South Africa must endorse and proceed toward the implementation of certain fair employment principles. As a matter of policy, the ExIm Bank has not extended direct loans for U.S. exports to South African purchases since 1964.[11] The United States has never provided economic or developmental assistance to South Africa.

Like the rest of the world, the United States has refused to recognize the creation in South Africa of the so-called independent homelands in Transkei, Bophuthatswana, Venda, and Ciskei. Because homeland policy is a fundamental element of the apartheid strategy of South Africa, any recognition to those homelands would be an affirmation of South Africa's policy of racial inequality and a confirmation of the policy of apartheid.

The United States endeavored to use its influence to encourage peaceful evolution of racial justice through the maintenance of contact with leaders of political groups and through encouragement of private American firms to improve the pay and working conditions of their black employees. The United States has been supporting various constructive measures against apartheid in the United Nations and other international organizations.

There are indications that Botha is personally willing to make minor modifications in South Africa's policy of apartheid. He has made some beginning by limiting discriminatory practices like segregation in some public facilities, lifting bans against mixed sports, and recognizing some black trade unions. The initial success of majority rule in Zimbabwe may encourage South Africa to move toward further changes in its racial attitude. The United States supports any policy that is conducive to the growth of racial justice. The dilemma is how to bring about such improvement without violence and force—both internal and external—while simultaneously maintaining relations with the government and credibility with the black population.

Increasingly, the United States is concerned and alarmed by the proliferation of nuclear weapons in the world. In Africa, particularly if South Africa develops its nuclear arsenal, such nations as Nigeria and Libya will go all out to develop or procure nuclear weapons. American policy in this regard is to prevail upon South Africa to cooperate with international nuclear nonproliferation goals.

NAMIBIA

The U.S. position on the status of Namibia has been stronger than its position on the racial situation in southern Africa. In 1974, the American delegation to the United Nations took the lead in attacking South Africa on the issue of Namibia.[12] In 1949, the United Nations, with U.S. support, asked the International Court of Justice for an advisory opinion on South Africa's legal obligation to place Namibia under international trusteeship. The United States argued that the League of Nations mandate was still in force and that the United Nations and the Trusteeship Council were heirs of the League and the mandate commission. Many legal proceedings designed to have South Africa withdraw from Namibia have been drawn.

South Africa challenged the opinion of the ICJ and said that it was not bound by it. Pretoria decided to proceed with the parliamentary elections in Namibia, and the nationalist representatives from the territory were added to the nationalist majority in the South African Parliament. The United Nations was busy with the Korean War and, taking advantage of the situation, South Africa modified its disagreements with Washington. Nevertheless, the United States in support of a resolution in the UN General Assembly opposed by South Africa, called for negotiations with the Pretorian government on Namibia. In 1951, the United States was one of the eight sponsors of a resolution regretting South African policies on Namibia and urging that they be changed.[13]

This positive attitude of the United States was undercut by its hesitation in granting a visa to the Reverend Michael Scott, who wished to speak for the Namibians before the United Nations. The American representatives at the United Nations opposed Scott's appearance before the Trusteeship Committee, arguing that it would fog the World Court's decision. The NAACP appealed to the U.S. government on behalf of Scott, but in vain. The Trusteeship Committee, by resolution, regretted further that the South African government refused to present the Namibian chief with any travel documents to meet with the committee in New York.[14]

Each year the United Nations has fruitlessly condemned South Africa for its failure to live up to the terms of the charter. In 1966 the UN General Assembly revoked South Africa's mandate, and in 1971 the ICJ stated, in an advisory opinion, that South Africa was obligated to withdraw its administrator from Namibia.

At the 1975 Turnhalle Conference of representatives from most elements of the territory's population, South Africa sought to engineer a unilateral internal settlement based on a weak federation of ethnic groups. Since this plan was not internationally acceptable, the five Western members of the UN Security Council began a cooperative effort in 1977 to find a way to implement Security Council Resolution 385 for ensuring free and fair elections in Namibia under UN supervision. The Western five (the United States, Britain, France, West Germany, and Canada) have persisted, despite the fact that South Africa refuses to allow a United Nations-supervised election. South Africa insists that a precondition to any United Nations-supervised election is that no SWAPO forces be quartered within Namibia and that guerrilla bases in neighboring countries be carefully monitored.

Although on occasion it seems that a settlement of the Namibian question is imminent, South Africa continues to vacillate by insisting on conditions that neither SWAPO nor the United Nations and the Western nations would accept. America's plan for Namibian independence calls for assembling an expert panel to write a national constitution that would guarantee rights to the white minority. Only then would national elections be called. The framework of this scheme was outlined by Secretary of State Alexander M. Haig during South African Foreign Minister Botha's May 1981 Washington visit. But before the ink on the blueprint was dry, Sam Nujoma, the leader of the main guerrilla group fighting for Namibian independence, accused the United States and other Western nations of conspiratorial efforts to deviate from the UN plan.

The United States has been deeply involved in the problem of Namibia, the last major item on the agenda of African decolonization. The five Western nations, also known as the contact group, formulated a plan that was approved in 1978 as UN Security Council Resolution 435; it was provisionally accepted by South Africa, SWAPO, and Namibia's neighbors--the frontline states of Angola, Botswana, Mozambique, Tanzania, Zambia, and Zimbabwe.

Under the plan, a UN transitional assistance group, with civilian members, would be established in Namibia during the transition to independence; a constituent assembly would be elected and charged with drafting and adopting a constitution; South African troops would be progressively withdrawn, national elections held, and independence proclaimed. South Africa initially agreed to these principles, but Pretoria expressed growing reservations and finally broke off negotiations in Geneva in 1981.

Recognizing that independence for Namibia in the near future was impossible without South Africa's cooperation, in its first term the Reagan administration sought to regain the contact group initiative by addressing South African concerns more directly. In September 1981, a new phased plan for implementing Resolution 435, with features designed to satisfy all parties, was introduced. This proposal called for agreement on a set of constitutional principles to guide the drafters of the constitution and to ensure that the interests of all Namibians would be protected; agreement on the composition and size, as well as the operation, of the UN transitional assistance group, on the disposition of all troops during the transition period, and on measures relating to UN impartiality; and initiation for the transition procedure set forth in Resolution 435.

Since 1981, the United States and its contact group partners have obtained South Africa's recommitment to arrangements for bringing about Namibian independence through adherence to Resolution 435--the only internationally acceptable basis for solution; obtained the agreement of SWAPO, the United Nations, and the concerned neighboring African states to the arrangement negotiated with South Africa; and rejected South Africa's inclination to seek its own internal settlement in Namibia, which would inevitably guarantee many more years of regional turmoil. The United States considers the South African government's 1985 action in establishing an interim government for Namibia to be null and void and without standing.

The Reagan administration, as would be the case for any American government, faces difficulties in southern Africa. On the one hand, the continued existence of apartheid in South Africa and Namibia and the weak governments in other countries of the region encourage guerrilla actions and invite civil war. On the other hand, the stance taken by the African governments toward other issues, such as East-West confrontation, will be determined in part by their judgments concerning the stance of the United States toward dismantling apartheid and promoting the economic welfare of the black people in southern Africa.

ZIMBABWE

On November 11, 1965, the circumstances of Rhodesian politics were irrevocably altered by the declaration of independence by Prime Minister Smith. This act was considered illegal by the United States, Britain, and the whole of Africa and the outside world. The U.S. government, at the United Nations and elsewhere, denounced the discriminatory racial policies adopted by the Rhodesian government and deplored the "unilateral action of the white minority government of Rhodesia in illegally seizing power."[15] The United States decided to recall its consul general in Rhodesia and terminated the activities of the United States Information Service there.[16] The consulate was not closed until 1970.

On the second day of the Rhodesian declaration of independence, the U.S. representative at the United Nations, Arthur J. Goldberg, announced a series of American policy measures that included an arms embargo; restrictions on American private travel (Americans were urged to obtain British, not Rhodesian, visas); suspension of sugar imports from Rhodesia; and actions on application for American government loans, credits, and investment guarantees.[17] Very little enthusiasm was found among American officials for stronger measures, such as military intervention. This was because American officials disagreed with Africans on at least two counts: The U.S. government doubted that racial discrimination in Rhodesia constituted a threat to international peace, and there were doubts about the success of foreign military action and embargoes.

Nevertheless, the American position at the United Nations had been to support the United Nations and the British in their efforts to arrange compromises with the African delegations and thus ensure the success of the United Nations. Here the U.S. delegate had the Congo crisis in mind and was cautious about urging any action that might embarrass the Americans or the British. They, therefore, agreed that the United Nations should be involved in the Rhodesian crisis. The Nixon administration moved to deny recognition to Rhodesia and closed the American

consulate in Salisbury.[18] Soon the U.S. government condemned racial discrimination in southern Africa and pledged
to bring it to an end.

Against a backdrop of growing conflict in Rhodesia,
the Ford administration began a major change in U.S. foreign policy in Rhodesia. Secretary of State Henry A. Kissinger set forth the particular line of the policy in the
course of a speech delivered at Lusaka, capital of Zambia,
on April 27, 1976. He stated that the situation in Rhodesia
required the most immediate attention within the context of
the new U.S.-African policy. Intensive negotiations in
African capitals and in Geneva sought to compel the Rho-
desians to produce a plan acceptable to the black majority.

The Lusaka speech provoked an immediate response
in the United States. Supporters viewed it as a move
likely to enhance the American position throughout Africa.
Some saw it as a major diplomatic setback for the Soviet
Union. Opponents argued that America should intervene
more directly to unseat the white minority government in
Rhodesia. The American government had ignored racial
confrontation in southern Africa. "Only the Angolan affairs, bringing with it Soviet-Cuban military intervention,
alerted Washington to the need to compose a more attentive
policy."[19]

The Ford administration's position on Rhodesia
rested on ten points: (1) support of the British proposals
for a majority rule; (2) no diplomatic or material help to
Rhodesia; (3) fulfillment of obligations, under international
law, to observe mandatory economic sanctions; (4) negotiation of a settlement leading to majority rule; (5) denial
of official representation in Rhodesia; (6) assistance to
Mozambique where closing of the borders with Rhodesia for
the purpose of enforcing economic sanctions had resulted
in economic hardship; (7) alleviation of economic hardship
for any countries neighboring on Rhodesia that decide to
enforce sanction by closing their own borders; (8) humanitarian assistance to refugees who have fled in distress
from Rhodesia into neighboring countries; (9) support of a
program of economic, technical, and educational assistance
in cooperation with the world community to aid the newly
independent Zimbabwe; and (10) creation of a constitution
that would protect minority rights and a secure future for
both blacks and whites.[20]

In his inaugural address, President Carter stated
clearly and forcefully his own personal commitment to human

rights.[21] He repeated this commitment in remarks made at
the United Nations on March 17, 1977: "This week the government of the United States took action to bring our country into full compliance with United Nations sanctions
against the illegal regime in Rhodesia. And I will sign
that bill Friday in Washington."[22]

After years of promising an internal solution to
Rhodesia's racial trouble, Smith offered elections on the
basis of one man, one vote. The "pressures induced by
American diplomacy in a crisis area (Rhodesia) have helped
provoke an unexpected but welcome local initiative."[23] Although the United States had been committed to a British
initiative for a peaceful transfer of power in Rhodesia, the
American government, finding itself in a helpless position,
offered to support the initiative taken by Smith. The Department of State said Smith's move "is a step in the right
direction. However, it appears to be a conditional one."[24]
At the United Nations, Ambassador Andrew Young dismissed
Smith's offer as "no proposal for a settlement. If anything, this sort of thing would intensify the fighting."[25]
However, the basic trend of American policy--support of
the British initiative for a peaceful settlement and majority rule in Rhodesia and an immediate end to the guerrilla
warfare and pursuit of a negotiated settlement in which
blacks and whites could coexist and cooperate--toward
Zimbabwe remained unchanged.

On March 3, 1978, the Smith regime and three black
nationalists signed the Salisbury Agreement, which provided
for qualified majority rule. The Patriotic Front denounced
the settlement. After elections in April 1979, Bishop
Muzorewa was installed as the first black prime minister
of Zimbabwe. Following the election of a new conservative
government in Britain in May 1979, the British government
undertook a new initiative. This effort culminated in the
Lancaster House settlement, signed December 21, 1979 by
all concerned, including the Patriotic Front. The United
States fully supported the settlement.

Under the plan Robert Mugabe was elected prime
minister. The United States urged the various parties to
make necessary compromises that were eventually required
for a final solution. The United States assisted in the
British airlift to Salisbury of material used to monitor the
cease-fire. The United States immediately offered $15 mil-
lion in economic aid to the new nation of Zimbabwe and
became the first nation to open an embassy there.[26]

UNITED STATES ATTITUDES

The U.S. attitudes toward South Africa's policy of apartheid have never won much applause from either blacks or whites. Blacks see the United States as failing to take logical steps--economically, politically, and diplomatically-- to isolate and weaken the white government and thus hasten black rule. U.S. trade and investments in South Africa are seen by blacks as extensions of American policy. Black antagonism to American policy also stems from their belief that the United States refuses to give money and arms to black exile groups. On the other hand, whites in South Africa believe U.S. policy is based on an expedient attempt to win favor in the Third World. To them, American policies spell the end of white rule and supremacy in South Africa.

To the surprise of many observers, the Reagan administration is discouraging assumptions that it will rush to embrace the white government in South Africa. However, it is apparent that evenhandedness is the dominant theme, as enunciated by Reagan's chief adviser on African affairs, Chester Crocker, when he toured Africa, including South Africa, in April 1981. Nevertheless, the South African government is buoyant with expectations about improved relations with the United States.

Its hope for closer ties flows from a series of encouraging signs: official American comments on the need to halt Soviet expansion and international terrorism; a visit to Washington by Prime Minister Botha (now president); suggestions that the Reagan administration might offer assistance to anti-Marxist guerrillas in Angola; willingness of U.S. officials to meet with South African-backed political parties in Namibia; Reagan's statement that America cannot abandon South Africa and the administration's use of veto against the UN Security Council Resolution on August 31, 1981 (the United States, in a break with its allies, vetoed a resolution condemning South Africa for its raid into Angola); and last, but far from least, the indication that the United States now favors altering a Western-designed UN plan for independence of Namibia and calls for the establishment of a constitution before election. South African officials welcome this proposal, one they have promoted for some time.

In its six years of governance, the Reagan administration has made some efforts to develop friendly relations with the new nation of Zimbabwe. However, there have been many ups and downs: U.S. officials expressed annoyance over Zimbabwe's abstention on the U.S. Security Council vote condemning the Soviet downing of a Korean Air Lines jet, and its cosponsorship of a Security Council resolution denouncing the U.S. intervention in Grenada. U.S. relations with Zimbabwe have deteriorated, and the Reagan administration cut foreign aid to $40 million from the original $75 million. Although there is a precipitous move toward a one-party state, Zimbabwe gives every indication of remaining the main southern African recipient of American economic aid and technical assistance.

NONGOVERNMENT ORGANIZATIONS

The most active interest displayed by a nongovernment organization in the United States toward African or southern African affairs emanates from the American Committee on Africa (ACOA). Formed in 1953 by a group of civil rights activists, with headquarters in New York, the ACOA has been the leading organization among those that consistently protest against American collaboration with southern Africa. It has pressed for U.S. disengagement in southern Africa. Representatives of the NAACP, the Congress of Racial Equality (CORE), the Urban League, and the National Conference of Negro Women (NCNW) supported the efforts of the ACOA, which was motivated by concern over race relations more than any longstanding policy in southern Africa.

The special interest that these and other groups of black American citizens show toward the southern African crisis is due to a concern for the people of Africa in general and the oppressed people of southern Africa in particular. Their potential power may be illustrated by the success in 1967 of the American Negro Leadership Conference in forcing a shift in government policy at South African ports of call by U.S. naval vessels.

The ACOA has been publicizing its objectives as including active, tangible support to the African forces of liberation from colonialism, racism, and other forms of sociopolitical and economic exploitation. The group's Africa Today (turned over to the University of Denver in 1966) emphasizes the issue of apartheid and discourages all forms of cooperation between the United States and southern Africa. The ACOA has led and participated in protests and demonstrations against white supremacy in southern Africa. The ACOA and CORE picketed the South African consulate in New York to protest the Sharpeville massacre.[27] They have also protested against American banks and corporations doing business with southern Africa.

The ACOA has organized a World-Wide Day of Protest against apartheid, Human Rights Day against racism, Africa Freedom Day urging Americans to boycott southern African goods, and nationwide public meetings to make Americans aware of the consequences of the primacy of an aristocracy of color in southern Africa. The ACOA has supported a series of conferences on the general theme of apartheid and the rigid hierarchy of racial castes in southern Africa.

Following the establishment of the OAU, the ACOA formed a Consultative Council on Southern Africa, composed of some 75 labor, church, civil rights, and student organizations in the United States. Before the Consultative Council dissolved, it held two conferences in Washington. The ACOA helped organize the American Negro Leadership Conference and the Committee of Conscience Against Apartheid.

The ACOA has enabled black Africans to visit the United States, providing them with financial support and helping with visa problems. By way of its Africa Defense and Aid Fund, created in 1956, the ACOA has also provided legal and financial assistance to political prisoners, their families, and refugees in southern Africa. Despite many problems, the ACOA has remained one of the most important nongovernment organizations focusing on antiapartheid in the United States. It has demonstrated devotion to its cause and has helped retain an interest in southern Africa among black Americans. The major civil rights groups, such as NAACP and CORE, have often attacked the policy of apartheid in southern Africa. They have also joined the campaigns against apartheid organized by the ACOA. Together, these organizations may hold the key to the future strength of the antiapartheid movement in the United States.

PRIVATE INDIVIDUALS

Dr. Martin Luther King, on occasion, attacked apartheid in public statements. He also called for sanctions

and boycott of South Africa by the United States. In 1966
Dr. King was refused a South African visa, preventing him
from visiting South Africa to address a student gathering.
He took part in the American Negro Leadership Conference
on Africa.

Dick Gregory, the black comedian and political activist, spent much of his Thanksgiving Day in 1977 in a
Washington, D.C., jail.[28] He, his wife, and Bill Ownes,
a state senator from Massachusetts, were arrested for demonstrating within 500 feet of the South African embassy in
violation of a District of Columbia Law in Washington that
prohibits demonstration within such areas. They were
leading a group of about 50 people protesting the involvement of U.S. corporations in South Africa. At a press conference in front of the White House earlier in the day
Gregory said: "We ask you (the Carter administration) to
move swiftly to demonstrate to the ruler of the world's
most wicked government that our nation will no longer help
to subsidize human degradation which is an obscenity before God."[29]

South Africa's racial problems may affect the United
States internally and externally, since the plight of the
nonwhites elicits sympathy from American civil rights
groups. However, thus far there is evidence of only limited interest in the problem among black Americans. Pressure for stronger U.S. action against South Africa comes
mainly from other liberal, humanitarian, and academic
groups.

South Africans are used to hearing criticism of their
policy from abroad, but when outspoken attacks came from
a black American visitor in their own land it had a gal-
vanizing effect. The Reverend Jesse L. Jackson, the
Chicago-based black activist, called South Africa a "terrorist dictatorship"[30] and compared apartheid to the "un-
godly acts of Hitler."[31] Initially South Africa turned
down Jackson's visa request, but changed its mind under
pressure from the Carter administration. During his two-
week stay in South Africa, protected by its police, Jackson
deplored the factionalism among black leaders. He stirred
anxieties among whites with his efforts to promote unity
among blacks. The South African government accused him
of usurping the role of the country's own black leaders.

The current American relationship with South Africa
is far from normal. The significant embargoes and restrictions already in place on U.S. trade and limited co-

operation in the military and nuclear weapons areas, as well as reluctance to pursue certain corporate commercial relationships, demonstrate in a tangible way, that the United States finds apartheid repugnant. American arms sales to South Africa have been banned under the UN mandatory arms embargo of 1977.

On occasions the U.S. government has called for an end to apartheid in South Africa, but the most significant action taken was on September 9, 1985, when Ronald Reagan announced further restrictions on U.S. ties with Pretoria. This measure included restrictions on nuclear and computer sales and on bank loans to the South African government, a ban on arms imports from South Africa, a ban on importing Krugerrands, and a new requirement that U.S. firms operating in South Africa adhere to the Sullivan code of fair employment. American firms in South Africa have voluntarily set the pace among all foreign and domestic companies in supporting black advancement and have spent more than $115 million to date on black education and housing. The president also has increased American assistance to black education, black entrepreneurs, and black trade unions, as well as funds for human rights and legal assistance programs.

Many antiapartheid groups and individuals protest and get arrested outside the South African embassy in Washington quite frequently. Congress and the president have blamed apartheid as being largely responsible for the 1984-86 violence in South Africa. The White House has toughened its rhetoric toward South Africa recently by calling upon the government there to lift its state of emergency. But this action appears to underscore the lack of success of the Reagan administration's policy of "constructive engagement" or quiet diplomacy, in dealing with racially troubled white-ruled South Africa (American diplomatic initiatives are discussed in Chapter 9).

CHURCH GROUPS

Black interest in southern Africa has continued to grow rapidly within many churches in the United States. The World Council of Churches (WCC), composed of about 200 Protestant and Eastern Orthodox denominations from around the world and the United States, is a constant opponent of racial injustice in southern Africa. The WCC

believes that any form of segregation based on race and
color is prejudicial to the interest of humanity and contrary to the principles of Christianity. A WCC conference
in 1960 attacked apartheid and called for direct representation of the black people in southern Africa.[32] In 1965,
the WCC appealed for funds to support victims of discrimination in southern Africa, and by 1971, the churches in
the United States had raised $320,000.[33] In the same
year, the WCC called on its members to work for a ban on
all arms sales to South Africa and to stop white immigration there.

The National Council of Churches (NCC) has been
working for racial justice and self-determination in southern Africa. The NCC is involved in campaigns against
U.S. economic ties with southern Africa. In 1977, the NCC
called upon its 30 constituent denominations to withdraw
all their funds from banks and other financial institutions
conducting business with southern Africa. The NCC's action followed an address by UN Ambassador Young, who
described as prophetic the role of religion in the worldwide quest for an end to racial discrimination.[34]

The United Presbyterian Church presently calls on
churches in South Africa to persuade its government to
abandon apartheid and asks the U.S. government to cease
all material support to southern African governments.

The first American church to take meaningful action
in South Africa was the United Methodist Church. It with-
drew its $10 million investment portfolio from the First
National City Bank, which was aiding South Africa by its
participation in a credit consortium with other banks.
The United Methodist Church has donated money to the
South African Institute of Race Relations and the National
Union of South African Students. Other denominations,
such as the Protestant Episcopal Church and the United
Church of Christ, have put increasing pressure on the
United States to adopt a racially progressive business
practice in southern Africa.

The growth of black pressure within various churches
has given a particular focus to racial aspects of the problems existing in southern Africa. The churches have generally taken a position of first urging more progressive
business practices and, failing that, disengagement.
Furthermore, black church officials are pressing their
executives for divestment in American businesses that have
commercial relations with southern Africa.

ACADEMIA

As the crisis in southern Africa rises in intensity and scale, the academic community, both faculty and students, has tried to promote American interest in southern African affairs. The American Association of University Professors has passed resolutions and given money to support South African academics opposing apartheid.[35] The African Studies Association (ASA), the professional organization of Africanists in the United States, prefers to maintain academic neutrality on policy issues. The African Heritage Studies Association (AHSA) has been established to work outside the ASA.

Although southern African politics has never caught on with large numbers of students as a protest issue, unlike Vietnam, there has been some activity. The National Students Association and Students for a Democratic Society have made some efforts to organize sustained student interest in the affairs of southern Africa. As demonstrations have become a less frequent form of campus protest, emphasis is now on the academic study of the U.S. involvement in southern Africa.

The African-American Institute, supported by foundations, has been cautious in adopting antiapartheid policies. The United States South Africa Leadership Exchange Program, a voluntary organization, has been working to develop a mutual basis of cooperation among professionals in all fields in the United States and South Africa. It supports, among other things, conferences and exchange programs.

The campus conflict over divestment in South Africa began at Harvard University in 1976. The first college divestment in April 1977 followed a building occupation by students at Hampshire College, Massachusetts. The divestment movement reached an almost critical stage in 1985–86, when frequent riots erupted in South Africa. Harvard University, with its $400 million portfolio of companies active in South Africa, agreed to a compromise in order to satisfy liberal elements; the university set up a million-dollar fund to aid black South African education.[36] On the national scene, while some campuses withdrew funds completely, others adopted bureaucratic solutions: partial divestment, committee studies of divestment, faculty council recommendation, and delayed disinvestment. The debate goes on as trustees in many American universities are attacked for holding stocks in corporations doing business with South Africa.

Interest group activities in the United States have induced American companies having business interests in South Africa to adopt the Sullivan code of fair practice in business. At the same time, many Americans and South African blacks maintain that the Sullivan principles only sustain apartheid and delay the inevitable destruction of the unique and unjust system of race relations. Be that as it may, antiapartheid protests and rhetoric in the United States stand to intensify on campuses, and many universities and foundations are likely to sell shares in corporations operating in South Africa (see divestment action in Appendix B).

BUSINESS COMMUNITY

One of the oldest of American interests in southern Africa is the business community. Although they are becoming increasingly important to antiapartheid activity, the 260 American companies doing business with South Africa must be reckoned with by American policymakers in any decisions on southern Africa.

As pointed out earlier, the United States has almost always had a favorable balance of trade with South Africa, and American business interests have never been very adversely affected. U.S. corporations doing business in South Africa know they face continuing pressures for disengagement. The points of view of the business community were illustrated by the president of the Chase Manhattan Bank:

> If we consider the receiver of a loan to be financially responsible we do business with him, regardless of his nationality, religion or political views. A loan to the Republic of South Africa is considered sound banking business, and we feel it would be unwise and unfair if we, as a bank, made judgments that were not based on economics. This does not mean, however, that the Chase Manhattan Bank endorses the political decisions of the government of the Republic of South Africa, or any other country

which receives a loan from us. On the
other hand, we believe it would endanger
the free world if every large American
bank deprived developing countries of the
opportunity for economic growth. If one
hopes for changes in the Republic of South
Africa, or elsewhere, it would do little
good to withdraw economic support.[37]

Many concerned organizations and individuals would not
agree with this statement, but it clearly explains the attitude of the American business world.

In November 1977, more than 130 U.S. firms set up
an American Chamber of Commerce in South Africa to spur
its trade and commerce with the United States.[38] The newly created Chamber wants to get across in Washington "a
more balanced view of what American business is doing in
South Africa."[39]

The American multinationals in South Africa are
coming under increasing fire in the United States. The
NAACP, hardening its stand, now calls for a total withdrawal of American firms from southern Africa. The Reverend Leon Sullivan, a black minister and a director of
General Motors, has been urging a strict code of conduct
for U.S. companies operating in South Africa.

It may be that American businesspeople unwittingly
have helped stimulate interest in southern African crises
by assisting the development of African studies programs
in American universities and giving financial aid to African students studying in the United States. The extent to
which such support has helped to elicit positive interest in
southern Africa (which donors want) is hard to judge.
Undoubtedly, it has helped to create opposition to southern
Africa's repressive policy of apartheid.

For years, American corporations professed to believe that South Africa was a place where they could earn
profits and do good business. U.S. corporations raised
black wages closer to white levels, desegregated plants
and offices, and fought against divestment advocates at
home. The reasons that the American companies are now
leaving South Africa are many and varied. What stand
out are the deteriorating economy in southern Africa,
American economic sanctions, the escalation of violence,
and the unrelenting pressure from antiapartheid groups in
the United States. The divestment campaign has only begun

to show its full impact.   U.S. business enterprises dependent on good public and university relations cannot afford
to do "business as usual in South Africa."   Any company
with a consumer product that can be boycotted could be
the target, sooner or later.

NOTES

1.   For a discussion on American missionary, phil-
anthropic, and educational activities, see Vernon McKay,
Africa in World Politics (New York: Harper & Row, 1963),
pp. 250–60.
2.   Cecil V. Crabb, Jr., American Foreign Policy
in the Nuclear Age (New York: Harper & Row, 1972), p.
297.
3.   Ibid.
4.   U.S. Department of State, Secretary of State,
U.S. Policy Toward Africa, July 1, 1977.
5.   New York Times, March 18, 1977.
6.   Time, June 15, 1981.
7.   Waldermar A. Nielsen, The Great Powers and
Africa (New York: Praeger, 1969), p. 278.
8.   John H. Willington, South West Africa and Its
Human Issues (London: Oxford University Press, 1967),
p. 405.
9.   New York Times, May 24, 1951.
10.   John P. Cope, South Africa (New York: Praeger,
1967), pp. 193–94.
11.   U.S. Department of State, Bureau of Public Affairs, Sub-Saharan Africa and the United States (Washington, D.C., August 1980), p. 28.
12.   New York Times, September 26 and 27, 1947.
13.   Ibid., December 7, 1951.
14.   Ibid.
15.   Anthony Lake, The "Tar Baby" Option: American Policy Toward Southern Rhodesia (New York: Columbia
University Press, 1976), p. 81.
16.   Ibid.
17.   Ibid., pp. 81–82.
18.   Crabb, American Foreign Policy, p. 303.
19.   Washington Post (editorial), April 25, 1977.
20.   See Secretary of State, Henry A. Kissinger's
speech in Lusaka, Zambia, as reported in Washington Post,
April 28, 1976.

21. New York Times, January 21, 1977.
22. Ibid., March 18, 1977.
23. Washington Post (editorial), November 26, 1977.
24. Washington Star, November 26, 1977.
25. Ibid.
26. New York Times, April 19, 1980.
27. Ibid., March 24, 1960.
28. Washington Star, November 25, 1977.
29. Ibid.
30. William F. Buckley, Jr., "When Jesse Jackson Visits South Africa," Washington Star, August 9, 1979.
31. New York Times, August 2, 1979.
32. Ibid., December 15, 1960.
33. Ibid., January 17, 1971.
34. Ibid., November 11, 1977.
35. Ibid., January 11, 1960.
36. Nation, March 1, 1986, p. 227.
37. Africa Digest, April 1965, p. 131.
38. Washington Post, November 24, 1977.
39. Ibid.

8
Economic Collaboration

Broadly speaking, the United States considers it
vital to its national interest and national security to expand the market for American products in the developing
Afro-Asian and Latin American countries. It follows from
this assumption, based on postwar realities, that the primary American interests in southern Africa are economic.

SOUTH AFRICA

It is usually American economic interests that prevent the United States from pressing southern African countries on apartheid--fear lest the market be lost. As a
former Pentagon historian says:

> Without the American money poured into
> South Africa in the form of investments,
> and without the United States' shielding of
> South Africa in the United Nations against
> sanctions and other strong measures to
> bring down apartheid as demanded by the
> great majority of nations, the brutal South
> African white dictatorship could not stand
> for long.[1]

An examination of U.S. economic interests in South
Africa shows that they have increased rapidly. Before
World War II, U.S. exports to South Africa were $66 million

annually. In 1946, they reached $230 million.[2] By 1948, the trade balance reached $300 million a year, in favor of the United States.[3] To remedy the situation, South Africa sought to attract U.S. capital and intensified its efforts to raise loans from the ExIm Bank and private American sources. The South African finance minister visited Washington and the ExIm Bank offered a loan. But South Africa rejected the loan because it could not agree to the conditions--a gold deposit as security.

In 1946 a three-year $10 million revolving credit was arranged with private American banks, but it was soon replaced by a $20 million revolving credit with eight banks--Bank of America, National City Bank of New York, Central Hanover Bank and Trust Company, Bankers Trust Company, Chemical Bank and Trust Company, New York Trust Company, Bank of the Manhattan Company, and First National Bank of Chicago.[4]

Under the Eisenhower administration, U.S. investment in South Africa grew from $212 million to $350 million.[5] South Africa remained a good market for U.S. exports, creating another foreign exchange crisis for Pretoria during the early years of the Eisenhower administration. American exports to South Africa rose from $249 million in 1958 to $427 million in 1960.[6]

The United States maintains normal commercial relations with South Africa; however, it avoids giving the appearance of closeness to the South African regime and neither encourages nor discourages American investments in South Africa. The U.S. government realizes that "There is reason to believe that wide and adverse publicity accorded race relations and political discord in the Union (of South Africa) discouraged many potential investors."[7]

But many American investors, bankers, and businesspeople are not discouraged by the political crisis in South Africa. The U.S. government encourages American firms operating in South Africa to establish employment conditions in those South African plants consistent with standards in their home plants. The government itself refrains from undertaking certain highly visible trade promotion activities in South Africa but does not discourage private American companies from participating in trade fairs or other promotional activities in South Africa.[8]

The period following the Sharpeville incident in 1960 produced South Africa's most severe foreign exchange crisis in history. In the first seven weeks after the incident,

as foreigners began to withdraw their holdings, the gold
and foreign exchange reserve dropped $64 million. Soon,
however, American corporations began to express confidence
in South Africa's future stability, and American capital
again began to pour into South Africa's economy. In 1961,
a year after the Sharpeville crisis, U.S. companies had
increased their investments in South Africa by $23 million.
Loans from Chase Manhattan Bank, First City Bank, and
other American banks and from the World Bank and its affiliates were made available to South Africa to save it
from disaster. Within a year South Africa's economic
crisis was over.

While the New York Times reported that South African businesspeople were putting pressure on their government to make some concessions to the black people to head
off confrontation, American investments, accompanied by
funds provided by the World Bank and its affiliates, relieved the South African government from the necessity of
liberalizing its policy of apartheid.[9]

Although the American government maintains "neutrality" toward American investment in South Africa, the
U.S. Department of Commerce issues occasional reports on
market conditions in South Africa that are favorable to
American investors. Commercial officers at the United
States embassy and its consulates in South Africa assist
potential investors in every way possible.[10] As a result
of this increased cooperation between the government departments and officials and American business, American
companies earned $72 million in South African profits in
1962. This profit was almost twice the average rate of
profit on investment in other countries.

The Kennedy and Johnson administrations moved beyond Truman and Eisenhower policies in expressing displeasure at apartheid, but the basic U.S.-South African
economic collaboration remained unchanged. The United
States continued its collaboration with South Africa, with
the exception of commerce in those items covered by the
arms embargo and economic sanction. In 1965, the United
States had a $200 million favorable trade balance with
South Africa. By 1968, American investment in South Africa
was about five times the value of that in 1960.[11] Normal-
ly some of the American oil companies handle nearly half
of South Africa's oil requirements, and American oil firms
have been in the forefront of those that have been granted
oil-prospecting concessions in South Africa.

Largely because of the new two-tier gold market arrangement of 1968, aimed at reducing upward pressures on the price of gold, South Africa faced a serious foreign exchange deficit in 1969. Negotiators representing the United States, South Africa, and the International Monetary Fund (IMF) reached an agreement in December 1969 that gave South Africa a most favorable gold marketing position.[12] This agreement preserved the American proposal of two-tier arrangement. It served South Africa's interest by granting it the right to sell gold at $35 per ounce to official buyers, even though the market price was below $35. South Africa could also sell gold higher when the free market price was up.[13] The Washington Post reported that during the first six months of 1970 South Africa made some $307 million in gold sales to the IMF.[14] The American balance of trade with South Africa remained favorable. U.S. private investment continued to grow.

In addition, beginning in 1970, the Nixon administration was strongly urging American business to invest in neighboring black states of South Africa. It was believed that this kind of investment in black Africa would help improve the image of American investors in Africa and consequently bring about an improvement in business. An increased economic upturn would probably encourage American businesses to undertake improvement of working conditions for nonwhite employees in South Africa.

In 1972 the United States had a favorable trade balance with South Africa. South Africa's export to the United States amounted to $324.7 million and imports from the United States amounted to $597.1 million.[15] Major exports to the United States consisted of diamonds, precious stones, metals, and sugar; imports included machinery, electrical equipment, chemicals, textiles, precision instruments, and papers.

Following the lead of the previous administrations, the Ford administration condemned South Africa's racial policy of apartheid by which a 14 percent minority limits most of the prosperity and economic development to whites only. South Africa remained an active trading partner and economic collaborator of the United States in 1975. U.S. trade with South Africa amounted to about $1.3 billion in exports and about $849 million in imports. About the same period (1975), American private investment totaled $1.46 billion, or about 40 percent of America's total investment in Africa.[16]

The Carter administration pursued a policy of retaining access to the mineral wealth of southern Africa. It visualized a very substantial growth in two-way trade under the proper political circumstances.[17] Spelling out the government's intentions toward southern Africa, William E. Schaufele, assistant secretary for African affairs, said: "Our policy toward Southern Africa is guided by our ideals of liberty and equality and by our commitment to oppose racial and social injustice. We believe that the minority governments in Rhodesia, South Africa, and Namibia violate fundamental human rights as spelled out in the UN Declaration of Human Rights."[18]

There are about 260 American-owned firms with investments and other business interests in South Africa.[19] Economic and commercial involvement between the United States and South Africa remains substantial and is valued at more than $14 billion.[20] Nearly one-third of all U.S. exports to the whole of the African continent, representing 50 countries, is with South Africa alone.[21] For the United States, economic partnership with South Africa has been most profitable. Next to the British investments in South Africa, which are at least three times as large as American, investments and trade with South Africa "represent a much more deliberate desire on the part of American investors to profit from apartheid."[22]

SOURCE OF SUPPLY

South Africa remains an important source for the United States of such items as diamonds, chemical chrome, asbestos, platinum, gold, and uranium. These commodities are very useful and almost indispensable in some cases. Of course, the United States could do without these imports from South Africa, but it would cause hardship to some industries and perhaps heartbreak to gem-loving American women.[23] The depletion of natural and mineral resources in the United States may lead to continuing dependence on such countries as South Africa.

In the last few years a great deal of attention has been focused on U.S. economic relations with South Africa, almost always profitable for the United States. South Africa is regarded as "one of those rare and refreshing places where profits are great and problems small. Capital is not threatened by political instability or nationalization. Labor is cheap, the market booming, the currency hard and convertible."24

U.S. exports to South Africa increased 30 percent in 1979. American investment in South Africa continues to expand gradually, reaching $2.5 billion. The outlook for U.S. exports to South Africa is very favorable, due to rapid growth taking place in the South African economy. Sophisticated capital equipment for mining and manufacturing should have particular market potential, as will data processing equipment and various chemical products. Obstacles exist--such as the absence of ExIm Bank's guarantee--but these are not expected to prevent continued growth in American exports to South Africa. Except for the arms embargo and restrictions on commerce on sensitive technologies, the United States maintained normal commercial intercourse with South Africa until September 9, 1985, when President Reagan announced further restrictions on relations with Pretoria.

Opposition to apartheid is no recent development. During the Carter administration, and in the six years of the Reagan administration, the U.S. government has expressed disapproval in one way or another of South Africa's oppressive regime. Nevertheless, as unrest increased among the victims of apartheid, the need for the administration to acquire a definite stance on the issue became more apparent.

In his first term Reagan appeared to believe that the South African government was "reformist" and during that period he condemned their racial practices. But in late 1985 he changed his attitude toward South Africa and imposed restrictions on nuclear and computer sales and on bank loans to the South African government, a ban on arms imports from South Africa, a ban on importing Krugerrands, and a new requirement that American firms operating in South Africa adhere to the Sullivan principles of fair employment practice.

In 1984, South Africa was America's most important trading partner in Sub-Saharan Africa. In 1985, South Africa continued, as in previous years, to be a well-established and prominent export market for U.S. goods and services. The United States regained first place as both a supplier of South African imports and a purchaser of that country's exports. American firms in South Africa have set the pace among all foreign and domestic companies in supporting black advancement and have spent

more than $115 million in the last eight years on black
education and housing.

Despite the strong foreign competition caused by its
high exchange rate, American technology is still much
sought after.   The foremost products are computer hardware, software, equipment, and service.   The local market
is constantly searching for high-quality new products to
update and automate operations.   South Africans are becoming increasingly concerned about American sanctions
against supplying these vital commodities and it is choosing British and other foreign suppliers.   Britain did not
impose any sanction on South Africa in 1985.

Unwilling to abandon South Africa, a country that
is essential to the free world's dependence on its minerals,
the Reagan administration is likely to ignore appeals for
American disinvestment as long as African governments
continue to trade with Pretoria.   At the same time the U.S.
government may request the adoption of fair employment
practices in southern Africa.   Nevertheless, American investors and businesspeople, and indeed, all foreign investors, would do well to note that there exists in South
Africa a crisis of relationship between the white minority
and black majority.   Increasingly, this crisis is taking
the form of guerrilla warfare and a struggle for equality
and independence for blacks.   Ultimately, one must assume,
the majority will prevail and the change in government,
as in Zimbabwe, may take place sooner than expected.

NAMIBIA

The U.S. government presently discourages Americans
from investing in Namibia.   The official announcement de-
clares: "Prospective investors should be aware that the
U.S. nationals who invest there on the basis of rights
acquired from the South African Government after October
27, 1966, will not receive U.S. Government assistance to
protect such investments against the claims of a future
lawful government of that territory."[25]

Most American investments in Namibia have been in
the oil and mining industries.   Oil is South Africa's most
critical lack in its drive for self-sufficiency, and the
terms of the concessions and grant options must be taken
up and explored speedily or relinquished.   In 1971 three
American companies--Exxon, Caltex, and Gulf--relinquished

their offshore oil concessions in Namibia. They were replaced by Aracca Exploration, Continental, Getty, and
Phillips, all of which were given short-term concessions
with an initial investment of $1.2 million.[26]

American corporations and their capital play a strategic role in the mining of base minerals. The American
firms most deeply involved have been American Metal Cli-
max and Newmont Mining, which jointly control the Tsumeb
Corporation. Tsumeb alone accounts for more than 80 percent of base mineral production in Namibia and for more
than 20 percent of all Namibian exports. Other American
corporations in Namibia include U.S. Steel, Bethlehem,
Nord Mining, Navarro, Zapata, Phelps, Dodge, and Tidal
Diamonds. The total American investment in Namibia is
about $50 million.[27]

The U.S. Department of Commerce regularly releases
integrated statistics on trade with Namibia and South
Africa; there are no separate statistics on trade with
Namibia alone. The United States is an important market
for the pelts of the rare Namibian Karakul sheep, used
for women's fur coats. When separate statistics on the
U.S.-Namibian trades were last available, in 1969, they
showed that Americans purchased Karakul pelts worth $7
million. Some of the other major Namibian exports to the
United States are fish products, diamonds, and copper.[28]

A pledge of greater economic assistance to bring
about an independent Namibia would possibly come as part
of a larger effort by the Reagan administration to revamp
U.S. assistance policies.

ZIMBABWE

Of all the countries of the world, Zimbabwe constituted the most blatant example of exploitative racism.
Whites, who made up only 4 percent of the population,
ruled the remaining 96 percent black population and generally lived in colonial-style luxury, while the black
majority lived in ill-health, was ill-clad, and was ill-fed.

American investments and trade with pre-Zimbabwe
Rhodesia were reduced following the adoption of UN sanctions (which were supported by the United States) in 1966
and 1968. Before Rhodesia's unilateral declaration of independence and the sanctions, there were 53 United States-
owned and -related companies operating there; in 1969,
only 31 remained.[29]

The UN sanctions on Rhodesia included a complete trade embargo as one of the mandatory provisions. American adherence to the sanctions was formalized through two executive orders issued by President Johnson. Because of the humanitarian exceptions to the sanctions, the U.S. government made frequent decisions about the purposes of export goods, and allowed licenses for export goods that would go to humanitarian, religious, medical, and educational institutions. In 1971 the U.S. Congress enacted legislation that had the effect of permitting importation of certain strategic materials, chiefly chrome, from Rhodesia. Congress took this action despite the Nixon administration's opposition, because of the dominant position in the chrome market held by the other world supplier, the Soviet Union. The Nixon administration was embarrassed by the passage of this so-called Byrd Amendment.

With the exception of strategic materials imported since that legislation took effect in January 1972, the United States had supported most of the balance of the sanction programs; however, the Byrd Amendment had since been repealed. There were some business-as-usual transactions--through the use of credit cards, advertisements, banks, hotels, car rentals, touring companies, and so on.[30] Some of the American companies were still active in pre-Zimbabwe Rhodesia in violation of the U.S. law, but there is no useful evidence to prove this.

Following the independence of Zimbabwe, the Carter administration planned to increase assistance to the Mugabe government to $75 million, virtually doubling the amount it had managed to extend soon after the country gained its independence.[31] But with the new Reagan administration and the inclination of Congress to cut foreign aid, the fate of this increase was uncertain. However, Zimbabwe's performance has heartened the United States and Britain; there is evidence that the two nations have encouraged the transition to black self-government. Virtually all Zimbabwe's support has been from the West. In March 1981 an international conference in Salisbury (now called Harare) pledged more than $1 billion in aid to the new nation, about 90 percent of it from the West. The United States pledged $225 million over the next three years.[32]

Businesspeople with experience in Zimbabwe have been concerned about outbreaks of fighting between rival factions. Many American businesspeople are taking a wait-and-see attitude toward Zimbabwe; they remain skeptical of the country's stability. Although a number of U.S. corporations have investigated prospects, only one major project has been undertaken—a $30 million expansion of chrome operations by Union Carbide.

In a situation of crisis in southern Africa it is impossible for U.S. corporations engaged in business in the area to play a neutral role. From this brief examination of major American economic involvement in southern Africa, it seems clear that such business activity cannot be said in any way to further what appears to be the legitimate struggle of the majority people of southern Africa. On the contrary, it plays an important role in bolstering the minority regimes in the southern African subcontinent. (For further information on economic collaboration see Chapter 5.)

POSTSCRIPT

Whenever a paroxysm of unrest grips South Africa, peoples all over the world ask, short of military action is there a way for the black majority to force the Pretoria government to change its racial policy? One such peaceful action was the imposition of economic sanctions by the U.S. Congress on October 2, 1986. In a sharp repudiation of President Reagan's policy toward South Africa, the Republican-controlled Senate overrode the president's veto of the congressional sanctions bill. The overwhelming senatorial vote (78-21) for the rejection of Reagan's veto meant that the United States had to put into place the most far-reaching and punitive measures against Pretoria imposed by any Western government. Earlier, the veto was crushed in the Democrat-controlled House of Representatives by a vote of 313-83. It was the first time in six years of the Reagan presidency that Congress overturned a veto on a critical foreign policy bill.

Following are the main provisions of the South Africa sanctions legislation; most of them are effective immediately. (The sanctions would be lifted if South Africa meets certain conditions, including the freeing of Nelson Mandela, head of the ANC, and other political prisoners, allowing the formation of political parties, and lifting the state of emergency.)

--Bans new U.S. loans to South African businesses, the South African government and entities controlled by it,

and forbids new U.S. investments in South Africa. The
investment prohibition does not apply to reinvestment of
profits earned in South Africa.

-- Halts the imports of South African iron, steel, coal,
uranium, textiles and agricultural products. The measure also bans the import of items produced by govern-
ment-controlled firms in South Africa except for strategic
materials needed by the U.S. military.

-- Severs the U.S. landing rights of South African Airways
and prohibits U.S. airlines from entering South Africa.

-- Prohibits U.S. banks from accepting deposits from South
African government agencies except for one account for
diplomatic purposes.

-- Bans the export to South Africa of crude oil, petroleum
products, weapons, and munitions.

-- Transfers South Africa's U.S. sugar import quota to the
Philippines.

-- Bars U.S. government agencies from cooperation with the
South African military, from purchasing items from South
African government-owned companies, and from promoting
trade or tourism in South Africa.

-- Authorizes $40 million in aid to disadvantaged South
Africans regardless of race. The bill also authorizes
$4 million per year in scholarship funds for victims of
apartheid.

-- Calls on the African National Congress to suspend "terrorist activities" and commit itself to a free and democratic
postapartheid South Africa.

-- States, as U.S. policy, that additional sanctions will be
imposed if substantial progress toward dismantling apartheid is not made within a year.

The chief reason for President Reagan's defeat in
Congress was his deep personal opposition to sanctions designed to pressure South Africa to end apartheid. Reagan
said sanctions would hurt the black South Africans they
are intended to help. He also worried that sanctions might
drive South Africa closer to Soviet influence.

Many observers maintain that any measure aimed at
damaging or undermining the South African economy would
be counterproductive and likely to lead to an increased
polarization of attitudes and removal of all possibility of
peaceful change. Political change and economic growth
run together in South Africa. The best hope of a solution
lies in economic growth over many years. The substantial

inflow of capital required for this purpose will only be forthcoming if there is solid evidence that fundamental political reform and the abolition of apartheid is underway.

While laden with symbolism, the U.S. economic sanctions against South Africa may not have much direct impact on South Africa's economy or on American corporations operating there. The sanctions affect about 10 percent of South Africa's trade with the United States and a much smaller portion of South Africa's total external trade.

From the beginning of his administration, Reagan staked out a policy of constructive engagement toward South Africa, seeking to bring about change by persuasion rather than by coercion. But that policy came under intensified attack in response to the violence and resistance in South Africa.

The fact that constructive engagement was an attempt to reform the South African government's racial policies was taken more seriously by Pretoria in 1986. For example, petty apartheid--discrimination in restaurants, clubs, hotels, public conveniences, and means of transportation--was abolished. The Immorality Act has been abandoned and interracial marriage is no longer illegal. Some universities are admitting black students. Blacks may benefit from recent legislation regarding housing, which enables them to buy and own property and private homes (but not all residential areas are integrated). At least one main factor influences negative reaction to the reform program: radical factions within ANC are not interested in partial reform. They insist on completely dismantling apartheid, a process which would then enable them to assume power.

One of the greatest tragedies of our time is the failure of world powers to exercise constructive influence on events in southern Africa. If it were not so sad, the irony of it would have been bitterly funny.

NOTES

1. William J. Pomeroy, <u>Apartheid Axis: The United States and South Africa</u> (New York: International Publishers, 1973), p. 9.

2. <u>New York Times</u>, September 9, 1947.

3. Ibid., April 9, 1948.

4. Ibid., October 8 and November 26, 1949; January 24, 1951.

5.   Ibid., April 1, 1960.

6.   Ibid.

7.   Ibid., November 26, 1953.

8.   U.S. Department of Commerce, Overseas Business Reports: Market Factors in South Africa, March 1977.

9.   New York Times, May 7, 1960.

10.   U.S. Department of Commerce, Overseas Business Reports.

11.   George Houser, in Charles C. Diggs and Lester L. Wolff, Report of the Special Study Mission to South Africa, August 1-30, 1969, pp. 98-99.

12.   Stephen Goodman, "What Future for South Africa's Gold," Africa Report, June 1970.

13.   Ibid.

14.   Washington Post, September 8, 1970.

15.   George Houser, "U.S. Policy and Southern Africa," in U.S. Policy Toward Africa, ed. Frederick S. Arkhurst (New York: Praeger, 1975), p. 104.

16.   See Gist on United States Foreign Relations, U.S. Department of State, Bureau of Public Affairs, 1976.

17.   U.S. Department of State, United States Relations in Southern Africa, April 16, 1977.

18.   Ibid.

19.   U.S. Department of Commerce, "Foreign Economic Trends and Their Implications for the United States," January 1977.

20.   Brooke Baldwin and Theodore Brown, Economic Action Against Apartheid (New York: American Committee on Africa, n.d.), p. 1.

21.   U.S. Department of Commerce, "Foreign Economic Trends."

22.   Pomeroy, Apartheid Axis, p. 15.

23.   Andrew W. Kamarck, "The African Economy and International Trade," in United States and Africa, ed. Walter Goldschmidt (New York: American Assembly, 1958), pp. 118-19.

24.   John Blashill, "The Proper Role of U.S. Corporations in South Africa," Fortune, July 1972, p. 49.

25.   U.S. Department of Commerce, Overseas Business Reports: Market Factors in South Africa, November 1984.

26.   Houser, Report of the Special Study Mission, p. 105.

27.   Ibid.

28.   Ibid.

29.   Ibid.

30. Ibid., p. 106.
31. New York Times, February 16, 1981.
32. U.S. News & World Report, April 20, 1981.

9
Power Games

As the momentum of liberation struggles in southern Africa continues to move the subcontinent to center stage of world politics, that part of the world is now on the list of potential global crises. Probably it is second only to the Middle East as the possible arena of bloody confrontation. An important element in the strife within southern Africa is the involvement of the superpowers and other interested parties.

Unless South Africa's racial policies are fundamentally redesigned, they are likely to lead to a catastrophic racial conflict that will have serious ramifications throughout the world. Many black and white Americans have intense feelings about the issues in southern Africa. The resulting debate could mobilize African political and economic pressures against the United States; it could divide the United States from its allies; and it could also lead to bitter racial trouble within the United States.

ZIMBABWEAN INDEPENDENCE

Southern Africa was in a state of heightened tension when the minority regime in Zimbabwe (formerly Rhodesia) proclaimed a unilateral declaration of independence in 1965.[1] Not a single nation supported the breakaway regime. Refusing to recognize the independence of its former colony, Britain initiated futile negotiations with Ian Smith's regime in an effort to force a new constitutional formula that would lead to black majority rule in Rhodesia.

In 1971 the British and Smith governments announced agreement on terms that were less advantageous to the blacks in Rhodesia than those that Britain had previously rejected. Majority black rule was relegated to the distant future. However, if the British proposal were approved, Britain was prepared to lift the United Nations-imposed economic sanctions. When a British commission visited Rhodesia to test the acceptability of the proposed agreement, it found vehement African opposition.

In the meantime, the black Rhodesian bishop, Abel Muzorewa, formed the African National Council, which sought to mobilize the general population in support of majority rule. Smith, under pressure from Britain, began to show a conciliatory attitude toward ZAPU and the ZANU-Patriotic Front (ZANU-PF). He released their leaders from jail and met with them in August 1975. However, the talks failed to produce any solution to the constitutional crisis.

British Foreign Secretary James Callaghan proposed a four-point peace plan: acceptance of the principle of majority rule; elections in 18 months to 2 years; independence only after majority rule is established; and no long, drawn-out negotiations. The Smith government rejected the British plan.

Then U.S. Secretary of State Henry Kissinger seized upon the rejected British plan and made it the basis of his shuttle diplomacy in Africa to avert racial war as well as to help Gerald Ford win the 1976 U.S. presidential election by securing the support of the black American votes. Kissinger's shuttle diplomacy was also aimed at preventing Soviet and Cuban intervention in Rhodesia. After consultation with the Rhodesian, South African, and British governments and the five frontline African nations (Tanzania, Zambia, Botswana, Mozambique, and Angola), the United States produced a modified version of the British plan for transfer of power to the black majority.

The major aspects of the American plan accepted by Prime Minister Smith were (1) majority rule to be effective within two years; (2) an immediate meeting of representatives of the Rhodesian government and black leaders to form a biracial temporary government composed of a council of state and a council of members to govern until achievement of majority rule through a new constitution and elections; (3) the head of the council of ministers to be a black and the group to have a black majority; (4) with establishment of the temporary government, economic

sanctions against Rhodesia to be lifted and the cessation
of guerrilla warfare mounted by nationalist factions; and
(5) an international financial trust fund to be established
outside the country to organize development and investment
programs in Rhodesia.[2]

South Africa was considered the lifeline of Rhodesia.
Since the United States believed that South Africa could
force Rhodesia to the negotiating table, Kissinger met with
Premier John Vorster of South Africa in Germany in June
1976 to explore ways of persuading Smith. They devised a
plan that would "compensate whites who chose to leave
Rhodesia before majority rule and would strengthen the
security of those choosing to remain by providing financial
and property guarantees. Highly professional whites would
be encouraged to remain; those whose skills compete with
Africans would receive financial and resettlement incentives
to leave."[3] Following another talk with Vorster in Zurich
in September 1976, Kissinger obtained from Smith a commitment to black majority rule within two years in return for
financial guarantees for white settlers in Rhodesia.[4] Smith
agreed to the black majority rule and the establishment of
an interim biracial government.

In the past, as was true of its overall African policy, U.S.-Rhodesian policy had suffered from benign ne-
glect. The United States considered Rhodesia a British
preserve and preferred that Britain take the diplomatic
initiative. However, following the Western debacle and
defeat in Angola, and the British failure to solve the Rhodesian crisis, the United States decided to take the peace
initiative in southern Africa. Kissinger undertook a trip
to southern Africa and, in Zambia, announced support of
the Lusaka Manifesto for the solution of the Rhodesian
crisis. Kissinger's ten points of American policy for Rhodesia positioned "the United States on the morally-right
and politically-compelling side of the major African issue
of black majority rule."[5]

After the enunciation of this new American policy, a
number of developments occurred as representatives of the
United States, Britain, and some black African countries
met upon various occasions. The most significant development was a conference held in Geneva on October 28, 1976,
to discuss the particulars of a changeover from white minority to black majority rule in Zimbabwe. The conference,
chaired by British UN Ambassador Ivor Richard, failed to
accomplish its objectives.

The main thrust of Anglo-American initiative in Rhodesia was directed toward achieving a peaceful settlement leading to free elections and black majority rule by 1978. To work out details, a joint consultative group was established in May 1977 under John Graham, deputy undersecretary at the British Foreign Office. From its base in Lusaka, the group held a series of consultations with the leaders of Zimbabwe's liberation movements and officials in the frontline countries, as well as South African and Rhodesian leaders.

The group failed to formulate an agreement acceptable to all the parties involved. The Rhodesian regime distrusted both the British and the nationalists; the nationalists were suspicious of both the Americans and the British. Another factor was the South African government. Although Vorster expressly supported the Anglo-American initiative and promised assistance toward achieving a settlement, he believed he was holding the trump card. He thought that if the West could accept his conditions on Namibia, he would be able to pressure Rhodesia. But the Smith regime insisted that a new constitution had to be drafted before an agreement could be reached on transition to majority rule.

The peace initiative in Zimbabwe reached yet another stage in September 1977. David Owen, the British foreign secretary, and Andrew Young, the U.S. ambassador to the United Nations, toured African capitals seeking support for a new set of Anglo-American proposals to end the war in Zimbabwe. Unlike the vague Kissinger proposals of the previous September, this Anglo-American plan was more specific. The proposal, which envisaged black majority rule and independence in Zimbabwe during 1978, was based on seven principles: (1) the surrender of power by the illegal regime and the return to legality; (2) an orderly and peaceful transition to independence in 1978; (3) free and impartial elections on the basis of universal adult suffrage; (4) the establishment by the British government of a transitional administration with the task of conducting elections for an independent government; (5) a UN presence, including a UN force, during the transitional period; (6) a constitution providing for a democratically elected government, abolition of discrimination, the protection of individual human rights, and the independence of the judiciary; and (7) a development fund to revive the economy of the country, which Britain and the United States viewed as predicated on the implementation of the establishment as a whole.

The five so-called frontline and key African nations formally approved the Anglo-American plan for a settlement of the Rhodesian dispute.[6] Smith, however, condemned the Anglo-American plan as an attempt to appease Communist-backed terrorist.[7]

After months of promising an internal settlement to Rhodesian racial troubles, Smith finally offered free elections on the basis of one man, one vote.[8] But, as was usual with Smith, there was a condition: He said he was willing to negotiate a settlement with black leaders who had renounced terrorism. Thus he was attempting to preclude negotiations with the guerrilla leaders who were opposed to his regime.

The fact that Smith conceded that one man, one vote could confer legitimacy on a government was, in itself, a welcome development in the racially troubled southern African subcontinent. As expected, the Smith offer was immediately rejected by the guerrillas. Smith claimed to have worked out his plan for negotiations leading to a constitution and elections with the three principal nationalist leaders operating inside Rhodesia--Bishop Muzorewa, the Reverend Ndabaningi Sithole, and Chief Jeremiah Chirau. He said nothing about bringing in two other important people, Robert Mugabe and Joshua Nkomo, leaders of guerrilla groups.[9]

> The principal difference between the Anglo-American plan and what Mr. Smith now proposes seems to be in nature of the transitional authority during the constitution-making and voting. The Anglo-American plan provides for a British caretaker and an armed force drawn from the present Rhodesian Army, the guerrilla forces and outside United Nations contingents.[10]

The agreement of internally based black nationalist groups to open negotiations with Smith posed a diplomatic problem for Britain and the United States. Smith succeeded in reaching an agreement with the moderate nationalists that might gain support of the black population.[11] (Such an arrangement would almost certainly be shunned by the ZANU-PF). The Front had the support of the five frontline black African states most concerned with the Rhodesian crisis and of most states in the OAU. Until the holding of an election on the basis of one man, one vote, all estimates of the various groups' support were speculative. Plagued with the heritage of failure, the odyssey for peace in Zimbabwe reached yet another stage when Britain and the United States expressed qualified support, in November 1977, for Smith's turnabout acceptance of the principle of universal adult franchise.[12]

What Smith had been trying to achieve was a safeguard for minority interests in black-ruled Zimbabwe, aimed at stopping an exodus of whites and retaining their confidence in the stability of law and order, their jobs, pensions, and property. The key factor was to retain white confidence. Exactly how Smith could achieve guarantees that a black government, with full executive power, would abide by negotiated agreements after it came to power, had never been made clear.

Apparently there was no outside support for Smith's decision to ditch the Anglo-American plan and proceed alone. The South African regime never openly backed it. The black frontline countries, from where the guerrillas attacked, were opposed. The main Anglo-American objection was that the war would not end unless the guerrillas and their political representatives were part of the deal.

If there was Anglo-U.S. support for internal settlement and for the black government it brought to power, then logically this agreement would include Anglo-American assistance in fighting the guerrillas. Black factionalism might pose an even greater threat to the creation of Zimbabwe than white intransigence. Personality clashes and conflicting loyalties presented major obstacles to black unity. Unless the differences could be resolved, prospects for forming a national government were not very encouraging. The alternative might be a civil war among various black groups, as in Angola; or war might come from guerrillas supported by the frontline nations. Such a war could spark outside intervention by South Africa, by Britain, by the United States, by the Soviet Union, and by Cuba.

The negotiation of a Rhodesian settlement was difficult, but the events of fall 1977 signified an erosion of the hitherto rigid position of the white minority in regard to the point of view of African nationalists: one person, one vote was the principle around which any peaceful settlement in Zimbabwe had to evolve.[13]

Britain and the United States had been pushing for quite a different kind of settlement, one intended to bring in Rhodesian guerrillas. The Anglo-American plan proposed that Smith return the power to Britain, which would then prepare for elections in which the guerrillas could take part. Otherwise, the British and American governments feared that the guerrilla war against the Smith regime would turn itself into a civil war among the competing black groups. The example of Angola was very fresh in their memories. That was why, reluctantly, both the British and American governments had welcomed the Smith settlement plan as a significant step in the right direction-- the direction of majority rule.

Things went awry for the Anglo-American plan. British and American diplomats met with leaders of the guerrilla movement in Malta to try to draw them nearer to a peaceful settlement. However, with the Malta talks ending inconclusively, events began to move suddenly in Rhodesia, where Smith reached an accord with the internally based black leaders.

Month followed month, in slow progress. Then disagreement ensued, and finally stalemate. On March 4, 1978, it was announced that Smith and the three black leaders had worked out a formula that would turn the government over to black rule by year's end. The negotiators formed an executive council and each key government position was to have one black and one white minister. Elections were held in April 1979. As expected, Muzorewa's party won the majority of seats in Parliament and he became the first black prime minister of Zimbabwe-Rhodesia. However, widespread dissatisfaction continued regarding the legitimacy of the new government and no nation recognized it.

Finally, at a Commonwealth Conference in Zambia in August 1979, Britain agreed to draft a new constitution and carry out new elections that would include the ZANU-PF. The British-drafted constitution stripped the whites of most of their influence in government, and their 28 seats in parliament were reduced to 20. A British governor was appointed--Lord Christopher Soames--and he arrived in Salisbury on December 12, 1979. After 14 years of rebellion, Rhodesia again became a British colony. The British government was in control and the promised election was held on February 27, 1980, which all parties (including the Patriotic Front) contested.

No one expected Mugabe's election victory to be so decisive—his party won 57 out of the 80 seats allocated to blacks. At last, on April 18, 1980, Zimbabwe became one of the black-governed nations of Africa.

During all these difficult years of negotiation, the U.S. government remained solidly behind the British proposals and it steadfastly refused to succumb to pressures to lift economic sanctions against Rhodesia. The reward had been a relationship, although guarded, free of acrimony. Prime Minister Mugabe, an avowed Marxist, has puzzled his critics by steering his new nation on a generally pro-Western course instead of pushing it into the Soviet orbit, as had been feared by many.

THE NAMIBIAN ISSUE

Discussions among the United Nations, the five Western nations, the frontline states, South Africa, and SWAPO continued at various levels throughout 1976-77. The United Nations repeatedly passed resolutions pressing for a settlement of the irritating problem. When the United Nations threatened reprisals against South Africa, the Western five presented an aide-mémoire to South Africa (on April 7, 1977) that urged it to arrange free elections in Namibia under the aegis of the United Nations leading that country to an internationally recognized independence. South Africa was pressed for a settlement consistent with UN Resolution 385 of 1976. To implement various UN resolutions the Western five then initiated proposals for a settlement that they placed before the UN Security Council on April 10, 1978. That proposal included among its key elements:

1. The holding of free and fair elections for a constituent assembly leading to independence
2. The cessation of all hostile acts by all parties
3. The restriction of South African and SWAPO armed forces to base and the subsequent phased withdrawal from Namibia of all South African troops—that withdrawal to be completed one week after the certification of elections
4. The administration of the territory during the transitional period leading to the elections by a South African-appointed administrator-general, with all acts affecting the political process under the supervision and control

of a UN special representative appointed by the secretary-general of the United Nations

5. The introduction of a UN civilian and military presence to ensure the observance of the terms of the settlement

6. The release of all Namibian political prisoners and detainees

7. The return of exiles

8. The establishment of conditions for free and fair elections, including freedom of speech, movement, press,
   and assembly, and the repeal of discriminatory or restrictive legislation[14]

On July 27, 1978, the UN Security Council took up
the Namibian problem and passed two separate resolutions.
The first resolution--adopted 13-0 with the Soviet Union
and Czechoslovakia abstaining--contained only three provisions creating machinery for carrying out the Western plan.
The resolution provided that the Security Council request
the secretary-general to appoint a special representative
for Namibia in order to ensure the early independence of
Namibia through free elections under the supervision and
control of the United Nations, and further request the
secretary-general to submit at the earliest date a report
containing his recommendations for the implementation of
the Western proposal. The second resolution, dealing with
Walvis Bay, was passed unanimously.[15] After declaring
its dissent to this resolution, South Africa agreed to proceed with the implementation of the first resolution. Even
on the first resolution, South Africa expressed grave reservations about many of the implications.

Secretary-General Kurt Waldheim issued a report
that provided for a detailed plan for carrying out the
resolutions passed by the United Nations. His recommendations included, among others, (1) cessation of all hostile
acts by all parties, and the withdrawal, restriction, or
demobilization of the various armed forces; (2) the conduct
of free and fair elections to the constituent assembly, with
preconditions including the repeal of restrictive laws, the
release of political prisoners and the voluntary return of
exiles, the establishment of effective monitoring by the
United Nations, and an adequate period for electoral cam-
paigning; and (3) the formulation and adoption of a constitution for Namibia by the elected assembly, to be followed by the entry into force of the constitution and the
consequent achievement of the independence of Namibia.[16]

In a letter to Waldheim, on September 6, 1978, Botha, the South African foreign minister, raised questions about the willingness of South Africa to accept the formula for implementing the Waldheim plan. He objected to the great size of the force designated for Namibia. Among other important unacceptable points raised by Botha was the introduction of a UN civilian police force into Namibia.

There were criticisms of South Africa both in England and the United States. The Economist charged South Africa with "brushing aside the achievement of all the long months of negotiation aimed at bringing Namibia to internationally recognized independence and, instead, to push ahead with its own solution."[17] The Washington Post editorially contended: "It is absurd and unforgiveable for South Africa to be quibbling over charges, if they are that, of such trivial dimensions, when quibbling means putting at risk the immense gains in security and respectability ensured by sticking with the U.N. plan."[18]

The situation in Namibia had been changing constantly and those changes threatened to unsettle the agreements that already had been reached. The most significant action inside Namibia was South Africa's creation of a so-called Council of Ministers, composed entirely of members of the Democratic Turnhalle Alliance, the party that won the South African-supervised elections of December 1978. These elections were boycotted by major internal political parties, as well as by SWAPO, and recognized by neither the five Western powers nor the United Nations.

Following the elections, the UN General Assembly took up the Namibia issue. The General Assembly unanimously passed two resolutions condemning South Africa and urging action by the Security Council. The first resolution urged the Security Council "to take effective measures, including sanctions . . . particularly the imposition of comprehensive economic sanction, including a trade embargo, an oil embargo, and a complete arms embargo."[19] The second resolution charged that the failure of South Africa to comply with previous UN resolutions and the Waldheim plan constituted a threat to international peace and security.

In May 1979 South Africa raised two principal objections to the secretary-general's plan for implementation. One objection concerned Waldheim's proposal that any SWAPO-armed personnel inside Namibia at the start of the cease-fire would be restricted and monitored by the United

Nations at designated locations. South Africa objected to this proposal on the grounds that it would provide SWAPO with bases inside Namibia. The other objection was its insistence on the monitoring by the United Nations of SWAPO bases outside Namibia. South Africa maintained this position despite the fact that there was no such proposal from the five Western nations.

There are many reasons for this sorry state of affairs in southern Africa. The West, the United Nations, SWAPO, and South Africa all differ on the goal of an independent Namibia; their goals are as divergent as their views on a proper negotiation process and the conduct of elections to grant independence to Namibia.

As in any negotiation, each side in the Namibian dispute has taken a position with a view to maximizing its bargaining leverage with the other. These positions will inevitably be altered once a final agreement is reached and implementation of the settlement plan begins. In insisting that SWAPO be denied that stature which it presently derives from its recognition by the international community, South Africa is, in effect, seeking to extract a major concession without committing itself to an agreement. There is considerable wariness on the part of SWAPO and its supporters in the international community--and on the part of South Africa--about surrendering advantages already negotiated. The task at hand for the United Nations and the Western five is to bring both sides to final agreement and to begin the implementation of the settlement plan.

Periodically fighting erupts along Namibia's northern border, with increasing losses to both SWAPO and South Africa. South African raids into neighboring states have become more frequent. The five frontline states have been cooperating with the United Nations and the Western five, but their willingness to implement the settlement plan cannot be taken for granted. The key to an internationally acceptable settlement in Namibia lies with the South African government, and the Western five are continuing their efforts to convince South Africa that such a settlement is in the best interest of the region.

Still another UN effort at settlement was torpedoed by the South African government. A conference on Namibia was to be convened at Geneva between November 12 and 15, 1979. South Africa, SWAPO, the Western five, and the frontline five were invited to participate by the UN secretary-general. South Africa wanted UN military experts to visit Namibia and get acquainted with the local situation before the Geneva talks took place. It also insisted that representatives of the local Namibia parties be represented at the Geneva meeting.

Since then the Western five have been drawing up new proposals to try to break the deadlock over Namibian independence. They are seeking resolution of the Namibian conflict by negotiating a constitution and other guarantees intended to persuade South Africa to stop blocking independence for Namibia.[20] This plan, reflecting the views of the Reagan administration, was approved by the Western five. The Western five, or the so-called contact group, seek to prevent Namibia from becoming a crisis issue between South Africa and black African nations. They are attempting to allay South African fears that Namibia, once independent, will fall under the domination of hostile and Communist forces.

The Namibians have been trying various peaceful and legal methods of gaining independence, but have been forced to take more militant approaches. It is still not clear what formula will eventually produce South African withdrawal from Namibia.

The Western contact group, in consultation with the frontline states, obtained agreement of all parties—including South Africa—to the UN plan for Namibian independence as set forth in Resolution 435. At the initiative of the United States, that plan was strengthened and appears to offer the best prospects for a fair and impartial result. However, South Africa has made clear its readiness to proceed only in the context of a parallel commitment to resolve the longstanding problem of the withdrawal of Cuban troops from Angola.

RECENT AMERICAN POLICY

The Carter administration saw its commitment to change in southern Africa within the context of the wider moral concern for human rights. Perhaps the relation to human rights and moral posture found symbolic meaning in the prominent role given to Andrew Young. Not only the American but the Western strategy in southern Africa was outlined by Young in Lusaka in May 1977. Young's outline comprised three elements: first, cooperation among the United States, Canada, France, Britain, and West Germany to obtain United Nations supervised elections in Namibia, thereby releasing it from South African control; second, cooperation of the United States and Britain in moving minority-ruled Rhodesia to independence under majority rule; and third, the transformation of South Africa's rule itself to majority rule. The five Western nations also wanted to call upon South Africa to use its influence to prod Rhodesia into settling its racial problems.[21] This was done to demonstrate that the West could produce movement in southern Africa to counter the diplomatic and military initiative that had been launched by the Soviets.

At one point President Carter announced that "we are now free of that inordinate fear of Communism which once led us to embrace any dictator who joined us in our fear."[22] This was read as meaning that American foreign policy would no longer be one of confronting communism abroad except when the United States might be directly threatened or when its interests were at stake. Such doctrine could mean that the United States would support black Communists against white non-Communists, as in Rhodesia, and neutrality in struggles between black Communists and black non-Communists, as in Angola.

At issue was whether American policy toward Africa will be subordinated to the U.S. overall relationship with the Soviet Union, as it was under Kissinger, or treated separately, with a focus on Africa. In southern Africa, the moment of choice came when Prime Minister Smith concluded a separate agreement with three moderate black leaders based inside Rhodesia; the power struggle among African nationalist factions was certain to escalate.

This was the point at which the United States had to decide whether to support Smith's agreement with the black leaders or to stick with the Anglo-American peace plan that gave the externally based guerrilla alliance, the Patriotic Front, a central role. The Soviets and Cubans decided to arm the guerrillas and train them. On these policy alternatives, there were two chief protagonists: President Carter's national security adviser, Zbigniew Brzezinski, and UN Ambassador Andrew Young. Young favored the Anglo-American plan and consequent vying with the Soviets and the Cubans; Brzezinski, who was more influential with the Carter administration, opted to support Smith's internal settlement.

Quoting one State Department source, the Washington Post reported that there were 19,000 Cuban troops in Angola, helping the Marxist government battle insurgents.[23] Instead of bringing stability to Africa, the presence of Cuban troops had introduced new tension and was causing worry to the American government, including Young. The latter revised his earlier stand, saying that the Cuban troops do not work as a stabilizing force in Africa, but are contributing instead to "the destruction and chaos of Africa."[24] The Cubans in Africa, reported to be about 19,000 to 20,000, serve as an extension of Soviet power where the American government had been avoiding a similar provocative extension of policy.

The Carter administration did not link its calls for majority rule in southern Africa to Soviet and Cuban threats, but it did set the Cuban withdrawal from Africa as the price of its normalization of relations with Cuba. This linkage could have possibly reinforced the belief that Americans are only interested in keeping out the Russians and, of course, their Cuban friends, rather than displaying sincere and unselfish interest in freeing blacks from white minority rule.

The Reagan administration's policy of constructive engagement had been important to the South African government's efforts to combat the divestment campaign. Advocating constructive engagement, the administration sought to encourage peaceful change through diplomatic channels and was strongly opposed to economic sanctions. The Reagan administration praised U.S. corporations as a positive force for change and urged them to adopt the Sullivan principles on a voluntary basis. However, in an abrupt reversal in September 1985, President Reagan abandoned the opposition to sanctions against South Africa and imposed partial sanctions.

Reagan's change of heart seemed to be a major concession to two political realities: He faced defeat in Congress if he continued to resist sanctions and he might have been able to continue resisting sanctions had there been any signs that President Botha was finally addressing himself to South Africa's political crisis in a decisive manner.

For all practical purposes constructive engagement is now dead. It is absent from the texts of administration speeches and of congressional testimony on southern Africa. Assistant Secretary of State for African Affairs Chester Crocker's 1980 contribution to the language of constructive engagement and diplomacy had taken on a life of its own:

It is being employed pejoratively by administration critics. From the beginning the constructive engagement was a failure by the single criterion that not enough antiapartheid leverage was brought to bear on South Africa.

SUPERPOWER RIVALRY

In the arena of superpower rivalry, the United States follows a reactive diplomacy and the Soviet Union pursues a diplomacy of polarization. It is usually the Soviet Union which gives support and supplies arms to a regime or a guerrilla movement, as it is doing in a small way in southern Africa. When the situation goes out of control, and when enough tension is created so as to unbalance the status quo, then the American government reacts to it.

Barring the Middle East, no other area of the world today presents such a challenge to peace as does southern Africa. What Vietnam was for American policymakers in the 1960s, southern Africa promises to be for the late 1980s.

With the failure of the so-called Kissinger concept of detente, it has become axiomatic that what is in the Russian interest is against American interest. It is obvious that Russian interest in southern Africa lies in supporting the black nationalists. At present, on a limited and selective basis, Soviet policy is beginning to strike responsive blows in African politics. This is accomplished by pursuing selective targets of opportunity, rather than large-scale interference. Nevertheless, the latter is a possibility in southern Africa, and in that situation we must ask whether the United States can afford to lag behind in its direct support of apartheid regimes.

Among those responsible for foreign policy planning it is generally assumed that denial of free access to South African markets would only come about as a result of Communist-controlled governments. If the southern African countries were taken over, one by one, by the Communists, American investments would be confiscated and its export-import would be affected. From such assumptions it appears that one of the threats to American interests in southern Africa is communism.

Since the United States looks to southern Africa as an area of export expansion, as well as a future source of raw materials (including those of military usefulness), the defense of southern Africa against communism is an important part of American strategic planning. Knowing that such an American advantage might weaken their influence in southern Africa, "the Soviets have engaged in a campaign to discredit the United States' efforts at conciliation and peaceful transfer of power to the black majorities in Namibia and Rhodesia."[25]

Impelled by considerations of power politics, the West set upon a course to improve its image in the region, as well as to undercut the possible spread of Soviet influence there. The involvement of former UN Ambassador Young, a black American with a deep personal interest in black Africa, was primarily motivated by the exigencies of Western interests and global politics within wider context of East-West detente.

The question is whether the West, and particularly the United States, could achieve diplomatic and political successes in southern Africa despite Young's ebullience. Even the probability of the continuance of that diplomatic tempo in southern Africa appears unlikely, given Washington's other pressing worldwide concerns. In the meantime, the Soviets continue to believe in the radicalization of southern Africa, which they think will be better achieved if independence is gained through armed struggle rather than negotiation. Although the Soviets have suffered some setbacks here and there in Africa, their power and influence remain predominant in strategic southern Africa. Throughout the subcontinent the Soviet Union is the prime arms supplier to the nationalist guerrillas who seek majority rule by any means, including violence.

The fundamental concern of President Reagan's policy in southern Africa, as indeed anywhere else, is the global contention between the United States and the Soviet Union, the strategic significance of the issue. Therefore, the main thrust of Reagan's policy is to pursue American economic interest in southern Africa and capitalize on Moscow's current isolation from most of the region. This may mean economic aid to Zimbabwe as well as trade with and investment in South Africa.

The American goal is to manage this high-priority theme of anticommunism in southern Africa--which is meant to blunt the influence of the Soviet Union and Cuba--without contributing to the kind of racial or regional strife that could wipe out whatever gains may be made against Moscow and Havana. How the Reagan administration treats

the regimes in southern Africa, that is, whether it continues the Carter administration's public pressure for
change or retreats somewhat in the name of overriding
strategic interests in Africa, remains a paramount issue.
Relations with South Africa will continue to present dilem-
mas. So will the establishment of an independent Namibia.

The United States, Britain, and France jointly cast
vetoes in the UN Security Council on April 30, 1981, to defeat four resolutions calling for sanctions against South
Africa for its failure to grant independence to Namibia.[26]
China and the Soviet bloc joined six Third World countries
on each of the four resolutions, providing the necessary
majority of nine votes. But the triple vetoes--the first
cast on this issue by the Western powers since 1976--sent
all four resolutions down to defeat. These votes represented the first open break between the Reagan administration and the Third World on an issue that black African nations have chosen to single out as the prime focus
of their concern.

Sanctions proposed by the Africans included a total
embargo on trade, travel, diplomatic representation, and
commercial credits and a specific proviso for an oil embargo. One of the resolutions also would establish a UN
committee to oversee compliance with the sanctions. All
three Western nations argued that the imposition of such
sanctions would have hurt the negotiating process, which,
they maintained, could still bring independence peacefully
to Namibia. But the Africans, suspicious of the Western
powers, particularly the Reagan administration's overtures
to South Africa, insisted on an assurance that the Western
consultations would not prove to be an excuse for delay
that would block the momentum generated by the UN debate.

Having failed to obtain UN sanctions against South
Africa, Namibia called for the OAU to denounce the United
States and other Western nations for obstructing the efforts
of the international community to achieve Namibian independence, and the 50-nation organization unanimously complied.
This may well signal stronger support for the Namibian
cause from the Soviet Union and Cuba.

The United States and the Soviet Union had talks on
March 6, 1986, in Geneva on a UN peace plan for Namibia
and on the withdrawal of Cuban troops from Angola. It
followed President Botha's proposal of March 4 calling for
implementation of UN Resolution 435, which would lead to
independence for Namibia on August 1, 1986. However,
Botha's rhetoric was not followed by action.

SOVIET OBJECTIVES

Heartened by their spectacular success in Angola and Mozambique, the Soviets enthusiastically viewed the opportunity to fish in southern African troubled waters. The Soviets have taken a course that not only has left the Americans and other Western powers in a mood to retaliate but that also has outwitted Chinese policymakers. Power games in southern Africa are being played cautiously, strategically, and discretely.

> France, Great Britain, and the United States are generating power and influence flows that penetrate the feeble and porous national defenses of the new states, envelop their leaders, and engulf their people. On a highly restricted and selective scale, Soviet diplomacy is beginning to strike responsive chords. Communist China, even more restricted and selective, though also pursuing targets of opportunity rather than systematic conquests, lags far behind the Soviet Union.[27]

The first phase of cold war having tempered, the second phase appears to be gripping Africa. On the one hand there is the fear of growing Soviet and Chinese influence, and on the other there is the continuing skepticism about Western interests.

The Soviet Union visualizes successful policy objectives in the following general areas:[28]

1. To implement Soviet political and economic influence in key countries in southern Africa
2. To encourage the establishment of Communist-oriented regimes
3. To expand the Soviet military presence by gaining access to port facilities and bases
4. To control the supply of raw materials from and around Africa

In the past the main challenge to the Soviet effort in southern Africa has emanated from China, with the United States, Britain, France, Belgium, Portugal, and other Western European nations contributing to the cold war. The failure of the United States and its European allies to take the lead in opposing the violation of human rights gave the initiative to the Communists, who were willing to act more aggressively.

Military aid is a principal instrument of Soviet assistance to the national liberation forces; the Brezhnev doctrine "encompasses a role for Soviet armed forces in 'national liberation' struggles in Third World regimes like Southern Africa."[29] Up to 1964, Soviet policy wavered, although its financial and technical assistance flowed both to moderate and radical nations in Africa. This produced some tangible results—the Soviets could build good relations with a number of new nations while getting involved in the national liberation struggles in southern Africa. The recipients of this assistance have been independent nations as well as national liberation movements fighting against whiteocracy in southern Africa. Under this policy "Moscow's interest is not so much in 'liberation' itself but in the support of specific revolutionary groups that can assume Soviet influence in the post-liberation environment."[30]

The Soviet Union cast the struggle in southern Africa in terms of a racist struggle. The Soviets hold that the racial issue is alien to the Marxist principles of class struggle. The Soviets are, therefore, in a better position than the United States to advocate the case of the black majority in southern Africa in international forums in the struggle between the black oppressed and the white oppressors. The U.S. interest in racial integration is looked down upon by the Soviets as a smoke screen to mask Washington's support for the policy of racism.

Much of the talk about the Communist threat in southern Africa has come from Rhodesia (Zimbabwe) and South Africa and their sympathizers in the West. For years these two governments have been capitalizing on raising the bogey of the Communist threat and by eliciting appropriate Western public support. Recently, notably during the Carter administration, Western diplomacy (especially that of the United States and Britain) took a turn toward balance. This change is partly because of an emerging desire to see a peaceful, rather than a bloody, change in southern Africa and partly because of America's expressed faith in human rights.

The Soviet Union anticipates the eventual growth of two contradictory elements in southern Africa—the progressives and reactionaries. The experiences of Angola and Mozambique confirmed the Soviets' appreciation of the radicalizing effect of national liberation movements. Soviet preferences for armed struggle in the remaining unliberated countries of southern Africa emerge as a reaction to the Western efforts to bring about a negotiated settlement. Needless to say, a negotiated settlement would weaken the Soviet position and strengthen Western efforts at conciliation and integration.

SINO-SOVIET COMPETITION

Diplomatically, in the 1970s, China came out of its isolation, not only at the United Nations but elsewhere—particularly in Africa. Generally the Soviets have held the upper hand in southern Africa, but the Chinese are making inroads toward acceptance there. Attacking Soviet policy in southern Africa, Chairman Hua Kuo-feng said on July 16, 1976:

> Particularly noteworthy at present is the fact that, while one superpower is bolstering the racist regimes in various ways the other superpower, which claims to be the "natural ally" of the African people, is carrying out in a more cunning way its expansion and infiltration in Southern Africa under the signboard of "supporting" the national liberation movements, its purpose being to gain control of the strategically important Southern Africa.[31]

China, though itself a developing country, has channeled foreign aid to southern Africa. Nothing has impressed the Africans more than the efficient completion of the Chinese-built Tanzam railway, linking Tanzania with Zambia. Neither the Soviets nor the Americans have matched this in magnitude. Thus the Soviets have to contend with two rivals in southern Africa, China and the United States.

The Soviets succeeded in rebuffing both the Chinese and the Americans in Angola. Both the Chinese- and American-supported factions lost the war in Angola, while the Soviet- and Cuban-backed Popular Movement for the

Liberation of Angola (MPLA) won. While the United States and its Western allies urge peaceful settlements in Rhodesia, Namibia, and South Africa, the Soviets support leaders who insist on intensification of armed struggle. Regarding this approach, the policies of both the Chinese and the Soviets in southern Africa do not differ fundamentally. Like the Soviets, the Chinese have provided revolutionary groups mostly with small arms, ammunition, light vehicles, and on-site training in guerrilla operations.[32] For heavier and sophisticated weapons, the warring factions have had to turn to the Soviet Union.[33]

However, "on balance the Chinese have as much prodded as hindered the expansion of Soviet influence"[34] in southern Africa. Once the level of a conflict rises, the Soviets gain the upper hand, as may be discerned in the following testimony: "The Soviet Union can easily trump anything that the Chinese can offer to African clients. This Soviet advantage becomes all the greater as the scenario shifts relentlessly toward such militarily more sophisticated targets as Rhodesia and ultimately, the Republic of South Africa."[35]

In southern Africa the Soviet Union is seen as a greater threat because of its capacity to support military operations at long range. Although the Chinese prefer a low profile (perhaps because of their inability to do otherwise), they generally support any armed struggle not backed by the Soviets. However, southern Africa has low priority for the Soviets as well as for the Chinese. That is why Western nations can afford to relegate southern African problems to tomorrow's crisis.[36]

CUBAN INTERVENTION

Cuba, working under Soviet direction in Africa, apparently has the inclination to revive aspects of colonial intervention that have been condemned almost universally. The presence of Cuban soldiers in southern Africa and elsewhere in the continent raises legitimate concern over neocolonial intrusion.

The arrival of the Cuban forces marked the first time that foreign Communist forces have openly intervened in Africa: "The Soviet Union deploys Cuban soldiers in places where it serves Soviet interests (as, for example, in Angola); it gets the Soviets around the dangerous task

of sending their own troops and running the risk of bringing the United States in the scene."[37]   The Cuban intervention in Angola could not have been conducted without
the support--logistically and materially--of the Soviet Union.
The presence of Cuban troops sharply altered the military
balance, giving the MPLA the advantage over its enemies.

The continuing presence of Cuban forces in Angola
has implications pointing toward Rhodesia and ultimately
to South Africa.   The American news media reported that
several hundred Cuban military advisers were in Mozambique to train Rhodesian guerrillas.[38]   It was convenient
for the Cuban forces to establish their "permanent" bases
in Angola and Mozambique to train Rhodesian guerrillas
and move from there to any trouble spots in Africa or the
Middle East--as indeed they did in Ethiopia.   The U.S.
Department of State cautioned Cuba that an expansion of
its new military role in Ethiopia would jeopardize prospects for a renewed relationship between Havana and Washington.[39]   Surprisingly, the next day Ambassador Young
separated his views from those of the State Department,
telling a press conference in London that Cuban forces in
Africa had a "stabilizing influence" there.[40]   He was later
corrected by President Carter himself, who sent Premier
Fidel Castro of Cuba a message urging the withdrawal of
Cuban troops from Africa.[41]

Within South Africa and abroad, it is becoming increasingly evident that time is running out for a peaceful
change and negotiated settlement.   But, at the same time,
South African blacks are not ready for a revolution in the
sense of completely destroying the prevailing order.   This
is because the "revolutionaries" lack adequate arms and
external bases from which to operate.   There is also the
problem of a united black leadership, presently lacking.

The resented influence of foreign powers in southern
Africa is a product of the political and economic weak-
nesses of the subcontinent itself.   Since it is a vast
storehouse of raw materials and minerals, southern Africa
is naturally coveted by both West and East; southern African disunity and division offers a tempting invitation for
foreign meddling.   While the Soviets welcome this instability in the region, Western strategists view South Africa as
the primary guarantor of southern African stability and as
the only bastion against Communist influence and infiltration.

NOTES

1. Wellington W. Nyangoni, African Nationalism in Zimbabwe (Rhodesia) (Washington, D.C.: University Press of America, 1977), p. 63.

2. New York Times, September 25, 1976.

3. Richard W. Hull, "The Conflict in Rhodesia," Current History, November 1976, p. 185.

4. Ibid.

5. Washington Post (editorial), April 29, 1976.

6. Ibid., September 25, 1977.

7. Ibid.

8. Ibid., November 25, 1977.

9. Ibid., November 27, 1977.

10. Ibid. (editorial).

11. New York Times, November 27, 1977.

12. Washington Star, November 26, 1977.

13. Frederick S. Arkhurst, ed., U.S. Policy Toward Africa (New York: Praeger, 1975), p. 3.

14. U.S. Department of State, Bureau of Public Affairs, Namibia: Review of Negotiations, September 9, 1980.

15. Walvis Bay is an enclave on the Namibian coast. The bay, 420 square miles, is Namibia's only functional access to the sea and the only deep-water port on the coast of southern Africa from Cape Town to Luanda. When South Africa assumed its mandate over Namibia in 1920, it (South Africa) proceeded to administer Walvis Bay as part of the annexed area. South Africa wants to retain the bay as part of its Cape Province. Namibia claims the bay as the integral part of its territory. The United Nations adopted Resolution 342 (1978) supporting the contention of Namibia.

16. Jeffrey B. Gayner, Namibia: The Road to Self-Government (Washington, D.C.: Council on American Affairs, 1979), p. 50.

17. Economist (London), September 30, 1978.

18. Washington Post, September 22, 1978.

19. Quoted in Gayner, Namibia, p. 76.

20. Washington Post, May 4, 1981.

21. Ibid., April 4, 1977.

22. Ibid., May 24, 1977.

23. Ibid., December 7, 1977.

24. See Stephen S. Rosenfeld, "Cubans in Africa: A New Colonialism?" Washington Post, December 9, 1977.

25. Walter F. Hahn and Alvin J. Cottrell, Soviet Shadow Over Africa (Miami, Fla.: Center for International Studies, University of Miami, 1976), p. 74.

26. New York Times, May 1, 1981.
27. Henry L. Bretton, "Patron-Client Relationship: Middle Africa and the Powers" (New York: General Learning Press, 1971).
28. For further details, see Hahn and Cottrell, Soviet Shadow, p. 55.
29. Ibid, p. xiii.
30. Ibid., p. 56.
31. Quoted in G. W. Choudhury, Chinese Perception of the World (Washington, D.C.: University Press of America, 1977), p. 64.
32. Cited in Hahn and Cottrell, Soviet Shadow, p. 59.
33. Ibid.
34. Ibid.
35. Ibid.
36. See Colin Legum and Margaret Legum, "South Africa in the Contemporary World," Issue, Fall 1973.
37. Quoted in Hahn and Cottrell, Soviet Shadow, p. 63.
38. Miami Herald, September 22, 1976.
39. Washington Post, May 26, 1977.
40. Ibid., May 27, 1977.
41. Ibid., December 7, 1977.

10
Policy Implications

In the past the United States neglected Africa. Even in the early 1970s, beyond displays of moral outrage and economic self-interest, the United States did not show much concern about Africa. The United States's "discovery" of Africa began with Secretary of State Kissinger's trip in 1976. Even then American concern was not primarily with the southern African crisis but with the possibility of growing Soviet influence in Africa.

Kissinger's Lusaka statement of April 27, 1976 carried two messages. One was obviously addressed to the Soviets and the other to the Africans. Giving the Soviets certain chiding, he said, "Africans cannot want outsiders seeking to impose solutions." An attempt by another country to "pursue hegemonial aspirations or bloc politics," Kissinger stated,[1] "will inevitably be countered" by the United States.[1] The other message was directed to the Africans, particularly to the southern Africans. It said: "We support self-determination, majority rule, equal rights and human dignity for all the peoples of Southern Africa--in the name of moral principle, international law and world peace."[2]

The Lusaka statement had new implications for U.S. policy: a determination to use American influence to avert racial conflict in southern Africa. Kissinger's other speeches, made at Boston, Philadelphia, and the United Nations, spelled out the policy implications further. As he lashed out in these speeches, peaceful negotiations between parties in Rhodesia would be followed by majority rule within two years of the 1976 Lusaka address. His plan included financial compensation to be given to neighboring states for funds lost to a Rhodesian blockade. These steps, coupled with diplomatic initiatives, led to the realization of a Zimbabwe governed by the black people of Rhodesia. United States support for this principle in Zimbabwe is not simply a matter of foreign policy but an imperative of American moral heritage.[3]

The concrete steps that the Lusaka statement enunciated as being necessary to avoid war and bring majority rule to southern Africa marked an important turning point in American policy toward Africa and other developing nations. It is understandable that white settlers in Rhodesia, having developed a successful capitalistic pattern of economy—by a combination of Western technology and capital and easily exploited black labor—was fearful of black majority rule. Nevertheless, no society in the present-day world can long exist with 96 percent of a population kept as slaves and 4 percent enjoying freedom. Belatedly, the United States realized this truth in Rhodesia.

A critical question the United States now faces in regard to its southern African policy is whether it can play an effective role in the resolution of the Namibian crisis; some amount of pressure might be needed to force successful negotiations. In this connection, the question of how pressure is to be applied is regarded as one of the key tests of U.S. policy. Many Africans regarded the repeal of the Byrd Amendment, which permitted U.S. imports of Rhodesian chrome ore, as a measure strong enough to bring Rhodesia to negotiation. But it did not.

Another source of pressure could be South Africa. Observers of the southern African scene, including many supporters of South Africa, believe that it is in South Africa's self-interest to negotiate Namibian issues and settle other matters with black South Africans. Other commentators argue that as a result of American pressure, South Africa (for the first time) actively discussed constitutional reorganization and gave Asians and Coloureds, but not the blacks, some degree of political rights and participation.[4]

The U.S. government has been an active associate of repressive governments in southern Africa. This policy places the United States in direct opposition to the legitimate aspirations of the people of southern Africa. The recent independence of Angola and Mozambique offered opportunity for the United States to abandon its support of the white minority regimes, but it did not want to intervene more directly to unseat those governments and establish black rule.

Meanwhile, a number of developments have taken place as representatives of the United States and Britain on various occasions discussed the situations in southern Africa. A conference in Geneva on October 28, 1976 sought agreement on how and when a changeover in southern Africa should take place. The conference failed to agree on the timetable to be established for the proposed government changeover. Could the U.S. initiative have succeeded had it begun earlier? On this the Washington Post had the following to say:

> Could the United States, by beginning years
> earlier its push for black majority rule,
> have disabused Salisbury of the expectation
> of an American bailout and thereby induced
> it to change course? Could the Ford ad-
> ministration have achieved such a result
> last year while Rhodesian negotiations
> were still in progress, if it had become
> unstrung by the Soviet-Cuban intervention
> in Angola? Quite possibly, but it is not
> much help now to speculate.[5]

Kissinger stated at Lusaka that the United States was "ready to help alleviate economic hardship for any countries neighboring Rhodesia which decide to enforce sanctions by closing their frontiers."[6] There are many examples of economic cooperation and interdependence that the southern African countries have had with each other. South Africa, as the only industrial economy in the sub-continent, exports its goods and technicians to the neighboring countries. The mineral resources of Zimbabwe, Zambia, and Zaire made possible the development of rail links with the Atlantic and Indian oceans. These are just two examples of the integrated economic collaboration among the countries in southern Africa. The economies of all the countries would be badly hurt if they applied sanctions against Rhodesia. Sensing this, the United States immediately pledged $12.5 million to Mozambique. Subsequently, the U.S. Congress authorized $75 million for southern Africa in the International Assistance Act of 1976.

Zambia and Zaire received $27.5 million in balance of
payments support. In addition, $20 million was undesig-
nated for potential uses to offset the impact of the sanctions on the Mozambique and Botswana economies and other
assistance programs.

A more important development took place on November
24, 1977, when, in a surprise turnabout, Rhodesian Prime
Minister Smith committed himself to black majority rule
based on one man, one vote, and offered to negotiate such
transfer of power with moderate black leaders.[7] The
agreement of internally based black nationalist groups to
open negotiations with Smith had reached an agreement
stage with the moderate nationalists but would be boycotted
by the Patriotic Front, which controlled the guerrilla forces
fighting against the Smith regime. In this situation the
main concern of the United States was that a settlement
should include all parties to the Rhodesian conflict--other-
wise Rhodesia's future would remain in doubt. On a possible settlement of the Rhodesian crisis, "There should be
no question of where the United States' moral and political
loyalties lie; on the side of the government freely chosen
by the people of Zimbabwe."[8]

Rhodesia was the most urgent, though by no means
the only, critical problem in southern Africa. The paramount fact is that the two governments involved, Rhodesia
and South Africa, have been almost universally condemned
by other nations. There is universal demand also that
South Africa remove itself from the control of Namibia,
which it has held in defiance of the United Nations and
the International Court of Justice. South Africa presents a
much more complicated situation than Rhodesia. One in 7
is white, compared to one in 25 in Rhodesia. Apartheid
in South Africa remains an issue of great concern to those
committed to racial justice and human dignity. The United
States has a vested interest lest racial tensions in southern
Africa flare into open conflict in the United States. The
possibility of conflict transforming itself into violence and
external exploitation is there.

The Carter administration made a central issue of
human rights, yet South Africa continued to violate all
fundamental human rights for its majority population.
President Carter's oft-repeated personal commitment to
human rights required the American government's firm and
clear opposition to racial and social inequality wherever
it existed: "A policy toward Southern Africa that is not

firmly grounded on this principle would be inconsistent with our national character and therefore would not command the support of the American people. Moreover, it would cast doubt on our commitment to social justice both here at home and elsewhere in the world."[9]

In the famous _Playboy_ interview of November 1976, Carter, then a presidential candidate, said: "The fact that I didn't crusade at a very early stage for civil rights in the South, for one-man, one-vote ruling, it might be that now I should drop my campaign for President and start a crusade for black majority rule in South Africa or Rhodesia."[10] This statement became Carter's foreign policy objective toward southern Africa. What he did not do as an American in his native South, he wanted to accomplish in the south of Africa. The problem is basically the same but in a reverse order: In the American South the forcibly imported black minority was reduced to slavery but was ultimately given its civil and political rights under the law. In southern Africa, the white minorities, smaller in numbers and percentages of total populations than American blacks in the South, have apartheidized the vast majority of the aboriginal black peoples.

From all accounts, President Carter, Vice President Walter Mondale, and Ambassador Young intensified their efforts to achieve black-white detente in southern Africa. The big question was, Would they put enough pressure on southern African governments? It all depended on the kinds of pressures that the Carter administration could bring to bear on the dehumanized governments of southern Africa.

In a rather comprehensive statement to black Americans on the Carter administration's policy toward southern Africa, Secretary of State Cyrus Vance called on South Africa to dismantle its apartheid system or face inevitable deterioration of its relations with the United States.[11]

Like the Jewish minority in the United States, which seems to play a most prominent role in American foreign policy formulation and implementation in the Middle East of late, black Americans are, for the first time, muscling their way to influence U.S. policy in Africa. Former U.S. Ambassador to the United Nations Young, a confidant of President Carter and a prominent black leader, openly identified with the African cause on black rule in southern Africa.

A most important, recent implication for American foreign policy in southern Africa is the growing interest of black Americans and others concerned with racial problems since the constitutional crisis and recurrence of riots in South Africa from 1985. Although South Africa has not yet become a major political issue in the United States, serious crises in the countries of apartheid could have severe repercussions in the United States.

If widespread racial conflicts develop within southern Africa, it is likely that the United States will become involved in the disputes. The question is, On which side? The answer would depend on whether the United States wants to maintain its economic interest with the whiteocracy or prevent genocide of the blacks in southern Africa. It appears that the United States would like to safeguard its economic interests. Another compelling reason for the United States to side with the apartheidists is political, a defense against communism. Any bloodbath in southern Africa will be exploited by the African and international Communists. This in turn will draw the sympathy of the humanitarian people everywhere in the world. The various humanitarian and church groups in the United States, including many white organizations, will be involved in opposing the atrocities in southern Africa. As a result, the United States is likely to face a crisis in its foreign policy in southern Africa.

U.S. policy toward southern Africa has been weak and reactive. The suddenness with which the issue of race burst into the American consciousness as a force finds the government acting cautiously. The justification for the low priority of southern Africa is that more important and pressing problems exist elsewhere and African nations are not pressing as hard in private contact with the U.S. government as is their public rhetoric.

The Carter administration succeeded in impressing upon Africa that, at least in principle, it considered human rights in southern Africa to be a question of magnitude. The weakest element of the Carter administration's policy toward southern Africa was on the issue of black majority rule. The Ford and Carter administrations indirectly strengthened the South African government by continuing to support the economy with U.S. trade and investment and by vehemently opposing those economic sanctions proposed by the United Nations.

The advocates of a tougher American policy favor total disengagement from South Africa until it abandons apartheid. Opponents of this policy contend that a tougher policy does not further America's interests; it gives comfort to the Soviets. They insist that weakening stable governments based on vigorous multiparty parliamentary systems, alienating moderates, and encouraging liberation movements, the United States creates a vacuum for Communist meddling.

This evaluation of U.S. policy toward southern Africa could not be complete without an examination of its impact on broader American interests. It is important to recognize that American policy in southern Africa has a profound effect on U.S. relations with 50 black African nations. These nations are particularly concerned about the continuation of whiteocracy in the African continent.

In the international forum, such as that represented by the United Nations, African nations have called upon the world community to help further the principle of human rights and dignity in southern Africa. American response to these appeals will be regarded as an indicator of the U.S. government's concern about human rights and self-determination in southern Africa. American violation of international sanctions against Rhodesia had seriously undermined the credibility of the commitment of the United States to the United Nations. However, by repealing the Byrd Amendment, the United States restored its credibility to a certain extent. The possibility of the American use of the military facility at Simonstown, South Africa, is viewed with apprehension, but the devastating effect on America's relations with the rest of Africa would be critical.

The new nations of the world have demonstrated how important they feel the southern African crisis to be in their introduction of numerous resolutions on Rhodesia, Namibia, and South Africa in the UN General Assembly. The United States, the oldest of the newest nations in the world, instead of supporting these resolutions, has acted upon them half-heartedly, while stringing along with the European nations.

What can America do? There is still time to demonstrate that South Africa will receive no diplomatic support from the United States under any circumstances if it continues to violate human rights. Further, the United States can encourage South Africa to free Namibia. America can also initiate discussion at the United Nations and elsewhere on future international peacekeeping operations against the possible outbreak of violence in southern Africa in the wake of majority rule there.

In determining future policy, what weight should the Reagan administration give to its short-term economic and security interests and its long-term interests of democracy and anticommunism? Can these interests be blended into one? If not, which should take precedence? The balance is vital.

A cursory glance at American policy toward southern Africa after Reagan became president shows that he is unwilling to abandon South Africa. Said he: "Can we abandon a country that has stood beside us in every war we have fought. . . ."[12] This reflects a common geopolitical world view shared by the United States and South Africa. In this context the Reagan administration may reconsider the idea broached a few years ago of a South Atlantic Treaty Organization (SATO) in which the United States, South Africa, Brazil, Argentina, Paraguay, and Uruguay would join as members.[13]

Most of Reagan's foreign policy advisers have been drawn from conservative think tanks. They have stated unequivocally that the issue in Africa, including southern Africa, will be considered in terms of cold war conflicts.[14] Richard V. Allen, Reagan's former National Security adviser, believed in recognizing the importance of South Africa as a key ally. Chester Crocker, the assistant secretary of state for African affairs, emphasizes the protection of American strategic interests in Africa. John Sears, a senior partner in Washington's Baskin and Sears law firm, was Reagan's campaign manager. Baskin and Sears was hired by the South African government to represent its interests and lobby in the U.S. Congress for South Africa. Phillip Hare, a South African-American, is another partner in this firm. The law firm is paid $500,000 a year, plus expenses, for its services to South Africa. Sears has strong pro-South African views and he is close to President Reagan.[15]

Many other agents for the Pretoria government are busy working in Washington and New York to create favorable opinion for South Africa in the United States. Among such lobbyists are those from the law firms of Smathers and Symington, Marion Smoak, and Carl Shipley. Organizations like Freedom House in New York and the American Security Council also are actively lobbying for South Africans. The president of the American Security Council, John Fisher, invited the South African military intelligence chief and other military officers to hold meetings with Reagan administration officials, including former UN Ambassador Jeane Kirkpatrick. Their visit to the United States was in violation of a 1962 corollary to the arms embargo placing restrictions on visits to the United States by ranking South African personnel down to brigadier.[16]

The orientation of President Reagan and his advisers suggests a strong pro-South African bias. Their public statements on Africa proclaim a repeated preference for countries with free market economies. While some will be attracted by ideological support for South Africa, others certainly will be influenced by lucrative business deals and other economic interests.

Several important southern African issues will necessarily require decisions by the Reagan administration. One of these is the attempt by the Western five to negotiate for the United Nations a settlement of the Namibian issue between South Africa and SWAPO. South Africa, it will be recalled, has persistently declined to accept the terms offered for a cease-fire, elections, and independence for Namibia.

With a view to obtaining South Africa's cooperation for negotiations on Zimbabwe and Namibia, the Carter administration took no firm measure to offend South Africa for its policy of racial apartheid. How will the Reagan administration's policy differ from that of the previous administration? President Reagan and his advisers are more sympathetic toward South Africa. The strongest impetus for a tilt toward South Africa is the heightened concern of the Reagan administration with the supply of strategic minerals. On a 1980 visit to South Africa, Allen observed that there were strategic reasons for closer U.S. relations with South Africa. The argument continues that because South Africa holds a special place among African raw materials exporters, the United States should follow an aggressive commercial diplomacy, including trade and investment in the region. This will help balance America's foreign trade. Crocker believes the United States can neither embrace South Africa in its current form nor walk away from the problem.[17]

Embargoes on weapons and nuclear fuel supplies will continue. At the same time specially targeted economic sanctions will be enforced as a clear signal to the

South African government of U.S. dissatisfaction with the pace of reform. Reagan's southern African policy will have to take into account the fact that South Africa does not exist in a vacuum. The United States cannot befriend South Africa without incurring massive diplomatic, political, and economic damage, not only in Africa but in the entire Third World, and thereby will risk severe domestic polarization and racial trouble.

In the face of such jeopardy, the Reagan administration announced a policy of "constructive engagement" with South Africa after two days of talks with Botha in May 1981.[18] Although President Reagan has labeled South Africa's racial policy as "repugnant," there has been no public drive by the U.S. administration to demand reforms. A policy of constructive engagement rather than one of confrontation has been chosen as the best way to bring about progress. With a successful Namibia settlement, there would be a foundation for a more constructive bilateral relationship. The assertion that the Reagan administration regards any such improvement in relations as dependent upon South African cooperation on the Namibia issue appears to be a firm signal to black Africa that Washington is not willing to improve relations dramatically with the South African government without regard to other U.S. interests in Africa and the Third World.

Before concluding, we will try to formulate the following important issues likely to have some impacts on U.S. foreign policy in southern Africa:

1. Despite appearances to the contrary, southern Africa is inherently unstable. South Africa has made anti-government activity both difficult and dangerous, but the threat to its survival remains. The U.S. government cannot ignore this realism in southern Africa.

2. The policy of apartheid expresses the determination of the whites to retain their privileged socioeconomic status at all costs. Apartheid is an insult not only to black people but also to all human beings everywhere. Minority rule by any color is irreconcilable with the American concept of governance.

3. The liberation forces and the white supremacists in southern Africa will ultimately tangle, perhaps in Namibia, forcing genocide in the subcontinent. In all likelihood it would be a black bloodbath in southern Africa, with dangerous involvement of black Africa on the side of the nationalist forces.

4. A race war in southern Africa would involve the world powers. The Communist nations are likely to support the blacks, while the Western powers, including the United States, in order to protect ecostrategic interests, may join the white regime.

5. U.S. multinational corporations have helped, shaped, and profited from the current oppressive situation in southern Africa. A policy of complete economic divestment from South Africa could seriously challenge white rule there.

6. Many black Americans, churches, and academics have begun to question the propriety of investments that support discrimination. The continued turmoil in southern Africa will inevitably result in the destruction of foreign investment and business interest.

7. Americans recognize from their own national experience that to abandon the legalized structure of racism is but the first step taken in a much larger battle toward freedom and equality for all. Nowhere else in the world are people confined to putative homelands because of their skin pigmentation. The first step to abolish legalized racism in South Africa has not been introduced. The United States, instead of furthering the elimination of discrimination, has preferred to depend on repressive regimes to block the wheel of change.

NOTES

1. New York Times, April 28, 1976.
2. Ibid.
3. Ibid.
4. George W. Ball, "Asking for Trouble in South Africa," Atlantic, October 1977, p. 48.
5. Washington Post (editorial), April 29, 1976.
6. Ibid., April 28, 1976.
7. Ibid., November 25, 1977.
8. Ibid., November 26, 1977.
9. U.S. Department of State, "Southern Africa in the Global Context," March 3, 1977.
10. Playboy, November 1976.
11. Secretary of State, Department of State, "U.S. Policy Toward Africa," July 1, 1977.
12. Africa, May 1981.
13. Ibid.

14.   Africa Report, July–August 1980.   They were questioned before Ronald Reagan was elected president.

15.   Africa, May 1981.

16.   Ibid.

17.   Africa Report, January–February 1981.

18.   Washington Post, May 17, 1981.

11
Conclusions

The crisis in southern Africa, which broke into the public consciousness in the fall of 1984, persists. Politics remains polarized and shrill, making it difficult for moderates on both sides to meet, much less negotiate. Violence and repression occur at levels that disturb many people who hope for peaceful change in the subcontinent.

South Africa is the most important country in southern Africa. It is a divided country in which suspicion and mistrust abound. White and black South Africans tend to look at their country and see two different realities. For the whites, the glass is seen to be filling at an unprecedented pace; for the blacks, it remains nearly empty.

White South Africans emphasize how much change has taken place in recent years and to what degree the government has lately made concessions: The state of emergency has at last been lifted; power sharing and negotiations are called for, and apartheid is branded as outdated. The government has also announced that political domination, petty discrimination, economic and educational inequality, and the pass laws, no longer enforced, are to be eliminated altogether. An undivided South Africa, a common citizenship, and a universal franchise--these are political commitments from a National party government, commitments that would have been unthinkable a few years ago. To many white South Africans these changes appear rapid, even revolutionary. Such change inspires fear in some, and in others it provokes resistance. To many it offers the promise that a more just society can be peacefully achieved.

Looking at these events, many black South Africans see something quite different. Such changes as have taken place appear marginal and grudging to them. Whatever concessions have been made or promised, blacks still lack citizenship; they still cannot vote in national elections; they are forced to send their children to inferior schools; and they are confined to black areas where crime, intimidation, and the presence of security forces are too common. Black contract laborers still must leave their spouses and families behind in the homelands.

In these circumstances, after more than two years of violence (as of November 1986) and 11,000 detentions and over 1,700 deaths, it is hardly surprising that politics has polarized. Nor is it surprising that the South African government should find dismantling apartheid far more difficult than imposing it.

An economic downturn has produced new strains. High inflation, running at nearly 20 percent, and budgetary austerity have cut into funds available for social expenditures, affecting all sectors of South African society. Blacks, at the lowest end of the economic scale, are hit hardest. Higher unemployment and sharply increased costs for housing, transportation, and food clearly have hurt blacks much more than whites. External economic pressures have increased as well, leading to the debt standstill and a plummeting currency in the fall of 1985. This debt crisis is unusual in that it traces more to politics than to economic causes--yet another indication of the true nature of South Africa's problems.

The southern African crisis is by no means the most difficult one the world is facing, but it is the most disgraceful one. Never in the history of humankind has the color of skin prejudiced people's thinking and actions as much as in southern Africa. And seldom in world history (save in certain colonies) has the minority of population ruled an overwhelming majority and denied its basic rights. It may be inaccurate to use the analogy of Hitler's Germany when describing South Africa, but both represent situations in which human beings became victims on the grounds of their race.

The most disturbing internal problem of southern Africa is racial unrest. People are suffering indignities and nourishing hatred mainly because of skin pigmentation. Discrimination policies and laws of minority white governments have brought ill repute to the name and interests of southern Africa in the world. By these laws nonwhites are denied inalienable opportunities of gaining the basic needs of life. For decades they have suffered, and continue to suffer, a repression that impoverishes them and is a humiliating affront to their humanity.

Despite the mounting array of injustices afflicting blacks in southern Africa, nothing substantial has changed in the subcontinent. So far there is no real physical threat to white lives and little threat to white political power. White South Africa is well equipped; it has the capacity to repress township revolts with military might and cruelty. The blacks have virtually no urban and rural guerrilla capacity, practically no guns, and few safe havens within South Africa. It is still premature to talk about the overthrow of Afrikanerdom in the near future. But is it wise to assume because white physical power is unchallenged that the white will to govern is likely to remain constant? Not any more. It is the will, not the physical strength, that is under question.

White South Africa faces a growing threat from beyond its borders as well. Until recently South Africa was shielded from the rest of the African continent by the Portuguese colonies of Mozambique and Angola and by white-ruled Rhodesia. A black Marxist government, allied to Moscow, took over in Mozambique. The Soviet Union installed another pro-Russian regime in Angola. Rhodesia became the independent Zimbabwe.

Stripped of its white-controlled buffer states and faced with a hostile black Africa of 50 nations, South Africa finds itself in a beleaguered position. The black population is restive, and many people are joining guerrilla forces outside the frontiers of South Africa and Namibia.

Whatever confidence the whites of southern Africa had in their ability to defend themselves indefinitely is diminishing as white emigration increases. The dilemma of southern Africa's whites seems insurmountable. In the end they will have to devise a policy that is based on consent rather than force. This means that if they want to integrate the majority of the black population into the white economy, they will have to give nonwhites those political rights commensurate with their economic status.

In considerations of the future it is important to avoid succumbing to two fallacies advocated by opponents of pressure. The first is the contention that pressure should be relaxed because it only rigidifies and solidifies the whites in their resistance; the second is the wishful thinking that if pressure is relaxed, economic integration will kill apartheid and solve the problem of race relations. Time, it is argued, will dampen the fires of internal revolt, since the region's economic growth will raise the standard of living of the blacks and provide them with a vested interest in the status quo. But, alas, time is running out.

The status of human rights in southern Africa could not have been worse at any time than it is now. The very idea of human rights presupposes the basic acceptance of human equality. Every aspect of southern Africa's state organizations is inconsistent with the concept of human equality and freedom. But this is not simply an internal matter. Without the kind of practical support that the southern African governments have been and are still receiving from the Western countries, the present apartheid structures could not stand for long and minority rule could not continue.

The problems of the contemporary world are too complex to center on the single issue of race, but most observers believe that everything feasible should be done to prevent the polarization of conflict in southern Africa. Though Western governments deplore southern Africa's racial policies, they know that if it were to come under Communist sway, the region would be a crucial loss to the West.

In southern Africa terror has become commonplace; terror is conveyed effectively by the use of extraordinary power. There is an increasing use of force and arbitrary decree--the banning of persons from membership in organizations and attendance at meetings; deportation, exile, and mass trials; police intimidation and violence; secret summary trials within prison walls; and the practice of incarceration without trial.

The key fact about southern Africa is the power of the whites and their will to use it to maintain white domination. South Africa is the bulwark of the white redoubt because of its military power, economic power, and the willpower of its white leaders.

Majority self-government in southern Africa can only be denied by force. Negotiation of the issues is the only deterrent to civil war in southern Africa. The Soviet Union, which sponsors guerrilla operation in southern Africa,

stands to gain from the intransigence of majority and minority leaders in the area.

Because of limited interests in southern Africa, the
position of the United States has customarily been expressed in verbal generalities and in perfunctory moves
for UN resolutions condemning apartheid. American investment in southern Africa has more than tripled in the last
decade. Western investors profit from apartheid and the
discriminatory wage structures and thus have an interest
in sustaining it. But by identifying themselves in practice with the apartheidist regimes, Western investors are
liable to bring about the very thing they most fear--the
growth of Communist influence. In offsetting these liabili-
ties, South Africa, which already controls the West's supply of gold, is fast becoming its major source of enriched
uranium and other valuables such as diamonds.

Can the United States force any solution to the
southern African crisis? Before this question is answered,
another question seems relevant. Can the United States
avoid sacrificing any of its vital stakes in southern Africa? One school of thought believes, and with some justification, that the only solution to the southern African
crisis is black majority rule through revolution or civil
war. These proponents of conflict argue that to be consistent with American morality and philosophical principles,
based on the belief that all persons are created equal,
the United States should sever its ecopolitical relations
with the regimes of apartheid.

Another school of thought is that the United States
should cultivate friendly relations with southern African
governments and attempt to liberalize the system through
persuasion. Moreover, they say that through better com-
munication and assistance to encourage economic growth in
southern Africa, the moderate force of social change can
be brought to bear on the policy of apartheid. Protection
of human rights will follow.

This second school of thought neglects the view that
racial prejudice is an attitude--and a sentiment--like nationalism. Both seem equally unalterable, but the former
is a vice, whereas the latter is a virtue. The most in-
destructible component of southern African whiteocracy is
apartheid on which the dehumanized regimes are dependent
for their survival. South African Foreign Minister Botha
said that his country's whites "never ever" would accept
black majority because that would be "negotiating our own
destruction."

Such an attitude is not at all conducive to a peaceful settlement of the southern African crisis. Whatever the attitude of the minority white regimes in southern Africa, the solution of the crisis lies in majority rule. This must come about if democratic institutions are to have any hope of success in the countries of the Third World where minorities may be considering a power takeover.

The destruction of southern African whiteocracy is inevitable. The important two-part question is how it will come about. The destruction of the South African government cannot come through negotiation as the apartheidists do not want negotiation. It appears that at some point the racist regimes in southern Africa will choose war as a last resort to retain their hold on the land of affluence. Negotiations would delay their self-destruction; civil war or war would hasten it.

Many countries fighting for independence in Africa in recent years have won their freedom through Soviet support. It seems that, in most Afro-Asian struggles, the side that is supported by the United States loses. Recent examples include Angola, Bangladesh, Mozambique, and Vietnam. Therefore, if a situation of war develops in southern Africa and the United States supports the regimes of whiteocracy there, then the war may be won by the black majority people of southern Africa.

Southern Africa is an arena in which the major powers are competing for influence. If the United States loses, client states of the Soviet Union could control a vast area in southern Africa. Namibia is in immediate danger of falling. South Africa is not threatened immediately, but if winter comes, can spring be far away?

Southern Africa can be compared with an ancient Chinese puzzle in which there are three boxes. In this case the boxes are Zimbabwe, Namibia, and South Africa. The first box, Zimbabwe, is exposed on all sides, its lacquer chipped and lusterless. Open up the lid and there is the second box. Namibia is exposed to the same danger as the first box. Zimbabwe has already fallen, and when Namibia falls, which is inevitable, the days of South Africa will be numbered. It appears that South Africa is the last of what could truly become a row of falling dominoes.

What is happening in southern Africa has meaning for all people who believe in social and human justice. Today this search for social justice is under increasing challenge, and Americans are beginning to show some understanding of the human dimension of the system. American interests lie, as in the settlement of the Zimbabwe crisis, in coming to terms with the inevitable course of events. They lie in seizing what opportunities remain to shape that course in ways that will pressure and extend the rights and the interests of both whites and blacks.

It will be most difficult to work toward a stable society in South Africa under any form of government in which whites and blacks can live together in peace and to the benefit of all. But the chances of that outcome will be made infinitely worse if peaceful means fail.

Can the United States influence any solution to the southern African crisis? Acting alone, it cannot. But working in concert with the West European countries and the Third World nations, the United States could conceivably bring South Africa to its knees. If they fail to fashion a peaceful settlement in southern Africa, the consequences for 5 million whites will be disastrous. They will have to flee their homes and seek asylum in Europe, North America, and Australia. This could be a most tragic human upheaval in the history of refugee migration.

To be sure, the mass departure of more than a million Frenchmen from Algeria and some 800,000 Portuguese from Mozambique and Angola constituted one of the rapid migratory phenomena of white populations from Africa in recent times. This record should bear testimony and warning that we may indeed expect a painfully large refugee movement among whites in southern Africa also, once serious racial violence or civil war develops.

For many American corporations in South Africa, the choice may well turn out to be between getting more deeply involved in the country's affairs or getting out. A persuasive argument for deeper involvement is made by some of the contributors to business with South Africa. They have collectively made a powerful case for the proposition that apartheid is not doomed because it is cruel and unjust nor because world opinion will no longer stand for it, but because it is fundamentally incompatible with a modern industrial economy such as in South Africa.

South Africa has emerged as the most powerful actor in southern Africa by overwhelming its neighbors and ignoring the signs of American displeasure. Despite internal unrest and turmoil, South African overlordship in the region is expected to continue for some time longer.

A beneficial solution to the problem in southern Africa, reached by a realistic and sympathetic American foreign policy, is the alleviation of the suffering of millions (on both sides of the Atlantic) for many years to come. The people to the south of the Atlantic will suffer as a result of possible civil war in southern Africa, and the people to the north of the Atlantic will suffer as a result of racial riots and damage in the United States. It is a subject that deserves further attention of South African and American leaders today.

American influence in southern Africa--not insignificant--is still limited. The Reagan administration starts from the premise that a blueprint for greater racial justice and harmony can emerge only out of political dialogue and negotiations between the South African authorities and the authentic leaders of its black community. For the United States, the question in South Africa is not whether it should strive to end apartheid; that is a given. Apartheid is morally unacceptable to many Americans--it is contrary to their basic principles and violates America's sense of fair play. The practical and ethical question that Americans face is how they can be most effective in speeding the demise of apartheid and promoting the evolution of a more just society in southern Africa.

Appendixes

Statement of Principles of United States firms with affiliates in South Africa.

Principle I   Non-Segregation of the races in all eating, comfort and work facilities.
    Each signator of the Statement of Principles will proceed immediately to:

-- Eliminate all vestiges of racial discrimination.
--Remove all race designation signs.
--Desegregate all eating, comfort and work facilities.

Principle II   Equal and fair employment practices for all employees.
    Each signator of the Statement of Principles will proceed immediately to:

-- Implement equal and fair terms and conditions of employment.
-- Provide non-discriminatory eligibility for benefit plans.
-- Establish an appropriate and comprehensive procedure for handling and resolving individual employee complaints.
-- Support the elimination of all industrial racial discriminatory laws which impede the implementation of equal and fair terms and conditions of employment, such as

abolition of job reservations, job fragmentation, and apprenticeship restrictions for Blacks and other non-whites.

-- Support the elimination of discrimination against the rights of Blacks to form or belong to government regis-tered and unregistered unions and acknowledge general-ly the rights of Blacks to form their own unions or be represented by trade unions which already exist.

-- Secure rights of Black workers to the freedom of associa-tion and assure protection against victimization while pursuing and after attaining these rights.

-- Involve Black workers or their representatives in the development of programs that address their educational and other needs and those of their dependents and the local community.

Principle III   Equal pay for all employees doing equal or comparable work for the same period of time.
     Each signator of the Statement of Principles will proceed immediately to:

-- Design and implement a wage and salary administration plan which is applied to all employees, regardless of race, who are performing equal or comparable work.

-- Ensure an equitable system of job classifications, in-cluding a review of the distinction between hourly and salaried classifications.

-- Determine the extent upgrading of personnel and/or jobs in the upper echelons is needed, and accordingly imple-ment programs to accomplish this objective in representa-tive numbers, insuring the employment of Blacks and other non-whites at all levels of company operations.

-- Assign equitable wage and salary ranges, the minimum of these to be well above the appropriate local minimum economic living level.

Principle IV   Initiation of and development of training programs that will prepare, in substantial numbers, Blacks and other non-whites for supervisory, administrative clerical and technical jobs.
     Each signator of the Statement of Principles will proceed immediately to:

-- Determine employee training needs and capabilities, and identify employees with potential for further advancement.

-- Take advantage of existing outside training resources and activities, such as exchange programs, technical colleges, and similar institutions or programs.
-- Support the development of outside training facilities, individually or collectively, including technical centers, professional training exposure, correspondence and extension courses, as appropriate, for extensive training outreach.
-- Initiate and expand inside training programs and facilities.

Principle V   Increasing the number of Blacks and other non-whites in management and supervisory positions.
    Each signator of the Statement of Principles will proceed immediately to:

-- Identify, actively recruit, train and develop a sufficient and significant number of Blacks and other non-whites to assure that as quickly as possible there will be appropriate representation of Blacks and other non-whites in the management group of each company at all levels of operations.
-- Establish management development programs for Blacks and non-whites, as needed, and improve existing programs and facilities for developing management skills of Blacks and non-whites.
-- Identify and channel high management potential Blacks and other non-white employees into management development programs.

Principle VI   Improving the quality of employees' lives outside the work environment in such areas as housing, transportation, schooling, recreation and health facilities.
    Each signator of the Statement of Principles will proceed immediately to:

-- Evaluate existing and/or develop programs, as appropriate, to address the specific needs of Black and other non-white employees in the areas of housing, health care, transportation and recreation.
-- Evaluate methods for utilizing existing, expanded or newly established in-house medical facilities or other medical programs to improve medical care for all non-whites and their dependents.

-- Participate in the development of programs that address
the educational needs of employees, their dependents,
and the local community. Both individual and collective
programs should be considered, in addition to technical
education, including such activities as literacy education, business training, direct assistance to local
schools, contributions and scholarships.
-- Support changes in influx control laws to provide for
the right of Black migrant workers to normal family life.
-- Increase utilization of and assist in the development of
Black and other non-white owned and operated business
enterprises including distributors, suppliers of goods
and services and manufacturers.

Increased Dimensions of Activities Outside the Workplace

-- Use influence and support the unrestricted rights of
Black businesses to locate in the urban areas of the
nation.
-- Influence other companies of South Africa to follow the
standards of equal rights principles.
-- Support the freedom of mobility of Black workers to seek
employment opportunities wherever they exist, and make
possible provisions for adequate housing for families of
employees within the proximity of workers' employment.
-- Support the ending of all apartheid laws.

With all the foregoing in mind, it is the objective
of the companies to involve and assist in the education
and training of large and telling number of Blacks and
other non-whites as quickly as possible. The ultimate impact of this effort is intended to be of massive proportion,
reaching and helping millions.

Periodic Reporting

The Signatory Companies of the Statement of Principles will proceed immediately to:

-- Report progress on an annual basis to Reverend Sullivan
through the independent administrative unit he has established.
-- Have all areas specified by Reverend Sullivan audited by
a certified public accounting firm.

-- Inform all employees of the company's annual periodic report rating and invite their input on ways to improve the rating.

Reprinted with permission of International Council for Equality of Opportunity Principles, Inc., 1502 North Broad Street, Philadelphia, PA, 19122.

APPENDIX B: DIVESTMENT ACTIONS ON SOUTH AFRICA
BY U.S. COLLEGES AND UNIVERSITIES

School	Amount Affected	
¶ Amherst College	16,876,850	1978–85
§ Antioch College	NA	1978
§ Arizona State University	3,100,000	1985*
§ Barnard College	945,000	1985*
§ Bates College	5,000,000	1986*
¶ Boston University (1st)	6,600,000	1979
¶ Boston University (2nd)	195,480	1985
¶ Bowdoin College	1,800,000	1985
¶ Brandeis University	350,000	1979
¶ Brown University	4,600,000	1984
¶ Bryn Mawr	700,000	1986*
§ California State University (Northridge)	2,300,000	1985*
¶ Carleton College	295,000	1979
§ City University of New York	10,000,000	1984
§ Clark University	5,000,000	1986*
¶ Colby College (1st)	2,600,000	1980–84
¶ Colby College (2nd)	6,500,000	1985*
¶ Columbia University (1st)	2,700,000	1979
§ Columbia University (2nd)	39,000,000	1985*
¶ Dartmouth College	2,000,000	1985
¶ Delta College	NA	1985*
¶ Duke University	1,640,000	1985*
§ Evergreen State College	NA	1985
§ Fairfield University	4,000,000	1985*
¶ Florida State University	2,000,000	1985
¶ Franklin and Marshall College	1,000,000	1985*
¶ Georgia Tech University	500,000	1985*
¶ Grinnell College	9,000,000	1985*
§ Hampshire College	40,000	1977
§ Hartford Seminary	5,000,000	1985*
¶ Harvard University (1st)	50,900,000	1981
¶ Harvard University (2nd)	1,000,000	1985
¶ Harvard University (3rd)	2,800,000	1985*
¶ Haverford College	NA	1982
¶ Hebrew Union Theological Seminary	NA	1986*
¶ Hobart and William Smith Colleges	650,000	1985*
¶ Holy Cross	NA	1985
§ Howard University	8,000,000	1978
§ Iowa, University of	2,500,000	1985*
¶ Iowa State University (1st)	130,000	1985*
§ Iowa State University (2nd)	120,000	1985*
§ Kentucky, University of	1,500,000	1985*
§ Louisville, University of	9,000,000	1985*

(continued)

School	Amount Affected	
§ Lutheran School of Theology	NA	1981
§ Maine, University of	3,000,000	1982
§ Massachusetts, University of	600,000	1977
§ Miami, University of	17,000,000	1985*
¶ Missouri, University of	5,000,000	1985*
§ Minnesota, University of	35,000,000	1985*
§ Minnesota Foundation, University of	5,000,000	1986*
¶ Eastern Michigan University	2,500,000	1980
§ Michigan State University	7,200,000	1979-80
¶ Michigan, University of (1st)	306,117	1979
¶ Michigan, University of (2nd)	35,400,000	1984
¶ Michigan, University of (3rd)	5,800,000	1985
¶ Middlebury College	1,500,000	1986*
§ Western Michigan University	200,000	1983
¶ Mount Holyoke College (1st)	459,000	1981
§ Mount Holyoke College (2nd)	14,480,487	1985*
¶ New Brunswick Theological Seminary	NA	1981
¶ New Hampshire, University of	400,000	1985*
¶ New York, State University of	4,000,000	1985*
§ New York, State University of	11,000,000	1985*
¶ New York, State University of (Oneonta)	80,000	1978
§ New York, State University of (Stonybrook Foundation)	80,000	1985
¶ Northeastern University	7,000,000	1985*
¶ Notre Dame	10,000,000	1985*
¶ Oberlin College	NA	1980
¶ Ohio State University (1st)	250,000	1978-79
§ Ohio State University (2nd)	10,800,000	1985*
§ Ohio University	60,000	1978
¶ Pace University	40,000	1986*
¶ Pennsylvania, University of	800,000	1983
¶ Pittsburgh, University of	7,500,000	1986*
§ Rhode Island Foundation, University of	868,000	1985*
§ Roosevelt University	NA	1986*
¶ Rutgers University (1st)	NA	1980
¶ Rutgers University (2nd)	7,000,000	1985
§ Rutgers University (3rd)	7,500,000	1985*
§ Sarah Lawrence College	650,000	1985*
§ Seattle University	2,500,000	1986*
¶ Smith College (1st)	697,728	1977
¶ Smith College (2nd)	550,000	1986*
¶ Swarthmore College (1st)	3,000,000	1981-85
¶ Swarthmore College (2nd)	2,100,000	1986*
§ Teachers College	5,000,000	1985*

School	Amount Affected	
¶ Temple University (1st)	534,000	1985*
§ Temple University (2nd)	1,960,000	1985*
¶ Trinity College	800,000	1985*
¶ Tufts University	100,000	1979
¶ Union Theological Seminary (1st)	4,000,000	1980
¶ Union Theological Seminary (2nd)	2,603,537	1985
¶ Union Theological Seminary (3rd)	1,503,145	1985*
§ Vermont, University of	2,100,000	1985*
¶ Vassar College	6,500,000	1978
¶ Washington, University of (1st)	800,000	1985
¶ Washington, University of (2nd)	4,500,000	1986*
§ Wayne State University	NA	1984
§ Western Washington University	NA	1985
¶ Wesleyan University (1st)	367,000	1980
¶ Wesleyan University (2nd)	750,000	1985*
¶ Williams College (1st)	700,000	1980
¶ Williams College (2nd)	672,000	1983
§ Wisconsin, University of	11,000,000	1978
¶ Yale University (1st)	1,600,000	1979
¶ Yale University (2nd)	4,100,000	1984

Actions 1977 through mid-March 1986

Overall total	84 schools	470,253,344
Total divestment	41 schools	231,503,487
Partial divestment	43 schools	238,749,857

*Actions April 1985 through mid-March 1986

Overall total	52 schools	259,966,632
Total divestment	27 schools	191,403,487
Partial divestment	25 schools	68,563,145

(Note: Iowa State, SUNY, and Temple took partial and then total divestment actions since April 1985.)

Student Actions

¶ California, University of, Berkeley (Associated Students)	4,000,000	1979
§ California, University of, Los Angeles (Associated Students)	25,000,000	1980
§ New York University Law School (Student Bar Association)	11,000,000	1978

§ Total Divestment; ¶ Partial Divestment; *Since April 1985.

NB: Dollar figure is for amount affected, as in some divestment has not yet been completed.

Reprinted with permission of the American Committee on Africa, 198 Broadway, New York, NY 10038. Copyright 1986 The Africa Fund. March 18, 1986.

Selected Bibliography

Adam, Heribert. Modernizing Racial Domination: The Dynamics of South African Politics. Berkeley: University of California Press, 1971.

African National Congress of South Africa. Fuelling Apartheid. New York: UN Center Against Apartheid, 1980.

Albright, David E., ed. Africa and International Communism. London: Macmillan, 1980.

Arkhurst, Frederick S., ed. U.S. Policy Toward Africa. New York: Praeger, 1975.

Arrighi, Giovanni, and John S. Saul. Essays on the Political Economy of Africa. New York: Monthly Press, 1973.

Barber, James. South Africa's Foreign Policy, 1945-1970. London: Oxford University Press, 1973.

Benson, Mary. South Africa: The Struggle for a Birthright. New York: Funk & Wagnalls, 1969.

Berghe, Pierre L. Van Den. South Africa: A Study in Conflict. Berkeley: University of California Press, 1967.

Bissell, Richard E. South Africa and the United States: The Erosion of an Influence Relationship. New York: Praeger, 1982.

_____. Apartheid and International Organizations. Boulder, Colo.: Westview, 1977.

Bissell, Richard E., and Chester A. Crocker. South Africa into the 1980s. Boulder, Colo.: Westview, 1979.

Boulle, L. J. Constitutional Reform and Apartheid: Legitimacy, Consociationalism and Control in South Africa. New York: St. Martin's, 1984.

Bowman, Larry W. Politics in Rhodesia: White Power in an African State. Cambridge, Mass.: Harvard University Press, 1973.

_____. South Africa's Outward Strategy: A Foreign Policy Dilemma for the United States. Athens: Ohio University Center for International Studies, 1971.

Caradon, Lord. Southern Africa in International Relations. London: Africa Bureau, 1970.

Carey, John, ed. Race, Peace, Law, and Southern Africa. Dobbs Ferry, N.Y.: Oceans, 1968.

Carter, Gwendolen M. Which Way Is South Africa Going? Bloomington: Indiana University Press, 1980.

Carter, Gwendolen M., and Patrick O'Meara, eds. International Politics in Southern Africa. Bloomington: Indiana University Press, 1982.

_____. Southern Africa: The Continuing Crisis. Bloomington: Indiana University Press, 1982.

Cell, John W. The Highest Stage of White Supremacy: The Origins of Segregation in South Africa and the American South. Cambridge: Cambridge University Press, 1982.

Choudhury, G. W. Chinese Perception of the World. Washington, D.C.: University Press of America, 1977.

Cockram, Gail-Maryse. Vorster's Foreign Policy. Pretoria, South Africa: Academia, 1970.

Cohen, John P. Africa Addio. New York: Ballantine, 1966.

Cooper, Allan D.   U.S. Economic Power and Political Influ-
    ence in Namibia, 1700–1982.   Boulder, Colo.:   Westview,
    1982.

Cope, John P.   South Africa.   New York: Praeger, 1967.

Crabb, Cecil V.   American Foreign Policy in the Nuclear
    Age.   New York: Harper & Row, 1972.

Crocker, Chester A., ed.   The International Relations of
    Southern Africa.   Washington, D.C.:   Georgetown Uni-
    versity, 1975.

Danaher, Kevin.   In Whose Interest?   A Guide to U.S.-
    South Africa Relations.   Washington, D.C.:   Institute
    for Policy Studies, 1985.

_____.   The Political Economy of U.S. Policy Toward
    South Africa.   Boulder, Colo.:   Westview, 1985.

Davis, N. E.   A History of Southern Africa.   London:
    Longman, 1978.

Deshmond, Cosmas.   The Discarded People: An Account of
    African Resettlement in South Africa.   Harmondsworth,
    England: Penguin, 1972.

Duggan, William R.   A Socio-Economic Profile of South
    Africa.   New York: Praeger, 1973.

Duncan, Patrick.   South Africa's Rule of Violence.   London:
    Methuen, 1964.

Elazau, Daniel J.   Jewish Communities in Frontier Societies:
    Argentina, Australia, and South Africa.   New York:
    Holmes and Meier, 1983.

First, Ruth, Jonathan Steele, and Christabel Gurney.   The
    South African Connection: Western Investment in
    Apartheid.   London: Temple Smith, 1972.

Fisher, Scott.   Coping with Change: United States Policy
    Toward South Africa.   Washington, D.C.:   National De-
    fense University, 1982.

Foltz, William J. Elite Opinion on United States Policy Toward South Africa. New York: Council on Foreign Relations, 1979.

Frederickson, George M. White Supremacy: A Comparative Study in American and South African History. New York: Oxford University Press, 1981.

Gandhi, M. K. Satyagraha in South Africa. Ahmadabad, India: Navajivan, 1928.

Gann, Lewis H. Why South Africa Will Survive: A Historical Analysis. New York: St. Martin's, 1981.

Gavshorn, Arthur. Crisis in Africa: Battleground of East and West. London: Penguin, 1981.

Gerhart, Gail M. Black Power in South Africa: The Evolution of an Ideology. Berkeley: University of California Press, 1978.

Gibson, Richard. African Liberation Movements: Contemporary Struggles Against White Minority Rule. London: Oxford University Press, 1972.

Grundy, Kenneth W. The Militarization of South African Politics. Bloomington: Indiana University Press, 1986.

_____. Confrontation and Accommodation in Southern Africa. Berkeley: University of California Press, 1973.

Hahn, Walter F., and Alvin J. Cottrell. Soviet Shadow over Africa. Miami, Fla.: Center for International Studies, University of Miami, 1976.

Hance, William A., ed. Southern Africa and the United States. New York: Columbia University Press, 1968.

Hanks, Robert J. Southern Africa and Western Security. Cambridge, Mass.: Institute for Foreign Policy Analysis, 1983.

Hill, Christopher R. Change in South Africa: Blind Alleys or New Directions? Totowa, N.J.: Barnes and Noble, 1983.

Hoagland, Jim. South Africa: Civilization in Conflict. Boston: Houghton Mifflin, 1972.

Hoek, P. W. Southern Africa: Now and in the Future. Pretoria, South Africa: Haum, 1980.

Horrell, Muriel. A Survey of Race Relations, Annual Editions, 1953–1970. Johannesburg, South Africa: South Africa Institute of Race Relations, 1954–1971.

Hovet, Thomas, Jr. Africa in the United Nations. Evanston, Ill.: Northwestern University Press, 1963.

Hull, Richard W. Southern Africa: Civilizations in Turmoil. New York: New York University Press, 1981.

Johnson, R. W. How Long Will South Africa Survive? London: Macmillan, 1977.

July, Robert W. A History of the African People. New York: Scribner's, 1974.

Kantor, Brian. South African Economic Issues. Cape Town, South Africa: Juta, 1982.

Khapoya, Vincent B. The Politics of Decision: A Comparative Study of African Policy Toward the Liberation Movements. Denver, Colo.: University of Denver, 1975.

Koenderman, Tony. Sanctions: The Threat to South Africa. Johannesburg, South Africa: J. Ball, 1982.

Lake, Anthony. The "Tar Baby" Option: American Policy Toward Southern Rhodesia. New York: Columbia University Press, 1976.

Lapchik, Richard E. The Politics of Race and International Sport: The Case of South Africa. Westport, Conn.: Greenwood, 1975.

Leftwich, Adrian, ed. South Africa: Economic Growth and Political Change. New York: St. Martin's, 1974.

Legum, Colin. The Western Crisis Over Southern Africa. New York: Africana Publishing, 1979.

_____. *Dialogue: Africa's Great Debate*. London: Africa Contemporary Record Current Series, 1972.

Legum, Colin, and Margaret Legum. *South Africa: Crisis for the West*. New York: Praeger, 1964.

Leistner, Gerhard Max E. *Southern Crucible: South Africa: Future World in Microcosm*. Pretoria, South Africa: Africa Institute of South Africa, 1980.

Lemarchand, Rene, ed. *American Policy in Southern Africa: The Stakes and the Stance*. Washington, D.C.: University Press of America, 1978.

Leonard, Richard. *South Africa at War: White Power and the Crisis in Southern Africa*. Westport, Conn.: Lawrence Hill, 1983.

Lewin, Julius. *The Struggle for Racial Equality*. London: Longmans, 1967.

Libby, Ronald T. *Toward an Africanized U.S. Policy for Southern Africa: A Strategy for Increasing Political Leverage*. Berkeley, Calif.: Institute of International Studies, 1980.

Loney, Martin. *Rhodesia: White Racism and Imperial Response*. Harmondsworth, England: Penguin, 1975.

McClellan, Grant S. *Southern Africa*. New York: Wilson, 1979.

McKay, Vernon. *Africa in World Politics*. New York: Harper & Row, 1963.

McKown, Robin. *Crisis in South Africa*. New York: Putnam's, 1972.

MacLear, Ian. *Pattern for Profit in Southern Africa*. New York: Praeger, 1973.

Malherbe, Paul. *Multistan: A Way Out of the South African Dilemma*. Cape Town, South Africa: Philip, 1974.

Mandela, Nelson. *No Easy Walk to Freedom*. New York: Basic Books, 1965.

Mansergh, Nicholas, ed. Documents and Speeches on Commonwealth Affairs, 1952–1962. London: Dowsons of Pall Mall, 1968.

Mazrui, Ali A., and Hasu H. Patel, eds. Africa in World Affairs. New York: Third Press, 1973.

Meredith, Martin. The First Dance of Freedom: Black Africa in the Post–War Era. New York: Harper & Row, 1984.

Molteno, Robert. Africa and South Africa: The Implications of South Africa's "Outward–Looking" Policy. London: Africa Bureau, 1971.

Morris, Michael Spence L. South African Security: Some Considerations for the 1980s: Special Report. Cape Town, South Africa: Terrorism Research Centre, 1981.

Mutharika, B. W. T. Towards Multinational Economic Cooperation in Africa. New York: Praeger, 1972.

Myers, Desaix III, et al. Business in South Africa. Bloomington: Indiana University Press, 1980.

Nielsen, Waldermar. The Great Powers and Africa. New York: Praeger, 1969.

Nolutshungu, Sam C. South Africa in Africa: A Study of Ideology and Foreign Policy. New York: Africana Publication, 1975.

Nyangoni, Wellington W. African Nationalism in Zimbabwe (Rhodesia). Washington, D.C.: University Press of America, 1977.

Olatunde, J. C. B. Ojo, et al. African International Relations. London: Longman, 1985.

O'Meara, Patrick. Rhodesia: Racial Conflict or Coexistence? Ithaca, N.Y.: Cornell University Press, 1975.

Parker, Frank J. South Africa: Lost Opportunities. Lexington, Mass.: Lexington Books, 1983.

Phillips, Norman. The Tragedy of Apartheid. New York: David McKay, 1960.

Pifer, Alan J. South Africa in the American Mind. New York: Carnegie Corporation of New York, 1981.

Pomeroy, William J. Apartheid Axis: The United States and South Africa. New York: International Publishers, 1973.

Potholm, Christian P. The Theory and Practice of African Politics. Englewood Cliffs, N.J.: Prentice-Hall, 1979.

Potholm, Christian P., and Richard Dale, eds. Southern Africa in Perspective: Essays in Regional Politics. New York: Free Press, 1972.

Ramamurti, T. G. Fight Against Apartheid: India's Pioneering Role in the World: Campaign Against Racial Discrimination in South Africa. New Delhi, India: ABC Publishing House, 1984.

Razis, Vincent Victor. Swords into Ploughshares? South Africa and Political Change: An Introduction. Johannesburg, South Africa: Ravan Press, 1980.

Robertson, Janet. Liberalism in South Africa, 1948-1963. London: Oxford University Press, 1971.

Rogers, Barbara. White Wealth and Black Poverty: American Investment in Southern Africa. Westport, Conn.: Greenwood Press, 1976.

Roux, Edward. Time Longer Than Rope. Madison: University of Wisconsin Press, 1966.

Rubin, Leslie, and Brian Weinstein. Introduction to African Politics: A Continental Approach. New York: Praeger, 1974.

Rubinstein, Alvin. Soviet and Chinese Influence in the Third World. New York: Praeger, 1975.

Rupert, Anton. Priorities for Coexistence. Cape Town, South Africa: Tafelberg, 1981.

Sachs, Albie. Justice in South Africa. Berkeley: University of California Press, 1973.

Schmidt, Elizabeth. One Step in the Wrong Direction: An Analysis of the Sullivan Principles as a Strategy for Opposing Apartheid. New York: Episcopal Churchpeople for a Free Southern Africa, 1985.

_____. Decoding Corporate Camouflage: U.S. Business Support for Apartheid. Washington, D.C.: Institute for Policy Studies, 1980.

Shaw, Timothy M., and Kenneth A. Heard, eds. Cooperation and Conflict in Southern Africa: Papers on a Regional Subsystem. Washington, D.C.: University Press of America, 1976.

Sjollema, Baldwin. Isolating Apartheid: Western Collaboration with South Africa: Policy Decisions by the World Council of Churches and Church Responses. Geneva: World Council of Churches, 1982.

Spandau, Arndt. Economic Boycott Against South Africa: Normative and Factual Issues. Cape Town, South Africa: Juta, 1979.

Study Commission on United States Policy Toward Southern Africa. South Africa: Time Running Out: The Report of the Study Commission on U.S. Policy Toward Southern Africa. Berkeley: University of California Press, 1981.

Thompson, Leonard M. The Political Mythology of Apartheid. New Haven, Conn.: Yale University Press, 1985.

_____. Politics in the Republic of South Africa. Boston: Little, Brown, 1966.

Tutu, Desmond. Hope and Suffering: Sermons and Speeches. Johannesburg, South Africa: Skotaville, 1983.

_____. Crying in the Wilderness: The Struggle for Justice in South Africa. Grand Rapids, Mich.: Eerdmans, 1982.

UNESCO. Racism and Apartheid in Southern Africa. Paris, 1974.

Venter, Denis. South Africa and Black Africa: Some Problem Areas and Prospects for Rapprochement. Pretoria,
South Africa: Africa Institute of South Africa, 1980.

Walshe, Peter. The Rise of African Nationalism in South
Africa. Berkeley: University of California Press, 1971.

Western Massachusetts Association of Concerned African
Scholars, ed. U.S. Military Involvement in Southern
Africa. Boston: South End Press, 1978.

Williams, G. Mennen. Africa for the Africans. Grand
Rapids, Mich.: Eerdmans, 1969.

Willington, John H. South West Africa and Its Human
Issues. New York: Oxford University Press, 1967.

Wimer, S. E., et al. Zimbabwe Now. London: Rex
Collings, 1973.

Worrall, Denis, ed. South Africa: Government and Politics.
Pretoria, South Africa: Van Schaik, 1971.

Wyatt, Donald W., ed. Progress in Africa and America.
New Orleans, La.: Dillard University Press, 1972.

Index

About the Author

SHEIKH R. ALI is a professor of political science at North Carolina Central University. A prolific writer, Dr. Ali has published seven books in the areas of Third World and American politics. He has authored more than three dozen articles and reviews in national and international refereed journals, including the American Political Science Review and the Arab Journal of Social Sciences.

Dr. Ali holds a Ph.D. in international studies from American University and has three master's degrees--in government, political science, and international relations. He was a Fulbright scholar at New York University.

A former diplomat based in Washington, Professor Ali was a rapporteur for President Jimmy Carter's Commission on Foreign Languages and International Studies in 1979. He is a member of the Republican task force and has been awarded a Gold Medal of Merit by President Ronald Reagan.

Professor Ali is a member of many professional organizations, including the Southern Association of Africanists, American Political Science Association, and International Studies Association.